REGULATORY JUSTICE

REGULATORY JUSTICE

Implementing a Wage-Price Freeze

ROBERT A. KAGAN

New York
Russell Sage Foundation

PUBLICATIONS OF RUSSELL SAGE FOUNDATION

Russell Sage Foundation was established in 1907 by Mrs. Margaret Olivia Sage for the improvement of social and living conditions in the United States. In carrying out its purposes, the Foundation conducts research under the direction of members of the staff or outside scholars, in the general fields of social science and public policy. As an integral part of its operation, the Foundation from time to time publishes books or pamphlets resulting from these activities. Publication under the imprint of the Foundation does not necessarily imply agreement by the Foundation, its Trustees, or its staff with the interpretations or conclusions of the authors.

Library of Congress Catalog Card Number: 77–72498
Standard Book Number: 87154–425–3

To My Mother and My Father

Contents

Preface

"The law of the United States is today largely embodied in, shaped by, or effectuated through the rules, regulations, programs and policies of governmental agencies."* The legal decisions made by the hundreds of bureaus, boards, and commissions that dot the governmental landscape, however, are rarely reviewed by courts, or reported in newspapers, or examined by scholars. Most administrators' decisions are made informally, undramatically, deep in the recesses of bureaucracies. The records of the rights they recognize and those they deny lie buried in filing cabinets. Nevertheless, if we are to understand and evaluate the dynamics of our legal system as a whole, it seems important to find a way to extend our vision more fully into the inner workings of the administrative legal process.

This book is an effort in that direction. Its strategy is a detailed case study of a pair of closely-linked federal agencies, the Cost of Living Council (CLC) and the Office of Emergency Preparedness (OEP), which administered a nationwide wage-price freeze in 1971. Its purpose is not to assess the desirability of wage and price controls or the relative merits of regulation as compared to the free market, but to provide insight into the nature of the administrative legal decision process and the making and application of rules in regulatory agencies.

Of course, it is risky to speak of *the* administrative legal decision process or

---

* American Bar Foundation, *The Legal Profession in the United States,* 2nd Ed. (Chicago: American Bar Foundation, 1970).

to base an analysis of the way it *varies* on a single regulatory experience. Every administrative agency is in some ways unique, and the freeze agencies—short-lived and vast in jurisdiction—seemed in some ways more unusual than most. Whatever their special qualities, however, agencies as diverse as the Cost of Living Council, the Food and Drug Administration, a municipal zoning commission, and a county board of tax appeals also have a great deal in common. They make legal decisions within the traditions and restraints of the American legal system as a whole. A case study of any single agency casts light on the activities of others, insofar as it is consciously comparative in its mode of inquiry and presentation and focuses on *dimensions* of the legal process and the environment of decision that are common to all legal institutions. From that standpoint, the freeze agencies, by virtue of the intense and dramatic nature of their enterprise, turn out to be a surprisingly rich source of insight into the regulatory legal process in general.

My interest in studying the freeze agencies came almost by accident. I had long been interested in doing an observational study of the administrative legal process, especially an agency involved in economic regulation. I was stirred to action in August, 1971 as I watched President Nixon's television announcement of a new, anti-inflationary program including a price-wage freeze. The commentators who followed the announcement, I observed, had difficulty answering questions about what the freeze meant, how it would be enforced, how it would affect any particular industry. For all its apparent simplicity, the freeze promised to be quite complex. Consequently, I saw it as a massive *experiment* in economic regulation, in imposing centralized legal controls on a vast economy, and because of its limited duration, I thought it was an experiment that could be examined in its entirety. Within a few days, I was in Washington, attempting to get an inside view of the agencies that were assigned to conduct this experiment.

In 1971, Elmer Bennett, a lawyer with whom I had once served as co-counsel in an anti-trust case, was general counsel to the Office of Emergency Preparedness. His office was in charge of enforcing the freeze, of issuing interpretations of the rules promulgated by the Cost of Living Council (the chief policymaking body) as those rules applied to particular cases, and of reviewing OEP's proposals for new rules to be issued by CLC. Elmer was both sympathetic to my research goals and shorthanded. He gave me a job in his office, and this created extraordinary opportunities to participate in as well as to observe the administrative legal process.

I first worked with John Simpson, Bennett's aide in charge of management and coordination with other offices; thus I was able to develop contacts, on a working basis, with all the other offices in the national headquarters of OEP and with CLC as well. I quickly became involved in the process of rule interpretation, first in the decision of individual cases and then in the review of the work done by other lawyers. Soon I was assigned to meet with interested groups—trade associations, local government officials, landlords—who had questions about the freeze, and I became involved in the policymaking or rule formulation process as well. I prepared presentations and participated in meetings of the CLC's Executive Committee (Ex Comm), and I talked daily with OEP officials who regularly attended those meetings. After the freeze came to a close, I had the opportunity to serve as special assistant to C. Jackson Grayson, the chairman of the Price Commission, one of the agencies that took over Phase II of the Economic Stabilization Program; this experience gave me a valuable perspective on the characteristics of the freeze agencies that were common to the regulatory process in general.

To thank those who made this research possible is a ritual, but it is a worthy and meaningful one. Most indispensable, of course, were the many conscientious OEP officials who treated me as a trusted co-worker, who led me through the labyrinth of the bureaucracy, shared with me their problems and insights, and entrusted me with significant tasks. I must thank in particular Elmer Bennett; his deputies Dick Murray and John Simpson; Lee Butler, Scott Martin, and finally, General George Lincoln, Director of OEP. Special thanks are also due to Raymond Snead of the Internal Revenue Service who graciously helped me gain access to OEP records after they had been transferred to the IRS building, normally an impregnable bastion.

I would not have mustered the conviction to undertake this project at all without encouragement, at a crucial moment, from Professors Stanton Wheeler of Yale University and Herbert McClosky of the University of California, Berkeley. During the first long months of attempting to set down my observations in a coherent manner, Stan Wheeler again gave me unflagging encouragement and valuable advice. I received generous financial support from Russell Sage Foundation's program of residencies in law and social science. Albert J. Reiss, Jr., and Arthur A. Leff of Yale University, and my colleagues Sandy Muir and Nelson Polsby of the University of California, Berkeley, read various drafts and provided many helpful comments. The index was capably prepared by Elinor Lindheimer. My greatest debt, however, is owed to my wife Betsy, partly for her active assistance, but even more for her love and understanding.

Robert A. Kagan

REGULATORY JUSTICE

Part I:
Sources of
Regulatory Policy
and Legal Structure

CHAPTER 1

The Dilemmas of Regulation

In August 1971, pursuant to the Economic Stabilization Act of 1970, President Nixon issued an executive order imposing a ninety-day freeze on all wages, prices, and rents in the United States. Its stated objective was to stop inflation, prevent the continued erosion of real wages, and promote economic recovery. While these goals would appear to command universal support, the corridors of the administrative agencies assigned to implement the freeze were soon filled with corporation officers and labor union lawyers seeking exceptions—permission for a wage or price increase in their particular case. Strict interpretation or adherence to the order, these petitioners argued, would result in injustice or disruption of the normal economic functions of the firm in question.

From the standpoint of the freeze agencies, these arguments raised recurrent dilemmas of regulatory policy making and of law enforcement in general. To what extent should explicit and stringent regulatory laws be moderated in the interests of economic efficiency or fairness? Must authoritative legal rules be strictly applied, or should legal officials—be they regulatory commissioners or bureaucrats or policemen—interpret or suspend those rules in order to produce the results that appear most desirable or just in each particular case? This book is about those recurrent dilemmas, the way freeze agency officials dealt with them, and the forces that shaped their response. Fundamentally, therefore, it explores the capacity of regulatory bureaucracy to be effective, sensible and just.

One aspect of this inquiry concerns the inducements and deterrents to

5

legalism. Legalism is the literal application of a legal rule when the policy that gave rise to the rule would justify an exception or when common-sense notions of fairness and social utility would suggest a departure from the rule.[1] The risk of legalism often seems most acute in the administrative agencies that now bulk so large in the legal landscape, where the decision process is so often characterized by an emphasis on forms and detailed regulations, where crucial questions of legal policy—what remedy will be imposed for racial discrimination, what chemicals are so hazardous that they should be immediately banned—are made by narrowly specialized bureaucrats rather than legislatures or judges. The fear of legalism, in fact, has led many administrative agencies to foreswear the use of detailed rules, but the result, in the opinion of some observers, is an excess of administrative discretion, producing decisions that all too often are motivated by considerations of expediency or bias.[2] Sometimes explicit legal rules are necessary to prevent the arbitrary exercise of power, to create law which is clearly understandable and predictable, to enforce a controversial policy, or to protect an unpopular minority. The challenge is to develop the capacity in legal institutions to apply rules in a flexible, nonlegalistic manner, with sensitivity to the fairness and desirability of the consequences of decisions.[3] The question is how that can be done, especially in a bureaucratic setting.

A related problem, and a second underlying focus of this study, concerns the determinants of regulatory policy. To some critics, regulatory agencies have an inherent tendency to overregulate, to burden vital economic enterprises with arbitrarily stringent rules and reporting requirements, enforced with bureaucratic disregard for economic realities. To an antiphonal chorus of critics, the problem is just the opposite: regulatory agencies are not too stringent but overly accommodative to the businesses they are supposed to control; they become the "captives" of the dominant firms in the regulated industry, protecting their interests rather than preventing or redressing injuries to the public. These contrasting views often reflect rather one-sided conceptions of proper policy, but both sets of critics are sometimes right.

---

[1] See Philippe Nonet and Philip Selznick, *Law and Society in Transition: Toward Responsive Law* (New York: Harper Colophon, 1978) and the slightly different conceptions of legalism in Judith Shklar, *Legalism* (Cambridge, Mass.: Harvard University Press, 1964); John T. Noonan, Jr., *Persons and Masks of the Law* (New York: Farrar, Straus and Giroux, 1976); Lawrence Friedman, "On Legalistic Reasoning—A Footnote to Weber," 1966 *Wisconsin Law Review* 148.

[2] See Kenneth C. Davis, *Discretionary Justice: A Preliminary Inquiry* (Urbana, Illinois: University of Illinois Press, 1971); Henry Friendly, *The Federal Administrative Agencies: The Need for Better Definition of Standards* (Cambridge, Mass.: Harvard University Press, 1962); Charles Reich, "The New Property," 73 *Yale Law Journal* 778 (1964).

[3] See Mortimer Kadish and Sanford Kadish, *Discretion to Disobey: A Study of Lawful Departures from Legal Rules* (Stanford, Calif.: Stanford University Press, 1973); Philippe Nonet and Philip Selznick, *Law and Society in Transition*.

The reason is the enormous number and diversity of regulatory programs. Agencies vary greatly in the thrust of their policies, in the kinds of faults they display, and in the integrity and imagination with which they reconcile competing concepts of justice and social policy. The problem is to understand the *reasons* for these variations.

When can we expect a regulatory agency to define its regulatory mission stringently and stick to it, and when can we expect it to be more accommodative? What institutional arrangements are conducive of legalistic law enforcement? What conditions foster a more flexible and consequence-oriented method of rule application? For all the critical literature on regulatory agencies, the answers to these questions—which would seem so basic to realistic planning or reform—are not evident. One path to that kind of knowledge is the detailed observation and analysis of how legal decision makers behave in their natural habitat. In recent years, for example, observational studies of urban courts and prosecutors and police officers have illuminated the various ways in which "law in books" is translated into "law in action."[4] Relatively few observational studies, however, perform a similar function with respect to the lawmaking and law-applying activities of regulatory agencies.[5] There is still much to be learned about regulatory officials' thought processes and how their resolutions of legal problems are affected by organizational pressures inside the agency and by variations in the economic environment in which the agencies operate.

The freeze agencies were an apt laboratory for this kind of investigation. Standing at the center of a significant and controversial regulatory effort, they were a microcosm of the legal and regulatory process. In these agencies, the risk of legalism seemed especially salient: they were assigned to enforce a highly explicit and ostensibly single-purposed law; they were bureaucratically organized; they were dedicated to rapid decision making in accordance with detailed rules and regulations. But they were also subject to enormous pressures to avoid legalistic rule-application, to make accommodative modifications of the freeze order. Because of the dramatic nature of a freeze, the conflict between pressures for legalistic stringency and pressures for accommodation, as well as the forces that shaped official responses to those pressures, stood out with special clarity. Finally, the agencies were remarkably

---

[4] See, e.g., John Robertson, ed., *Rough Justice: Perspectives on Lower Criminal Courts* (Boston: Little, Brown, 1974); Jerome Skolnick, *Justice Without Trial* (New York: John Wiley & Sons, 1966); Albert J. Reiss, Jr., *The Police and the Public* (New Haven, Conn.: Yale University Press, 1971). The quoted phrases are from Roscoe Pound, "The Law in Books and Law in Action," 44 *American Law Review* 12 (1910).

[5] Some notable exceptions are Victor Thompson, *The Regulatory Process in OPA Rationing* (New York: Kings Crown Press, 1950); Peter Blau, *The Dynamics of Bureaucracy* (Chicago: University of Chicago Press, 1955); Philip Schrag, "On Her Majesty's Secret Service: Protecting the Consumer in New York City," 80 *Yale Law Journal* 1529 (1971).

accessible: I was able not only to observe policy makers and bureaucrats as they debated decisions but also to participate actively in their decision processes at all levels. The brevity of the freeze condensed the regulatory process into a small circle of time, enabling me to experience it virtually whole.[6]

Before stepping into the world of the freeze agencies, however, it will be helpful to place it in a broader frame of reference by discussing certain policy and legal dilemmas that are shared by regulatory agencies in general.

REGULATORY AGENCIES AS LEGAL INSTITUTIONS

Governments regulate private economic activity in a great variety of ways. They impose taxes to deter some activities and provide deductions or exemptions to encourage others. They induce desired behavior through grants and contracts with restrictive conditions. They influence investment, consumption, and employment by manipulating the total supply of money and credit and by adjusting the balance of government spending and taxation. I would prefer to reserve the terms *regulation* and *regulatory,* however, for a more limited method of government action, the control of economic activity by means of direct *legal orders*. Regulation in this sense occurs when businessmen are legally prohibited from practicing a trade without a license or from constructing buildings or processing milk except in accordance with governmentally prescribed health and safety standards. Typically, the detailed specification, enforcement, and application of these rules is entrusted to specialized regulatory agencies, established to concentrate on control of a particular industry or trade or a particular business practice.

The emphasis on legal rules and orders as a mode of control highlights the degree to which regulatory agencies are legal institutions. Regulatory officials are legal officials; they make and enforce and apply law. Their decisions are subject to challenge and review in the courts and to reversal for failure to adhere to the canons of legal justification.

"The law," of course, is not always clear and not always obeyed. As many authors have emphasized, or perhaps overemphasized, political pressure, bureaucratic convenience, ideological preferences, and even outright corruption are often significant factors in particular regulatory decisions. But regulatory officials, like other people, generally seek to justify their actions, and persuasive justifications must be grounded in the legal and moral values of their culture. To understand the context of regulatory policy making, therefore, one must be cognizant of the normative expectations and legal constraints that surround regulatory agencies in our political system. These can

---

[6] See Appendix for a description of the participant-observation and other research methods employed.

be discussed in terms of two fundamental problems faced by every agency—the problem of policy choice and the problem of legal method.

POLICY CHOICE: STRINGENCY VS. ACCOMMODATION

There is an old controversy in ethics between deontological theorists, who hold that moral rules should be followed categorically in all cases, regardless of the consequences, and teleological moralists, who hold that an action is right only if it leads to the best possible consequences, even if it means violating moral rules.[7] That choice is not dissimilar to one often faced by regulatory agencies. Launched on a wave of concern about a specific social problem, regulatory agencies typically are charged with a single publicly emphasized *police mission*.[8] They are called upon to attack air pollution, racial discrimination, coal mine disasters, or deception of consumers. The police mission, moreover, is often stated or justified in terms of a categorical ethical principle: the sanctity of human life and its prerequisites of health and safety; the fundamental immorality of fraud or of discrimination on the basis of race, sex, or wealth; the brutality of destruction of wildlife or forests. The same goals *can* be justified in utilitarian terms, and sometimes they are, but the primary emphasis in the demand for regulation is usually on the moral imperative.[9] Industrial accidents, defects in slum dwellings, and air pollution are viewed as inherently bad and therefore should be totally eliminated—without regard to the economic costs to the regulated businesses of doing so. In the face of an unqualified evil, there is no moral justification for making exceptions.

By contrast, the American legal tradition, taken as a whole, seems to favor a teleological approach, a utilitarian weighing of the relative magnitude of an evil against the costs of reducing it. Trained in the common law tradition, judges and lawyers have favored the pragmatic "balancing" of conflicting principles and interests and the adaptation of rules and policies in light of

---

[7] See Baruch Brody, ed., *Moral Rules and Particular Circumstances* (Englewood Cliffs, N.J.: Prentice-Hall, 1970), "Introduction."

[8] The term is adapted from James Landis, *The Administrative Process* (New Haven, Conn.: Yale University Press, 1938) and his analysis of the police function and the economic planning function. The concept of *police* in this context refers to the broad police powers of governments to enact laws to promote the general health, safety, and welfare.

[9] Some regulatory programs, of course, are explicitly based on the value of promoting economic stability and growth, as in the case of the Atomic Energy Commission, the Civil Aeronautics Board, and the Interstate Commerce Commission with respect to trucking. And some programs justified in terms of "moral" police-mission goals may in fact be inspired by business firms seeking economic stability. See Gabriel Kolko, *The Triumph of Conservatism* (New York: Free Press, 1963), for an extreme statement of this position. Most regulatory legislation, however, is supported or at least justified by strong, moralistic appeals. James Q. Wilson, "The Rise of the Bureaucratic State," 41 *The Public Interest* 77, 97 (1976).

their consequences in particular cases. They have a tradition of concern for
the requirements of entrepreneurial activity and values of economic
growth.[10] From this standpoint, regulators are expected to moderate
police-mission enforcement whenever it comes too strongly into conflict with
other important social interests and values, such as economic stability and
efficiency. Even if legislation states police-mission objectives in categorical
terms, it would be argued, the very adoption of regulation as the mode of
control (as opposed to abolition of the offending firms, for example) implies
that the community also cares about the continued existence and productivity of the businesses that are to be policed. If the golden goose is befouling its
nest, the regulator should try to clean it up without stopping egg production.

The contrast in approaches is revealed starkly by a report from the federal
Council on Wage and Price Stability which recommended the abandonment
of pending Labor Department regulations designed to eliminate cancer-
causing emissions from coke ovens. The report indicated that the cost of
compliance with the regulations would be $240 million per year and would
prevent an estimated twenty-seven cancer deaths annually. Therefore, the
council observed, the regulations would compel spending $9 million to save
each life, a price which was "extremely high, considering the amounts spent
in other health and safety areas." Those millions could save more lives, it
suggested, if spent on alternative programs. The United Steel Workers
Union, in response, criticized the council's report as "despicable." They
charged the council with "putting dollars ahead of human values" and with
suggesting that "the lives of coke oven workers aren't worth saving."[11]

The conflict between police-mission goals and values associated with economic efficiency and continuity is exacerbated by the fact that a regulatory
agency's principal weapon, the power of legal prohibition, is a limited one; it
is not the power of management of the regulated firms, and it does not enable

---

[10] See J. Willard Hurst, *Law and the Conditions of Freedom in the Nineteenth Century United
States* (Madison: University of Wisconsin Press, 1956); Laurence M. Friedman, *A History of
American Law* (New York: Simon and Schuster, 1973); Philip Selznick, "The Ethos of Amer-
ican Law," in *The Americans: 1976,* eds. Irving Kristol and Paul Weaver (Lexington, Mass.:
Lexington Books, 1976). On the adaptation of legal rules to the facts of particular cases, see
G. Edward White, "From Sociological Jurisprudence to Realism: Jurisprudence and Social
Change in Early Twentieth Century America," 58 *Virginia Law Review* 999 (1972); Mirjan
Damaska, "Structures of Authority and Comparative Criminal Procedure," 84 *Yale Law
Journal* 480 (1975).

[11] "Coke-Oven Emission Rules Are Opposed by Wage-Price Council Because of Costs,"
The Wall Street Journal, May 12, 1976, p. 4. The Council on Wage and Price Stability (an
advisory body only) did ask whether there were less costly alternative regulations, such as
limiting the time period workers were exposed to emissions each day or the use of respirators.

the agency to compensate firms for the cost of compliance with stringent police measures.[12] If enforcement pushes costs of compliance *too* high and the regulated firms are denied compensating price increases—either by price regulations designed to protect consumers or by market forces—stringent regulation can push low profit margin products or companies out of business. The resulting problem—whether or how far to moderate a stringent policy or a categorically stated police mission—is therefore not a simple choice between social justice and heedless materialism or between concern for the weak and deference to the powerful. If the enforcement of stringent anti-pollution or safety regulations requiring expensive remedial devices results in the shutdown of marginally profitable factories or mines, the result will be hardship for workers and their communities. If the enforcement of stringent housing code regulations sharply increases operating costs for slum landlords, the consequence may be increased rent charges to already poor tenants; if rent increases are also prohibited, the landlords may cut back on maintenance or abandon buildings, further advancing neighborhood disintegration. Suggested solutions—rent subsidies, tax abatement, government takeover—go beyond regulation (which attempts to put the cost of decent maintenance on the landlords) by shifting maintenance costs to the public treasury. Thus the choice between stringent or accommodative regulation actually involves fundamental problems of equity: what is the just allocation of the costs of ameliorative measures?[13]

Of course, the tension between regulatory stringency and values of economic continuity may be only slight in many cases, or even nonexistent. Will the factory really close down rather than install anti-pollution controls? Are landlords' profits so poor and maintenance costs so high that strict housing code enforcement really would produce the undesired effects? Or can the factory and the landlord, despite their protestations to the contrary, actually absorb the costs of compliance? Unfortunately, regulatory agencies are usually at a disadvantage in dealing with such questions. They are deeply

---

[12] The case is somewhat different where agencies have unusually extensive powers over an industry—including the power to restrict entry and prevent abandonment of services—such as the ICC with respect to railroads and the CAB with respect to airlines. To some extent, these agencies can subsidize the costs of regulation in one area by authorizing rate increases for other routes or services.

[13] See Bruce Ackerman et al., *The Uncertain Search for Environmental Quality* (New York: Free Press, 1974), pt. IV; Robert S. Smith, *The Occupational Safety and Health Act* (Washington: American Enterprise Institute, 1976) ch. 2; "Coal Controversy," *The Wall Street Journal,* March 17, 1971, p. 1; Bruce Ackerman, "Regulating Slum Housing Markets on Behalf of the Poor," 80 *Yale Law Journal* 1093 (1971); Neil Komesar, "Return to Slumville: A Critique of the Ackerman Analysis of Housing Code Enforcement and the Poor," 82 *Yale Law Journal* 1175 (1973).

dependent on regulated firms themselves for detailed information concerning the costs of compliance and the likely consequences of imposing restrictive controls. Alternative sources of information—consumer groups, academic experts, mandatory reports from the regulated firms themselves—are not always available and not always reliable. From the standpoint of the regulators, therefore, the point at which the pursuit of their police mission would actually become seriously disruptive is frequently unclear. Yet for the agency to *assume* bad faith on the part of the regulated firm, to automatically discount asserted risks to economic continuity, not only violates the tenets of due process of law but invites charges of unreasonableness and evasion by regulated firms. Resort to coercive enforcement of rules regarded as arbitrary rarely is wholly effective.[14]

Legal constraints on regulatory agencies, accordingly, usually include express or implied directives to attend to values of economic continuity. A statute that articulates a police mission in absolute, stringent terms will often include authorization to make exceptions, as in the "variance" procedures in land use zoning schemes. The constitutional prohibition against governmental "taking" of private property without compensation has sometimes been interpreted to prevent regulators from setting rates so low as to deny the regulated firm a fair rate of return on its investment.[15] The same position is implicit in regulatory statutes that command the agency to set "just and reasonable" rates.[16] Sometimes it is explicit; the Natural Gas Act of 1938, for example, instructed the Federal Power Commission to set natural gas prices at the "lowest possible reasonable rate consistent with the maintenance of adequate service in the public interest."[17] Courts sometimes

---

[14] See Robert Lane, *The Regulation of Businessmen—Social Conditions of Governmental Economic Control* (New Haven, Conn.: Yale University Press, 1954); Harry Ball, "Social Structure and Rent Control Violations," 65 *American Journal of Sociology* 598 (1960). See generally, Harry Ball and Lawrence Friedman, "The Use of Criminal Sanctions in the Enforcement of Economic Regulations," 17 *Stanford Law Review* 197 (1965).

[15] See *Smyth* v. *Ames*, 169 U.S. 466 (1898). The precise line between reasonable and unreasonable regulation and the handling of loss operations by regulated firms has been somewhat unclear in recent years. See, e.g., *Federal Power Commission* v. *Hope Natural Gas Co.*, 320 U.S. 591 (1944); Note, "Takings and the Public Interest in Railroad Regulation," 82 *Yale Law Journal* 1004 (1973); Frank Michelman, "Property, Utility and Fairness: Comments on the Ethical Foundations of 'Just Compensation' Law," 80 *Harvard Law Review* 1165 (1968). But even in recent decades, stringent land use regulations have sometimes been invalidated as uncompensated takings. See John Costonis, "Development Rights Transfer: An Exploratory Essay," 83 *Yale Law Journal* 75, 76 (1973).

[16] See *Yakus* v. *United States*, 321 U.S. 414 (1944), with reference to World War II price control legislation.

[17] 52 *Stat.* 825 (1938). The FPC, in fact, was widely criticized for setting rates for natural gas producers so low as to deter production and induce shortages. See, e.g., Paul MacAvoy, "The Regulation-Induced Shortage of Natural Gas," 14 *Journal of Law and Economics*, 167 (1971).

refuse to enforce agency orders which the judges see as overzealous or blind to competing equities.[18]

The regulatory agency's dilemma, however, stems equally from the risk of bending over too far in the direction of accommodation. Its *primary* duty, after all, is usually seen as implementation of a specific police mission and fidelity to the terms and intent of its authorizing legislation. Increasingly, victims of weak regulation—consumer and environmental groups, for example—are empowered and encouraged to file complaints and lawsuits to spur agencies toward greater stringency.[19] The slightest accommodation is often castigated by well-publicized critics and politicians as a departure from the agency's legal obligation and surrender to industry domination. Concessions to considerations of economic continuity at the behest of one firm or group of firms may lead others to see the agency as corruptible or as a paper tiger and tempt them to evade the law. Thus the legitimacy and continuing viability of the agency is also dependent on building a politically and legally defensible degree of stringency into its decisions.

THE PROBLEM OF LEGAL METHOD

A separate controversy has focused on the procedures by which issues of policy formulation and implementation should be resolved. Everyone agrees, of course, that agencies should proceed in an honest and equitable manner. The debate is about how the agency should be constituted and controlled to promote those ideals. It concerns the proper structure of participation, fact-finding, and accountability in the regulatory decision process.

One view, which we can call the *expert model,* goes as follows. Because the appropriate balance between stringency and accommodation is dependent upon the facts of specific cases, regulatory decisions should not be prescribed in advance either by legislation or fixed legal rules. Regulatory officials must be free to formulate policies in response to the problems at hand, adapting decisions to varied and changing situations on the basis of their accumulating

[18] See, e.g. *Reserve Mining Co.* v. *Environmental Protection Administration,* 514 F. 2d 492 (8th Cir. 1975), where the court balanced the social and economic harm to employees of defendant and their community against the environmental damage caused by defendant, and refused EPA's request for an injunction despite the defendant's violation of the applicable anti-pollution law.

[19] See Richard Stewart, "The Reformation of American Administrative Law," 88 *Harvard Law Review* 1669 (1975); Karen Orren, "Standing to Sue: Interest Group Conflict in the Federal Courts," 70 *American Political Science Review* 723 (1976). In a recent suit, for example, the Sierra Club challenged an exemption from federal clean water standards granted by the EPA to steel plants in Ohio's Mahoning River Valley. The U.S. Court of Appeals for the Third Circuit invalidated the exemption, which had been allowed to prevent "severe economic and employment disruptions." The court stated that the 1972 water pollution control law does not provide for outright exemptions. *Wall Street Journal,* September 19, 1977, p. 16.

knowledge, making intuitive judgments as to what result will maximize the public interest. In terms of Max Weber's well-known typology of modes of legal thought, the regulator should engage in "substantively rational" decision making: adaptive, unrestrained by formal procedures and legal classifications, and oriented to the requirements and equities of each case. The ideal of the regulatory process from this perspective is government not by formal law but by expert judgment.[20]

The expert model does not necessarily imply that that expertise, whether that of the economist or engineer or experienced civil servant, can define the public interest in an empirically verifiable manner. Advocates of the expert model today would recognize the evaluative or political elements in any regulatory decision, but they would argue that factual elements are a vitally important part of regulatory decision and that officials who are experts—in the sense of continuing attention to a problem and commitment to evaluating alternative decisions as rationally as possible—will do a better job of policy making and implementation than politicians or judges and bureaucrats who rely on pre-existing legal doctrines.[21]

A conflicting set of standards can be called the *legal model* of regulation. Whereas the expert model relies heavily on the good judgment of regulatory officials and on informal procedures, the legal model mistrusts such arrangements. It calls for formal controls, specific legally enforceable protections against the risks of arbitrariness and corruption. The legal model emphasizes accountability of regulatory officials to elected legislatures and to courts; predictability of decision and equality of treatment; decision according to systematized fact-finding procedures, such as court-like hearings, and according to explicit, known rules; and finally, fixed procedures for public participation in the agencies' decision processes. These ideals are reflected in the doctrines of administrative law under which aggrieved parties can contest agency rulings in the courts, and courts must reverse agency decisions if they are not in accordance with the terms of authorizing legislation, not supported by adequate findings of fact or articulated reasons, or reached in a procedurally unfair manner.[22]

Relatively few agency decisions, of course, are actually reviewed and reversed by a court. Reviewing courts generally defer to the policy judgments of agency officials, provided they meet minimum standards of evidentiary

---

[20] For Weber's typology, see Max Rheinstein, ed., *Max Weber on Law in Economy and Society* (New York: Simon and Schuster, 1967). On the *expert model,* see James Freedman, "Crisis and Legitimacy in the Administrative Process," 27 *Stanford Law Review* 1041 (1975).

[21] Ackerman, *The Uncertain Search,* and Stephen Kelman, "Regulating by the Numbers—The Consumer Product Safety Commission," 36 *The Public Interest* 83 (1974) are interesting analyses of the strengths and weaknesses of technical approaches to regulatory choice.

[22] See Stewart, "Reformation of American Administrative Law," and Louis Jaffe, *Judicial Control of Administrative Action* (Boston: Little, Brown, 1965).

support and rationality; in this regard the kernel of the expert model is incorporated in administrative legal doctrine. Moreover, the vast number of preliminary and informal regulatory decisions—the selection of cases for enforcement, the terms of settlements—are usually exempt from court review.[23] Nevertheless, regulatory agencies must rely upon legal forms and the potential coercive powers of the courts to transform their policy desires into authoritative command, especially in important contested cases. Administrative legal doctrine is reflected in the organizational structure and formal procedures prescribed in the legislation that creates regulatory agencies. Many agency officials are legally trained; almost all are advised by staff attorneys. The legal model thus provides a set of standards against which agencies are regularly assessed.

Every regulatory agency, in devising its methods of decision making, faces a dilemma raised by the conflicting ideals of the expert model and the legal model. An emphasis on strict adherence to specific rules and court-like adjudicatory processes helps to legitimate the agency's authority, symbolizing its intent to decide fairly and in accordance with known standards; but wherever formal rules are emphasized, there is a risk of legalism—rigid rule application—which impedes the adaptation of policy to unique and changing conditions and which frustrates and angers those who must deal with the agency. Wherever formal, participatory methods of adjudication and rule making are employed, there is the risk of enormous delay and expense and of paralysis of aggressive administrative action.[24] Avoidance of formal legal rules and procedures, on the other hand, in favor of an informal decision-making process, creates another set of risks. Informal and hence more "closed" procedures, reliance on agency officials to gather the information they think necessary and adjust policy to the situation as they think best, can easily lead to inconsistent and arbitrary decisions or the domination of policy implementation by informal relationships and plea bargaining between agency officials and regulated firms.[25] The problem, therefore, is to find an acceptable path between the Scylla of legalism and the Charybdis of uncontrolled discretion, a method by which decisions are made both promptly and consistently and rules are applied and adjusted in light of their actual consequences.

The problem of devising a fair and purposive legal method is obviously linked to the substantive problem of balancing stringency and accommoda-

---

[23] Davis, *Discretionary Justice.*

[24] See, e.g., President's Advisory Council on Executive Organization (The Ash Council), *A New Regulatory Framework* (Washington: Government Printing Office, 1971); Philippe Nonet, *Administrative Justice* (New York: Russell Sage Foundation, 1969); Richard Posner, "The Behavior of Regulatory Agencies, 1 *Journal of Legal Studies* 305 (1972); Stewart, "Reformation of American Administrative Law."

[25] See, e.g., Davis, *Discretionary Justice.* The issue is nicely discussed in Jeffrey Jowell, "The Legal Control of Administrative Discretion," 1973 *Public Law*, 178.

tion. An emphasis on decision in accordance with explicit rules—such as those which prescribe numerical standards for maximum prices or maximum pollution levels—helps meet the legal ideal of certainty and formal equality, but such universally applicable rules are likely to be unfairly harsh as applied to firms with special products or higher costs, or too soft on firms that can afford to comply with more stringent requirements.[26] On the other hand, decision methods or rules tailored to the particular factors of each case, such as detailed inquiry into each regulated firm's economic situation or rate of return, produce delays in administration and seem to increase the relative power of the regulated firms—especially larger ones with the resources to hire technical specialists in regulatory compliance and legal counsel who are sophisticated in manipulating rules and formal procedures.[27] In the early days of the World War II price control programs, for example, the statutory standard of "generally fair and equitable" prices was not given explicit definition by the Office of Price Administration on the grounds that the agency should not "tie its own hands" by issuing binding across-the-board rules. Prices should be set on a case-by-case basis, it was thought, in light of each specific firm's situation; but according to OPA Administrator Chester Bowles, this flexibility led to a plethora of inconsistent and inflationary decisions, as economically important firms threatened OPA officials with predictions of dire consequences for wartime production if price concessions were not made. Later, Bowles claimed, more explicit, fixed industry-wide rules minimized this problem. He failed to add, however, that an extensive mechanism was established for granting case-by-case exceptions to the fixed rules.[28] The tension between substantive and formal justice is never finally resolved. The problem, in fact, is keeping it alive.

[26] See, e.g., "The Catco Controversy" in Louis Jaffe and Nathaniel Nathanson, *Administrative Law, Cases and Materials* (Boston: Little, Brown, 1968), pp. 484–524, and annual supplements, involving the setting of area-wide prices for natural gas producers. An interesting theoretical analysis of the problem of rule specificity is provided by Isaac Ehrlich and Richard Posner, "An Economic Analysis of Legal Rulemaking," 3 *Journal of Legal Studies* 257 (1974).

[27] Allen Kneese and Charles Schultze, *Pollution, Prices and Public Policy* (Washington: Brookings Institution, 1975), Ch. V, outlines the dilemmas of choice between uniform nationwide standards for water pollution or permits tailored to the technology and economic capacity of individual polluters. As of 1974, some 33,000 plants had applied for permits; yet uniform standards promised to be both inflexible and unreasonably costly.

On the inherent advantages of "repeat players" in litigation and legal bargaining, see Marc Galanter, "Why the 'Haves' Come Out Ahead: Speculations on the Limits of Legal Change," 9 *Law and Society Review* 95 (1974).

[28] Chester Bowles, *Promises to Keep* (New York: Harper & Row, 1971), pp. 51–54; S. Sperling McMillan, *Individual Firm Adjustments Under OPA* (Bloomington, Ind.: Principia Press, 1949). Manuel Cohen and Joel Rabin, "Broker-Dealer Practice Standards: The Importance of Administrative Adjudication," 29 *Law and Contemporary Problems* 691, 715–716 (1964), argue that case-by-case adjudication *can* produce innovative, stringent regulation.

CONCLUSION: SOURCES OF VARIATION

The major purpose of our examination of the freeze agencies will be to identify the sources of variation in the ways regulatory agencies cope with the dilemmas of policy and legal method. To restate the questions raised at the outset, what induces an agency to adhere strictly to stringent policies, as opposed to making accommodations in the interest of economic continuity or other values? What induces an agency to use legal rules in a legalistic manner, or to employ a more flexible and purposeful mode of decision? And finally, where will we look for the sources of those variations? What factors matter?

Legal scholars have always tended to explain legal decision making by reference to authoritative legal sources—statutes and legislative reports, court opinions, and the arguments of counsel. Social scientists, on the other hand, have tended to picture legal institutions as responsive primarily to nonlegal factors. Political scientists, for example, have stressed the political background and personal ideology and career paths of legal decision makers (such as whether they are recruited from or "graduated to" the regulated industry); the configuration and strength of interest group pressures; and the attitudes of the legislative officials who control the agency's funding. Sociologists have often attributed legal outcomes to the dependencies that develop between lower-level legal officials and those with whom they interact on an everyday basis or to intra-agency bureaucratic patterns that lead lower officials to subvert official policy.[29] I see no reason to choose between these various approaches and every reason not to. It should be obvious that regulatory agencies, like all legal institutions, are simultaneously influenced by both legal and nonlegal factors.

The most vital legal influence on an agency is the legislation that it is called upon to implement. As emphasized by Herbert Simon, James March, and Richard Cyert, organizations confronted with conflicting goals and uncertain facts tend to seek simplified "definitions of the situation" to reduce the varied problems they encounter into a manageable set of categories and routine responses.[30] Relevant regulatory statutes, including the reports and proclamations of purpose that accompany their enactment, provide readily available, authoritative definitions of the situation. Adhering to those definitions provides the agency with guidance and with a measure of protection from legal and political attack. The definitions the statutes provide, of course, are not always clear. Some, not all, legislation is vague; even specific statutes

---

[29] For a useful summary of theories of regulatory performance, see Roger Noll, *Reforming Regulation* (Washington: Brookings Institution, 1971).

[30] See James March and Herbert Simon, *Organizations* (New York: John Wiley & Sons, 1958); Richard Cyert and James March, *A Behavioral Theory of the Firm* (Englewood Cliffs, N.J.: Prentice-Hall, 1963).

provide some interpretive leeway with respect to some cases, and competing legal values impose implied limits on statutes which by their terms allow for no exceptions. Not all statutory interpretations are plausible, however. Words can be defined and intentions construed. In any regulatory program, therefore, the rough boundaries of policy are likely to be charted by the legal arguments that can plausibly be linked to the authorizing legislation.

Implementing agencies, of course, are often presented with demands for alternative rules or decisions, each of which can plausibly be justified by reference to the authorizing legislation. Indeed, that is their normal bill of fare, because both the legally obvious questions and the legally implausible contentions tend to get settled without high-level official action. Within the range of legitimate choice, the interpretation selected, whether more stringent or accommodative, is inevitably influenced by the personal dispositions of the decision makers and by structural factors as well, such as the quality and source of information available, the attitudes of those on whom the agency is politically dependent, and bureaucratic pressures for cutting the workload. The relative importance of each of these factors, however, is not self-evident, nor are the different conditions under which each may rise to greater prominence.

The search for those conditions, in fact, seems to lead us full circle. Structural factors—such as the configuration of interest groups, the size and nature of the agency's case load—are the product, in large measure, of the specific content of the authorizing law. That is, the pressures brought to bear upon an agency stem from the particular groups which the law by its specific terms seems to threaten or assist. The size of an agency's case load and the quality of its information base are influenced by the powers and resources which the authorizing law confers upon it. There is a dialectic between legal and nonlegal factors. Each is continually shaping and being reshaped by the other. Our inquiry into policy formation and the struggle for legality in the freeze agencies is, at bottom, an effort to specify more carefully the interplay of legal and nonlegal factors in shaping legal decisions.

CHAPTER 2

The Freeze Agencies and Their Legal Structure

When President Nixon announced a wage-price freeze in August 1971, no administrative structure existed to communicate its requirements to the public, to detect and sanction violations, or to elaborate its application in particular cases. A new legal structure and set of legal procedures had to be created. Inevitably, they would shape the way in which freeze policy would be formed and implemented and the kinds of pressures for stringency and legalism that would be brought to bear on freeze agency officials.

THE ORIGINS OF THE FREEZE

Most governments in this century have faced—and some have been toppled by—the political and economic tensions engendered by inflation. They have resorted to a variety of control techniques: fiscal and monetary policy, currency revaluation, and simple appeals to businesses and unions to exercise restraint. In addition, many nations have adopted—at least for substantial time periods—incomes policies or direct legal controls on wage and price levels.[1] Mandatory controls have not been a favorite technique in the United States, however. Before the Nixon administration program, the federal gov-

---

[1] See Lloyd Ulman and Robert Flanagan, *Wage Restraint: A Study of Incomes Policies in Western Europe* (Berkeley: University of California Press, 1971); Murray Edelman and R. Fleming, *The Politics of Wage-Price Decisions* (Urbana: University of Illinois Press, 1965); Kenneth Karst and Keith Rosenn, *Law and Development in Latin America* (Berkeley: University of California Press, 1975), ch. IV.

ernment regulated wages and prices for the economy as a whole only during World War I, World War II, and the Korean War, periods in which the productive capacity of the national economy was severely strained and inflation was rampant.[2]

Despite some success in stemming inflation, the wartime programs were divisive and difficult to manage. During the Korean War controls, for example, labor representatives angrily resigned from the Wage Stabilization Board. A year later, after they had been lured back, industry representatives walked out.[3] Businessmen and consumers criticized the huge bureaucracies established to make and enforce pricing rules, complaining that they were unresponsive, inequitable, and inefficient. Black markets—secret sales at prices higher than the legally stipulated ceilings—were not uncommon.[4] Most economists condemned the idea of retaining mandatory controls in peacetime as a continuing check on inflation. Controls attacked only the symptoms of inflation, they argued, while creating distortions and inefficiencies in the productive system. As the crisis of war ended, controls were quickly abandoned.

When inflation reemerged as a political and economic problem during the late 1950s, direct governmental action against excessive wage and price increases was demanded, sometimes by business, sometimes by labor. Presidents did intervene on occasion, but by measures short of mandatory price and wage regulation. Federal officials sometimes participated in wage negotiations in major industries, such as railroads and steel. On one occasion, President Kennedy employed public exhortation and private threats to force the steel industry to roll back a large price increase. The Council of Economic Advisers under Presidents Kennedy and Johnson promulgated voluntary numerical guideposts for price and wage increases based on the theory that neither should increase at a rate higher than average productivity gains. But

---

[2] See Robert Cuff, *The War Industries Board: Business-Government Relations During World War I* (Baltimore: Johns Hopkins Press, 1973); Harvey Mansfield, et al., *A Short History of OPA* (Washington: Government Printing Office, 1949); L. Chandler and D. Wallace, *Economic Mobilization and Stabilization* (New York: Henry Holt, 1951); J. Kauffman, "The Problem of Coordinating Price and Wage Programs in 1950–1953," 24 *Indiana Law Journal* 499 (1953) and 30 *Indiana Law Journal* 18 (1954).

[3] Between those two walkouts, President Truman seized the steel mills (an action later ruled unconstitutional by the Supreme Court) in a dispute which concerned the extent to which steel companies should be allowed to pass on, in higher prices, the cost of wage increases approved by the Wage Stabilization Board. Craufurd Goodwin and R. Stanley Herren, "The Truman Administration," in *Exhortation and Controls: The Search for a Wage-Price Policy, 1945–1971,* ed. Craufurd Goodwin (Washington: Brookings Institution, 1975). Labor representatives also resigned from the Pay Board during Phase II of the Nixon administration's stabilization program. Arnold Weber, "Making Wage Controls Work," 30 *The Public Interest,* 28 (Winter, 1973).

[4] See Marshall Clinard, *The Black Market* (New York: Rinehart, 1952).

even when the guideposts were shattered by wage and price increases during the war in Vietnam, the Johnson administration did not seriously consider imposition of mandatory price and wage controls. President Nixon, too, repeatedly proclaimed his aversion to mandatory price and wage controls, as the wartime inflation persisted throughout the first two years of his administration.[5]

In 1970, however, patience with the orthodox antidotes to inflation was wearing thin in many quarters. Despite a pronounced slump in employment, industrial production, and construction, wages and prices continued to rise. The Federal Reserve Board's tight monetary policy seemed to be retarding economic recovery without stopping inflation. The conservative Business Council condemned the administration for failure to take more aggressive action against excessive wage and price increases. Congress passed the Economic Stabilization Act of 1970, which granted the president virtually unlimited discretion to impose direct legal controls, authorizing him to "issue such orders as he may deem appropriate to stabilize prices, rents, wages, and salaries."[6]

President Nixon at first proclaimed his disinclination to use his new statutory powers. In March 1971, however, he relied upon the act to establish the Construction Industry Stabilization Board to review and set aside labor agreements which provided for benefit increases "not supportable by productivity improvements and costs of living trends."[7] During the late spring and summer of 1971, pressures mounted for extension of similar controls to the rest of the economy, as large wage increases (10 percent annually) were announced in several basic metals industries. The Wholesale Price Index spurted upward. The nation's traditionally favorable balance of trade slipped into a serious and growing deficit, and there were large movements from the dollar into other currencies.[8]

In this uncomfortable posture, mandatory price and wage controls had some appeal even for an administration reluctant to use them. By artificially holding down domestic prices and wages, they could bolster the positive effect that a devaluation of the dollar would have on the balance of trade. Controls would also make possible a more stimulative monetary and fiscal

---

[5] William Barber, "The Kennedy Years: Purposeful Pedagogy," James Cochrane, "The Johnson Administration: Moral Suasion Goes to War," and Neil De Marchi, "The First Nixon Administration: Prelude to Controls," in *Exhortation and Controls,* ed. Goodwin.

[6] The President's orders, the act provided, were enforceable by injunction, and violations were subject to penalties of up to $5,000 each. 84 Stat. 799 (1970).

[7] Executive Order 11588, quoted in De Marchi, "The First Nixon Administration," p. 332.

[8] See Leonard Silk, *Nixonomics* (New York: Frederick Praeger, 1972); Ezra Soloman, *The Anxious Economy* (San Francisco: W. H. Freeman, 1975) (for an analysis of the roots of the inflation and trade deficit); and De Marchi, "The First Nixon Administration," pp. 338–348.

policy. Finally, they would provide a signal to the international economic community, to American business and labor, and to the electorate at large that the Nixon administration was sincerely committed to do something about inflation. And so on August 15, 1971, President Nixon appeared on television to proclaim a "new economic policy." The convertibility of dollars into gold was suspended (in effect permitting devaluation). He announced a temporary surtax on all imports and proposed tax credits to stimulate investment. Finally, the president stated, he had signed an executive order imposing a ninety-day freeze, backed by legal sanctions, on all prices, rents, wages, and salaries.

However, this venture into governmental regulation of prices and wages, the president emphasized, was to be a temporary expedient, a short detour from the straight road to an unregulated economy. The basic goal, he said, was to stop inflation without the "establishment of a huge price control bureaucracy" and "without the mandatory price and wage controls that crush economic and personal freedom."[9]

THE FREEZE AGENCIES: THE INITIAL STRUCTURE

The administrative structure created to implement the freeze reflected its reluctant genesis. Of primary importance was the Nixon administration's conception of the control program as a temporary and technical measure, rather than the beginning of a major commitment to centralized economic control and planning. If the controls were not envisaged as a major shift of power to the federal government or a device to redistribute income or restructure the economy, their implementation would require neither a large professional staff nor a large coercive apparatus. The freeze would be administered simply and enforced by persuasion and cooperation. In keeping with this conception, there had been virtually no advance administrative preparation. Only a handful of officials had prior knowledge of the freeze, for secrecy was thought necessary to forestall preemptive price and wage in-

---

[9] The text of the president's message is in Cost of Living Council, *Economic Stabilization Program Quarterly Report, August 15–December 31, 1971* (Washington: Government Printing Office, 1972), pp. 115–118. Executive Order No. 11615, 36 *Federal Register* 1527 (August 17, 1971) is reproduced in that report also.

The Economic Stabilization Program in fact lasted slightly over two and one-half years. The freeze was followed in November 1971 by Phase II. Phase III, beginning in January 1973, saw a substantial relaxation of controls, and a substantial rise in the inflation rate. A second freeze, only sixty days long, was announced in June 1973. The ensuing Phase IV rules were tighter than Phase III, but gradually exempted most sectors of the economy until the statutory authorization for the program expired, with the administration's willing consent, on April 30, 1974. See Marvin Kosters, *Controls and Inflation* (Washington: American Enterprise Institute, 1975), ch. 2.

creases. No plans for a new agency existed. No staff had been recruited to begin study of the policy issues, to establish mechanisms for monitoring the extent or effect of compliance, or to draw upon the experience of participants in the World War II or Korean War freezes. Rather, the approach was improvisational. In a flurry of last-minute activity, the leadership, administrators, and office space for the freeze agencies were borrowed from other federal agencies. To use Alvin Toffler's apt term, they were an "adhocracy."[10]

The president's executive order assigned primary policy-making responsibility to the Cost of Living Council (CLC). That body was designed, it would appear, to reassure the public that the controls would be administered in a "reasonable," evenhanded way. CLC's membership included an array of cabinet members ostensibly attentive to the interests of a broad range of competing, cross-checking constituencies—Treasury Secretary John Connally (chairman), Secretary of Agriculture Clifford Hardin, Secretary of Commerce Maurice Stans, Secretary of Labor James Hodgson, and Special Assistant to the President for Consumer Affairs Virginia Knauer.[11] Second, seats were assigned to professional economists with high government posts—Paul McCracken, chairman of the Council of Economic Advisers; George Schultz, director of the Office of Management and Budget; and Arthur Burns, chairman of the Federal Reserve Board. So composed, CLC was not a body of opinionated experts in price and wage regulation and certainly not a body that seemed dedicated to any radical movement toward government planning and control. It was a group of economic generalists and administrators, ideologically close to the president in their skepticism about massive governmental regulation, politically sensitive to traditional concerns and interests. The secretaries of Labor and Commerce could be assigned to seek voluntary cooperation from their respective constituencies, and, despite a few expressions of mistrust by AFL-CIO leader George Meany, they met with considerable success.

To formulate day-to-day substantive policy, CLC established a small executive committee with a more "expert" cast. "ExComm," as it was called, included Paul McCracken, Under-secretary of the Treasury Charls Walker, the director of the Office of Emergency Preparedness (General George Lincoln, a former political science professor at West Point), and the director of the CLC staff (Arnold Weber, a former professor of labor economics at the University of Chicago). CLC's small staff, never exceeding forty-five, con-

---

[10] Alvin Toffler, *Future Shock* (New York: Random House, 1970). On the preparations for administration, see Arnold Weber, *In Pursuit of Price Stability* (Washington: Brookings Institution, 1973).

[11] Later, George Romney, secretary of the Department of Housing and Urban Development, was added to CLC.

sisted of economists, lawyers, administrative personnel, and press relations people borrowed from other federal agencies, such as the Office of Management and Budget, the Treasury Department, and the Department of Labor.

Immediately, CLC delegated the job of implementing the freeze—disseminating the rules, answering the public's questions, monitoring compliance—to a small agency in the Executive Office of the President, the Office of Emergency Preparedness (OEP). Despite its promising name, OEP was hardly prepared for this kind of emergency. Previously, OEP's principal tasks had been coordination of relief during natural disasters, economic planning for potential national emergencies, management of stockpiled strategic materials, and administration of the oil import program. OEP did have three assets. It had ten regional offices linked to Washington by an excellent communications system. It had only 300 employees, and was therefore in no way reminiscent of the gigantic bureaucracies of prior price control programs, such as the 65,000-person OPA during World War II. Finally, OEP was not clearly identified with any constituency; it was likely to be seen as politically neutral.[12] The OEP leadership, under General George Lincoln, was heavily weighted toward military officers of an academic cast, but the main burden of day-to-day administration fell to OEP's staff of recruits borrowed from other agencies—a mixed bag of older, expendable civil servants, young military officers, government interns, and inexperienced lawyers. If any generalizations can be applied to this hastily assembled pickup team, it would be that they were reasonably well-educated but not brilliant, neither dedicated nor hostile to the idea of wage-price controls, without prior knowledge of the subject, and without ambitions for careers in the presumably temporary program.

The pressure of events soon proved too much for CLC and OEP alone. More help was needed, and more agencies were incorporated into the jerry-built freeze administration, most notably the sprawling network of Internal Revenue Service offices. The freeze agencies ultimately were shaped less by the administration's preconceptions than by the problems inherent in the management of the freeze. Before describing the agencies and their operations in any further detail, therefore, it will be helpful to analyze the demands and pressures to which they responded.

THE SOCIAL IMPACT OF THE FREEZE ORDER

Every new law, by its mere announcement, generates a set of demands for legal rulings, clarifications of the rights and obligations created by the newly

---

[12] See Harry Yoshpe et al., *Stemming Inflation: The Office of Emergency Preparedness and the 90-day Freeze* (Washington: Government Printing Office, 1972).

established law. The nature and number of those demands, however, and hence the day-to-day work of the legal agency that must make those rulings, are variable. They arise, as we will see with respect to the freeze order, from the characteristics of the new law, the ways in which it impinges upon the preexisting social order.[13]

Breadth of Jurisdiction

The freeze order applied to millions of individuals and business firms and a countless number of transactions. In this regard, it contrasted with regulatory laws that apply to one particular industry, thereby addressing a much smaller audience of firms. It also differed from laws that apply across many industries but refer to relatively infrequent transactions, such as the sale of new issues of corporate securities.

Moreover, the freeze order applied to virtually all the transactions engaged in by each regulated firm: it controlled not only the prices the firm charged, but the charges *to* the firm by its employees, its landlord, and its suppliers, and to the transactions of its competitors in related industries as well. The freeze agencies, consequently, had greater capacities for control than agencies that regulate only the prices charged by a firm for certain products or services, but not its cost factors or the actions of competing firms outside the agency's jurisdiction.

Restrictiveness and Cost of Compliance

The freeze order cut sharply into established norms and patterns of behavior. It demanded a suspension of the normal course of marketplace activity. It abridged the traditional freedom to seek higher wages and prices for services and products. It regulated action strongly believed to be properly within the autonomous control of management or of the collective bargaining process. Moreover, the cost of compliance with the freeze order's restrictions would be substantial. It commanded businesses to forego price increases that would make a difference between profit and loss. Households denied expected wage increases would, in many cases, experience a serious financial pinch. In this regard, the freeze order contrasted with regulatory enactments that simply codify the dominant normative beliefs and practices of a community and impose significant restrictions only on the deviant few.

On the other hand, the freeze order did not call for truly radical changes in

---

[13] While the Economic Stabilization Act of 1970 was technically the "authorizing law" for the freeze agencies, that act was totally without content and had no effect in itself. It merely authorized the president to legislate in the price and wage area. Hence the president's executive order of August 15, 1971, referred to here as the "freeze order," was in effect the operative legislation—the "new law"—creating immediate rights and obligations for citizens and guidance for the freeze agencies.

behavior, new techniques of production, or new and costly investments. It did not call for any fundamental redistribution of income or wealth or decision-making power *among* private groups. It called only for deferral of increases in income, applicable equally to all groups, and for a seemingly limited time period. According to nationwide opinion polls in December 1971, the restrictions called for by the freeze were generally regarded as legitimate—a harsh medicine, but worth taking for the future health of the system.[14] In this regard, the freeze order differed from restrictive regulations, the Volstead Act's prohibition against sales of alcoholic beverages being an extreme case, that are regarded as fundamentally unjust or illegitimate by a substantial portion of the regulated public, and it differed from laws, such as the Wagner Act, that threaten to produce a major redistribution of power or wealth.

Visibility of Noncompliance

Many regulatory laws restrict business practices that take place in secret, such as agreements in restraint of trade, or that cannot be seen by "victims," such as the use of dangerous chemicals in food processing. Similarly, where a law prohibits racial discrimination in employment but allows employers to insist upon bona fide occupational qualifications, a black person denied a job on grounds he is not qualified cannot easily discern whether that is so and whether the qualifications mentioned are also applied to white applicants.[15] Under these kinds of laws, illegal behavior is not readily and positively identifiable by those motivated to complain. For the most part, violators are vulnerable only to active governmental inspection or investigation.

The freeze order, by contrast, dealt with highly visible behavior. A market system relies on open communication of price increases. The changes are memorialized by enduring evidence, such as invoices and price tags. A price increase, be it legal or illegal, is not hidden from its "victims." More importantly, under the highly specific terms of the freeze order, the observer or recipient of a price increase was in a good position to ascertain its legal validity, because the freeze order regulated prices on a product-by-product basis according to an objective and visible standard—the price in effect for the same product prior to the freeze. In Phase II of the same Economic Stabilization Program, by contrast, the regulations forbade any price hikes that increased the seller's profit margin for his business as a whole; whether a price increase on any particular product was illegal, therefore, could not be ascertained without knowing all the seller's costs and hence without an examination of his financial records over an extended period.

---

[14] Yoshpe, *Stemming Inflation*, pp. 143–145.

[15] See Leon Mayhew, *Law and Equal Opportunity* (Cambridge, Mass.: Harvard University Press, 1968).

Mobilization and Voluntary Compliance

Because the population regulated by the freeze order was large, because the new law cut sharply into prior economic practices, and because violations were so visible, the freeze order was "mobilized," or called into play, at a very high rate.[16] It did not lie dormant in the *United States Code,* in the *Federal Register,* or in the libraries of law firms. The agencies were not forced into interaction with only a narrow segment of a single industry. Rather, the order was frequently, indeed incessantly, invoked by workers, consumers, and businessmen from all sectors of the economy. They urged the agencies to enforce the freeze against violators, to issue official interpretations of the freeze order, and to grant exceptions. Moreover, because of the economic significance of the order, newspapers, television networks, and trade magazines devoted extensive coverage to the program; this in turn produced a very high level of public awareness of the freeze.[17] This awareness, in combination with the visibility of noncompliance, led potential violators in all segments of the economy—sellers, employers, landlords—to try to forestall complaints by obtaining advance information about the terms of the law.

The freeze order's breadth of coverage, together with the restrictiveness of the behavior it demanded, also created a potentially impossible enforcement problem for the agencies. Even if agency officials initially had been oriented toward coercive enforcement, a high level of compliance could in fact be achieved only if most businesses *voluntarily* complied with the order. This fact, as we will explore in more detail later, dominated the consciousness of agency officials. Together, the high rate of mobilization and the forced dependence on voluntary methods of gaining compliance molded the decision processes adopted by the agencies.

THE LEGAL DECISION PROCESS

Decision making in a legal institution can be seen as occurring in four stages: the acquisition of a routine case load, decision of routine cases, activation of the policy-making process, and policy formulation. At each stage, the decision process can vary in degree of formality, and in terms of

---

[16] See Donald Black, "The Mobilization of Law," 2 *Journal of Legal Studies* 125 (1973), for an analysis of how legal agencies are affected by the way law is invoked or mobilized. Albert J. Reiss, Jr., *The Police and the Public* (New Haven, Conn.: Yale University Press, 1971) and Mayhew, *Law and Equal Opportunity,* are empirical studies that focus on the same subject.

[17] According to Yoshpe, *Stemming Inflation,* p. 146: "Public knowledge of the freeze was measured by Sindlinger & Co. to be 96 percent; the same firm found only 94 percent who were aware of the first moon trip." Even if the 96 percent figure is not credible, it does indicate remarkably broad and rapid diffusion of awareness of the freeze.

whether the agency proactively initiates the process or is more reactive and passive.[18] These concepts provide benchmarks for analyzing the legal decision process established by the freeze agencies.

Acquisition of Routine Cases: Inquiries and Complaints

Within hours after the public announcement of the order, CLC and OEP officials were besieged by telephone calls, telegrams, and letters. They came from trade associations, labor unions, and business corporations, from state and local government officials and congressional staff members, from individual wage earners, tenants, and consumers. These demands for action became the routine case load of the agencies. There were three kinds.

First were *complaints of violations*, primarily by ultimate consumers. They alleged, for example, that a retailer or gas station or insurance company had violated the freeze by increasing prices or that a landlord had illegally increased the rent. They demanded that the agency see to it that the increases were rolled back or the complainant's money refunded. Second, there were *inquiries*, requests for an official opinion or ruling concerning the requirements of the freeze as applied to a specific situation or transaction. Did the order ban the annual cost-of-living wage adjustment built into the collective bargaining agreement covering Ford Motor Company's assembly plant workers? Did it apply to the price of chemicals sold for shipment to Japan? Could a landlord increase the rent if he put new screens and storm windows in an apartment? Most inquiries sought agency permission for a planned price or wage increase, a letter from the agency that would serve as a declaratory judgment which could be used to justify the planned increases to any challengers. Some inquirers, however, were in the posture of complainant: they sought an official ruling that they could use to block increases threatened or demanded by their suppliers or landlords or employees. Third, there were *requests for exceptions*. Whereas an inquiry asked or argued for an interpretation of the order as it applied to a specific case, an exception request acknowledged that the desired wage, price, or rent increase was prohibited as a matter of freeze law as previously articulated, but asked for an exception on grounds of hardship as a matter of administrative compassion.

The volume of inquiries far overshadowed the other types of cases. According to official OEP records, some 50,000 complaints of violations and 6,000 requests for exceptions were processed in the ninety days of the freeze. But even these enormous figures shrink to insignificance beside the 750,000 inquiries which were received and answered by the agencies. The average weekly volume of inquiries remained close to 85,000 for almost the entire freeze period. Responding to inquiries became the preeminent work of the

---

[18] The terms *reactive* and *proactive* are taken from Black, "The Mobilization of Law" and Reiss, *The Police and the Public.*

agencies. Creation and maintenance of an efficient inquiry-response system became the principal organizational task.[19]

This was in part a deliberate choice. Legal agencies do have some capacity to control their case loads. They can establish priorities, reject or divert some requests for legal decision, and concentrate their energies on the cases and issues they think most important. In Phase II of the Economic Stabilization Program, business firms were divided into categories by size; the very largest corporations were required to submit detailed price and wage reports, and for the most part, the Price Commission and Pay Board focused only on those economic giants. Some agencies concentrate on problems identified not by complainants but by their own inspectors, who look for only the most serious breaches of agency rules. The freeze agencies, however, made no such investment in proactive enforcement and case selection.[20] The *continued* high volume of inquiries reflected their deliberate choice to welcome and be responsive to all inquiries, regardless of their economic importance. They did so because reactive inquiry-response was seen as a major enforcement strategy. Prompt response to all inquiries, it was assumed, was necessary to retain public support; an inquirer whose questions were not answered quickly might be alienated and more likely to evade the freeze. In addition, to be open to inquiries would help officials identify problem areas that could be made the basis of broader public education campaigns.

To facilitate rapid inquiry-response, OEP moved its regional offices from

---

[19] Official OEP records indicated that a total of almost 1,000,000 inquiries were answered during the freeze. A sample of the files in OEP's Washington office, however, indicated that 21 percent of the 24,000 letters and telegrams handled by that office and recorded as inquiries were merely protests, statements of opinion, or rhetorical questions. If that 21 percent figure were extrapolated to the entire reported total, the number of "true inquiries" would be reduced to 750,000 or 800,000.

By comparison, all the United States District Courts combined decided about 60,000 cases in the entire year of 1971. The State of New York processed 1,908,000 initial claims for unemployment compensation in that year, a rate of administrative legal judgments similar to that of the freeze agencies. *Statistical Abstract of the United States,* 93rd ed. (1972). The Internal Revenue Service in that year audited 1,650,000 tax returns, handled 35,000 requests for written interpretive rulings and 27,000,000 telephone or walk-in requests for taxpayer information. IRS, *Annual Report of the Commissioner, Fiscal 1971* (Washington: Government Printing Office, 1972).

[20] As a gesture toward proactive case selection, IRS agents were instructed to make spot checks of compliance with freeze rules in the course of their income tax audit rounds. Yoshpe, *Stemming Inflation,* ch. VI. However, the agencies' case load remained overwhelmingly citizen-generated. The problems resulting from that posture for other kinds of agencies are detailed in Alfred Blumrosen and Leonard Zeitz, "Anti-discrimination Laws in Action in New Jersey: A Law-Sociology Study," 19 *Rutgers Law Review* 184 (1963), Earl Johnson, *Justice and Reform: The Formative Years of the OEO Legal Services Program* (New York: Russell Sage Foundation, 1974); Douglas Rosenthal, Robert Kagan, and Debra Quatrone, *Volunteer Lawyers for the Poor: New York's CLO Program* (New York: Russell Sage Foundation, 1971).

suburban locations to new quarters in large cities and recruited personnel from other federal agencies. Its Washington staff mushroomed from 230 to 415, and its regional offices from 70 to 390. Even so, the backlog of unanswered inquiries quickly mounted. Other federal agencies were added to the team. OEP delegated front line responsibility for answering telephone inquiries to the Internal Revenue Service, with its 360 regional and district offices and thousands of employees. IRS was also given primary responsibility for investigation of complaints of violations. Simple inquiries that came to OEP or CLC in Washington by mail were referred to other federal departments—those related to wages, for example, were sent to the Department of Labor, routine price inquiries to Commerce, and uncomplicated queries about rents to HUD. Dedication to responsiveness thus transformed the small, centralized CLC and OEP staffs in Washington into the headquarters of a large, decentralized network of offices.[21]

Decision in Routine Cases:
Ex Parte Presentations and the Regime of Rules

Every complaint of a violation and every inquiry posed both a question of fact and a question of policy. A complaint would charge that a seller had illegally increased the price of Brand X. The question of fact was whether the seller had in fact increased the price during the freeze—perhaps he had increased it prior to the freeze and the complainant did not know that; perhaps the complainant had Brand X confused with the seller's other product, Brand Y; perhaps the seller *had* increased the price and claimed that he had not. The question of policy was whether, once the actual price changes in Brand X had been established, they should be allowed. Unlike complaints of violations, inquiries tended to be presented as questions of policy only. They took the form, "I sell Brand X. I announced a price increase on August 10, effective August 20. Under the freeze, which was announced on August 15, can I charge the higher price?" But in telling him "yes" or "no," an agency official implicitly had to judge whether the facts presented by the inquirer were true. For example, had the seller really announced the price increase on August 10?

Legal institutions employ a variety of procedures to deal with questions of fact, such as inspection or investigation by agency officials, adversarial hearings in which all interested parties participate, or simple acceptance of facts as asserted by the citizen or organization seeking a legal ruling. In the freeze

---

[21] Overall, the staff of the agencies most directly responsible for freeze administration—CLC, OEP, and the IRS Economic Stabilization Division—amounted to about 2,500 full-time workers. This figure was larger than most federal regulatory agencies—the ICC at the time had 1,800 and the CAB, 660—but it was much smaller than agencies, such as the IRS (70,000) and the OPA during World War II (65,000). See Roger Noll, *Reforming Regulation* (Washington: Brookings Institution, 1971), pp. 83 ff.

agencies, *complaints of violations* triggered an investigation by an IRS agent. Usually he simply telephoned the alleged violator and questioned him; if he felt it necessary, he visited the respondent's place of business and examined his records.[22] A series of formal procedures, however, stood between the investigation and the imposition of legal penalties. The alleged violator was first asked to give his version of the facts. If the IRS agent found a violation, the case was referred to OEP for review, and then to the Department of Justice for prosecution in a United States District Court. This route to prosecution and formal adjudication was rarely utilized, however. In 62 percent of the thousands of investigations, the IRS determined that there had been no violation. In most of the remainder, there was no dispute: the seller or landlord freely admitted violation and agreed to roll back his price or rent immediately. Only 214 cases developed into serious enough disputes to be forwarded to OEP for review. Ultimately only eight lawsuits were filed against recalcitrant violators. Hence, as in many other regulatory systems, while a formal adversarial procedure for the resolution of disputes and imposition of penalties was provided, the overwhelming proportion of cases was resolved informally, not through adjudicatory hearings, but by investigation of the facts by an agency employee.[23]

The agencies' approach to fact-finding for *inquiries* was even more informal. They sought to avoid all formal procedures and their usual corollaries—expense and delay. Persons or firms seeking a ruling from the OEP, for example, needed only to send a letter describing their situation and asking what the freeze order required. They did not have to hire attorneys, give notice to other parties who might be affected by their actions, or fill out special forms. They were not required to submit testimony or affidavits to certify the truth of the facts stated in their inquiries. This meant, of course, that there was no opportunity for adversarial confrontation between a landlord seeking permission for a rent increase and his tenants or between sellers and their customers. There was no opportunity for the agency officials to cross-examine the inquirer face-to-face. Almost all inquiries were decided on the basis of unverified ex parte presentations.[24] In agencies that stress en-

---

[22] The executive order required every business to "maintain available for public inspection a record of the highest prices or rents charged . . . during the thirty-day period ending August 14, 1971."

[23] See, e.g., Mayhew, *Law and Equal Opportunity* and Blumrosen and Zeitz, "Anti-discrimination Laws."

[24] For an example of what happened when other interested parties contested an ex parte ruling, see the Cincinnati Transit Case, pp. 130–132 herein.

It is important to recognize that decision on the basis of facts as asserted is not at all an unusual procedure. Such "advisory opinions" are regularly given by the IRS, see *Annual Report of the Commissioner;* and by the Securities and Exchange Commission, and other agencies. See Lewis Lowenfels, "SEC No-Action Letters," 59 *Virginia Law Review* 303 (1973). See generally, Glen Robinson and Ernest Gellhorn, *The Administrative Process* (St. Paul, Minn.: West Publishing Co., 1974), pp. 524–528, 785–790.

forcement, investigation, or adversarial confrontation, the greater part of official energy is devoted to resolution of factual issues. In the freeze agencies' inquiry-response system, as in appellate courts, the focus was almost exclusively on questions of policy or law, because the facts in each case were taken as given.

With respect to questions of policy, too, the agencies sought to avoid procedures that increased the risk of delay. Their goal was to have officials in the field offices issue rulings immediately. Concern for voluntary compliance, however, suggested that inquiry-responses should be not only prompt but consistent. Ad hoc policy decisions by the numerous, hastily recruited officials in the field, resulting in different decisions for similar cases, would invite mistrust of the fairness of the program, it was feared, and loss of public support. Lower-level officials, in fact, demanded definitive guidance from their superiors. A memo from an OEP staff member, for example, urged CLC to issue statements on certain policy issues, adding,

> If the Cost of Living Council won't answer these few questions, then how can the telephone operators and correspondents hope to answer the hundred questions they have? People want answers that are quick and responsive . . . uncertainty, delay and ambiguity and inconsistency cause the most trouble. They not only frustrate and anger the public, but they also aggravate our problems of getting the freeze to work effectively and efficiently.[25]

In response, CLC and ExComm met each day to formulate detailed written rules, articulating freeze policy with respect to a growing list of specific situations. Copies of the freeze order and CLC rules were disseminated to lower-level officials, who inserted them in loose-leaf manuals called Stabilization Program Guidelines and referred to them for answers to the inquiries they received. The inquiry-response system thus became a regime of rules in which policy questions were routinely transformed into questions of "correct" rule application. Formally, there was little scope for discretion or policy judgment on the part of the inquiry-response officials.

Activation of the Policy-making Process

Agency leaders recognized that the CLC rules would not provide clear and adequate answers for all inquiries. Novel situations would be presented, circumstances that did not seem to be covered by existing rules. In still other cases, it would not be clear which rule applied. In sum, freeze officials mentally divided the universe of inquiries into "easy cases" and "hard cases." Easy cases were to be decided by routine rule application. Hard cases, it was thought, demanded a more knowing, authoritative interpretation of the policy behind the rule or perhaps the formulation of a new policy or rule;

---

[25] ExComm Minutes, August 25, 1971.

indeed they were often referred to as "policy questions." To deal with them, a hierarchy of offices was established; successively "higher" offices were to specialize in progressively "harder" inquiries.

The transformation of a case into an occasion for more complex analysis or policy reformulation can be handled in a variety of ways. In most court systems, those decisions are made by private litigants; they appeal a lower-level decision at their own initiative and expense and ask higher-level judges for a change in law or policy. At the other extreme, selection of cases for policy making may be made only by high-level officials who systematically review lower-level decisions or patterns of results. In the freeze agencies, the process was predominantly one of *voluntary upward referral* by officials in the front line inquiry-response offices.[26]

In schematic form, the inquiry-response hierarchy operated as follows.

1) Primary responsibility for answering telephone inquiries was vested in local IRS and regional OEP offices. Written inquiries were handled by OEP's regional and national offices; they established Correspondence Sections to answer the routine ones.[27] The great majority of inquiries were answered, direct to the inquirer, by the initial office.

2) Whenever a front line official was uncertain as to a correct response to an inquiry under CLC rules, he was to refer it to higher level. IRS offices referred such hard questions to OEP regional offices. If the OEP regional office thought that the inquiry was particularly novel or legally difficult, it sent the question by telex to OEP's Washington office, where it was answered by OEP's Operations Center, with a review by the National OEP General Counsel's Office. Similarly, an inquiry sent by mail to the Correspondence Section in OEP national, if thought to involve difficult questions of rule application, was referred to the General Counsel's Office. Inquirers who expressed dissatisfaction with initial responses received from IRS or OEP's regional offices were told to write to the OEP national office for an official interpretive ruling.

3) The OEP General Counsel's Office was the final authority on questions of rule interpretation in specific cases. It issued almost 3,000 interpretive rulings in the course of the freeze. These responses, like those made directly by lower offices, were not published or distributed throughout the inquiry-response system but were transmitted to the inquirer only. Only responses by CLC or its Executive Committee (ExComm) were published and transmitted throughout the system, and thus only they were known and treated as rules.

4) When OEP lawyers could not agree as to the legally correct answer to an

---

[26] The appropriate analogy, with respect to courts, is the relatively infrequent practice whereby lower court judges on their own initiative "certify" questions of law to appellate courts when they feel they are sufficiently novel or difficult.

[27] The Correspondence Section in the OEP national office in Washington referred the very simplest written inquiries it received to other federal agencies—Labor, Treasury, Commerce, HUD, HEW.

inquiry under existing CLC rules or when another OEP national official encountered an inquiry seemingly not covered by existing rules, it would be
labeled a "policy question" and referred to OEP's Policy Analysis Office. Officials there made a judgment as to the importance of the issue, rejecting some,
sometimes combining separate inquiries that raised similar issues. They then
drafted an issue paper stating arguments for and against alternative answers to
the policy question and transmitted it to the Cost of Living Council for final
resolution.

5) Most policy issues referred to CLC were decided by ExComm, released
promptly to the press in the form of a question and answer and disseminated
throughout the inquiry-response system as a Stabilization Program Guideline.
The ExComm response was also rewritten in the declaratory form of a legal
regulation by the OEP General Counsel's Office and published in the *Federal
Register*.[28] Policy questions which ExComm considered particularly important
and politically sensitive were referred to the entire Cost of Living Council.
Altogether about 75 of the 415 rules issued by CLC during the freeze were
decided upon by the full council.

Of course, there were many exceptions to this general pattern. Some inquirers leapfrogged lower levels of the hierarchy by addressing their letters to
higher officials whom they or their lawyers knew personally. Congressmen and
newsmen talked on the telephone directly to public affairs officers at CLC
and OEP. Occasionally a department head, such as the secretary of Labor or
Commerce, thought that an inquiry addressed to his agency was particularly
significant and took it straight to CLC. For the vast majority of inquiries,
however, the general scheme outlined above and set forth graphically in
Figure 1 was followed.

The internal referral system in the inquiry-response hierarchy was the key
to the development of a body of increasingly specific rules, redefining and
tailoring the initial freeze order to the special problems of different industries
and trades. This adaptability was dependent on the ability of lower-level
decision makers to pick out routine inquiries that exposed vagueness or
rigidity in the existing body of rules and to transform those inquiries into
occasions for the elaboration of policy. On the other hand, to avoid overload
at the top of the system, it was necessary for the lower levels to filter out
unmeritorious demands for rule changes and treat them as matters of routine
rule application. Unlike systems that rely on litigants to activate policy
making by means of formal appeals and unlike systems that depend on
systematic review by superiors to keep the rules adaptive, the informal freeze
agency system necessarily relied upon the good judgment, conscience, and
dedication of lower and middle-level officials.

---

[28] Commerce Clearing House, a major legal publisher, established a Stabilization Program
Reporter, containing all the CLC rules.

Figure 1. CLC-OEP-IRS Inquiry-Response System

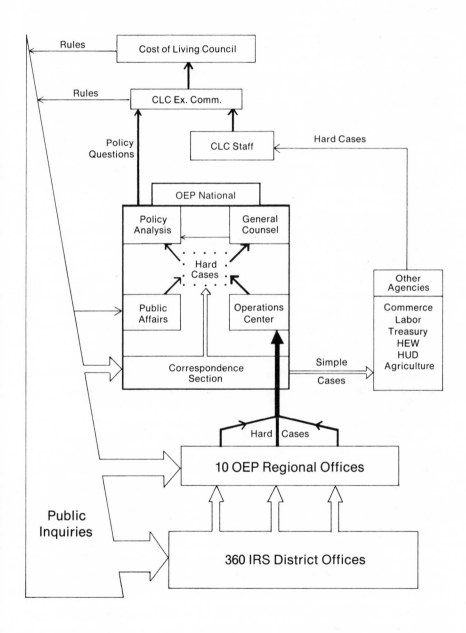

Policy Formulation

The dominant characteristics of the policy formulation process in the agencies were its emphasis on speed and its "closed" procedures. CLC and ExComm issued forty-nine questions and answers in the first week of the freeze, and 415 rules in the ninety-day period. Any delay in explication of the law of the freeze, they apparently thought, would alienate the regulated public or induce noncompliance. The procedures for policy formulation reflected this concern. It was an informal, rapid-fire, in-house operation. The inquirer whose problems and arguments had prodded lower-level officials to refer the case to CLC was not invited to participate in their deliberations, nor were firms or individuals who might have opposed the inquirer's position. Proposed rules were not published in advance of adoption for comment by the affected public.[29] There were no regularized procedures for consulting relevant government and academic experts or advisory committees of industry members. In sum, all of the formal mechanisms commonly employed to discover available policy alternatives and their likely impact—adversarial procedure, public hearings, multiple advocacy by experts, consultation with affected groups—were rejected on grounds that "there isn't time."

The sole attempt to produce more systematic analysis of policy problems was the staff-prepared issue paper, a device adopted some two weeks into the freeze. For the first two weeks, ExComm met each morning to consider a stack of proposed questions and answers. They were drafted for the most part by the OEP Policy Analysis Office in response to problems referred upward through the inquiry-response system. If the four ExComm members and the few aides who attended the sessions with them had doubts about the proposed answer, they sent it back to the staff for reconsideration. An OEP staff member then drafted an issue paper that included alternative answers or rules with the best arguments he could think of for or against each option. He usually consulted his colleagues. Sometimes he telephoned experts in other federal agencies or the inquirer whose problem generated the question, but that was done on an ad hoc basis. Eventually, the OEP Policy Analysis Office began to prepare issue papers in advance of every ExComm decision, and that procedure gradually brought greater order and deliberation to the rule-making process. Nevertheless, the process remained highly informal. There was little time for CLC members to read the issue papers. Minutes of the fast-paced deliberations were not kept, nor were votes recorded. CLC mem-

---

[29] The Federal Administrative Procedure Act, which has provisions requiring agencies to publish proposed regulations and consider the public's reactions in writing or at a public hearing, makes an exception for "interpretive rules" and situations where "the agency for good cause finds . . . that notice and public procedure thereon are impracticable, unnecessary, or contrary to the public interest." 5 *U.S.C.* Sec. 553. The CLC rules, issued under the time pressure of the freeze, arguably came within both exceptions.

bers did not write and publish opinions explaining or justifying decisions. Lawyers played a very minimal role in the deliberations and in drafting the decisions reached.

This kind of informal, rapid policy-making process generated great risks of inconsistency and of rules that would sweep too broadly, literally covering and calling for unintended results in transactions not envisioned by CLC. One hedge against these risks was to limit the scope and the authoritativeness of CLC rules. The questions and answers issued to the press and even the redrafted rules inserted in the *Federal Register* were not regulations with the force of law, it was stated, but only "policy guidance." (Their ultimate legal status was never fully clarified, although for the most part they were used internally and accepted by the public as binding regulations.) After the initial policy decisions during the first week or so of the freeze, most CLC rules were carefully limited to the facts involved in specific inquiries. They read much more like abstracts of court opinions than broadly applicable statutes or regulations.

CONCLUSION: THE SOURCES OF LEGAL STRUCTURE

To summarize the preceding account of the agencies' legal process, their overall posture was reactive. They dealt unselectively with a huge case load of questions concerning the applicability of the freeze order to specific situations. It was a case load selected by citizens, rather than by official priorities. The formal structure of inquiry-response was bureaucratic. Policy-making authority was formally vested in the Cost of Living Council, a body of appointed political officials and economists. Authority to answer routine inquiries was delegated to a decentralized but hierarchically coordinated network of offices, bound to follow written rules promulgated by CLC. Inquiries perceived as hard cases, not adequately answered by the rules, were referred to higher levels for more authoritative interpretation or sent to CLC for the promulgation of new and more carefully tailored rules.

The fact-finding and rule-making procedures, by contrast, were extremely informal. Individual cases were decided on the basis of unverified ex parte statements of fact presented by the inquirer. There were no provisions for public participation or comment on proposed rules, none of the careful economic study that would be called for by the expert model of regulation. CLC took little time for deliberation and did not justify its decisions by written opinions or statements of principle.

How does such a configuration of decision methods come about? Most regulatory agencies, Kenneth C. Davis asserts in a widely discussed study, refuse to formulate policy in the form of fixed and detailed rules.[30] The

---

[30] Kenneth C. Davis, *Discretionary Justice* (Urbana: University of Illinois Press, 1971).

uncertainties involved in taking a stand induce them to rely on discretionary judgment, decisions closely attuned to the factual details of each particular case. Why then would the freeze agencies, embarking upon a new regulatory program, create a regime of explicit substantive rules?

One contributing factor was the sheer volume of cases which the agencies had to decide—a product of the breadth, novelty, and financial impact of the law which they administered. Rules could provide guidance for the hundreds of officials who were recruited to answer the public's inquiries. But some agencies with a large case load do not rely heavily on formal rule application; like crowded urban courts, they do not hire hundreds of front line "judges," but make applicants for legal rulings wait or encourage them to negotiate their own dispositions. Two additional factors, therefore, stood behind the freeze agencies' emphasis on rules: (1) their felt compulsion to resolve cases both promptly and consistently, and (2) their desire to communicate official policy to the public quickly by articulating and disseminating it in the form of clear instructions. The goals of consistency and communication are shared, of course, by most regulatory systems, but in some they are especially crucial. Under a freeze—as with other laws that call for real sacrifices—a high level of compliance is both problematic and absolutely essential. Business firms left in the dark about their obligations might go ahead and increase prices; the perception of noncompliance in some sectors could lead to snowballing evasion. In that posture, freeze officials intuitively believed the requirements of the new law must be communicated clearly, specifically, and rapidly and in such fashion as to promote belief that the law was being applied consistently. Legal rules, of course, are traditional means to achieve precisely those ends.[31]

The informality of the fact-finding processes in the agencies, both with respect to routine cases and in policy making by CLC and ExComm, is also attributable in large part to the overriding impulse toward responsiveness and speed. Methods commonly employed to enhance the accuracy of legal fact-finding—adversarial hearings, public participation and comment, scientific study of the likely consequences of alternative decisions, justifying decisions on the basis of detailed findings of fact—all take a great deal of time and effort. Nevertheless, many agencies, despite the impulse to save that time and effort, do institute formal fact-finding procedures. Sometimes they do so through legal compulsion: their authorizing legislation commands it, or they experience court reversals of their decisions on procedural grounds. Sometimes they do so because of the recognition that decisions

---

[31] See Oliver Wendell Holmes, *The Common Law* (Cambridge, Mass.: Harvard University Press, 1881); Lon Fuller, *The Morality of Law* (New Haven, Conn.: Yale University Press, 1964), ch. 2.

based on unsystematic fact-finding can produce misguided policy and crumbling public support.

Freeze agency officials, however, were subjected neither to legal compulsions to adopt formal procedures, nor informal normative pressures to do so. In fact, the attitudes of the creators of the program encouraged the opposite view. The president and his chief economic advisers had no commitment to institutionalization of price and wage regulation as a permanent feature of government. The program was devised hurriedly and in secrecy. The freeze was pictured as a temporary expedient and as a relatively simple administrative operation. Its "authorizing legislation"—the freeze order—was totally devoid of procedural prescriptions for either lawmaking or case-by-case decision or for public participation in this decision process. The sense of temporariness, the sense that they had no long-term responsibility, provided agency officials with ready justification for emphasizing informal, speedy methods of decision and informal hunch rather than more detailed factual investigation and analysis.

CHAPTER 3

Freeze Policy

Most of the thousands of inquiries addressed to the freeze agencies were requests for permission to increase a price or rent or salary. Most inquirers argued passionately that to construe the freeze order so as to deny the increase would be profoundly unjust or detrimental to the economic health of the nation. The agencies were thus compelled repeatedly to decide whether to maintain an unremittingly stringent anti-inflationary policy or to make accommodations to competing values. The nature of their response—at the level of Cost of Living Council rules—is the subject of this chapter.

STABILIZATION POLICIES: PLAUSIBLE ALTERNATIVES

A realistic assessment of where a regulatory agency's policies fall on the stringency-accommodation continuum requires a preliminary assessment of the range of plausible alternative policies available to it. In the case of price and wage regulation, prior experience suggests several legitimate strategies of control.

The Perfect Competition Strategy

One readily available guide to policy formulation in price control schemes is the economic theory of pure competition. Price regulation, under this theory, is justified primarily to counteract the effects of market imperfection and inefficiency, such as that which results from monopoly or oligopoly power. The maximum price set by regulation should be that which would be charged by an efficient firm in a competitive market. That price presumably would cover an efficient firm's cost of production and capital formation. Price increases would be permissible if necessary to offset cost increases and maintain a reasonable profit margin; only those increases that exceed that level would be prohibited. To deny cost-justified price increases would be considered both punitive and counterproductive on the theory that producers will be induced to withhold products and services for which they are denied an adequate return, thereby distorting patterns of production and investment. The goal of preventing price increases per se is thus subordinated to concern for maximizing efficiency and continuity of production.

The perfect competition strategy suggests selective coverage. There would be no need for government regulation where price competition is strong and firms lack substantial market power as in most of the retail trade sector; controls should be aimed only at firms or unions that have substantial market power.[1] And in these markets, the logic of the perfect competition strategy would call for careful firm-by-firm regulation, attuning the allowable price to all the cost factors associated with the particular firm or product, much like the rate-of-return computations used in public utility regulation.

With respect to wage regulation, the closest approximation of the perfect competition strategy is a status quo "incomes policy" designed to maintain a steady share of the national income to the various economic sectors—labor, business, investors, and government. To maintain this balance, wages and benefits could be increased, but only as justified by increased economic productivity and profitability.[2]

Redistributive Strategies

Alternative approaches to price and wage regulation reflect dissatisfaction with the distribution of income resulting from prevailing market forces or even from a perfectly competitive market. Most commonly, the basic values advocated are egalitarian. Prices, wages, and salaries are regulated to benefit lower-paid workers in relation to management and investors, to provide

---

[1] Even ardent advocates of government price controls often urge that they be limited to large firms or the most imperfect markets. See, e.g., John K. Galbraith, *Economics and the Public Purpose* (New York: Signet Books, 1975). Analytic dimensions of price and wage control policies are nicely outlined by Arnold Weber, "The Continuing Courtship: Wage-Price Policy Through Five Administrations," in *Exhortation and Controls: The Search for a Wage-Price Policy, 1945–1971,* ed. Craufurd Goodwin (Washington: Brookings Institution, 1975).

[2] See, generally, Lloyd Ulman and Robert Flanagan, *Wage Restraint: A Study of Incomes Policies in Western Europe* (Berkeley: University of California Press, 1971); D. Quinn Mills, *Government, Labor and Inflation: Wage Stabilization in the United States* (Chicago: University of Chicago Press, 1975).

lower electricity rates for poor and elderly customers, or to fix rents in accordance with tenants' ability to pay.[3] A redistributive regulatory scheme, however, might seek the opposite, for example, to constrain wage increases and increase corporate profits so as to curtail present consumption and promote investment. Some pricing regulations compel the provision of electricity or transportation to rural areas at less than cost; the resulting cross-subsidation scheme is an urban-to-rural redistributive strategy. Thus any number of redistributive philosophies might be involved, based on perceptions of need, or merit, or a particular theory of social utility.[4] Like the perfect competition model, the logic of a redistributive strategy of price and wage controls would require attention to the specific situation of the individual firm seeking a price increase or to the individual worker or work group seeking a wage increase in order to determine where the applicant actually stood with respect to the characteristic—need, merit, social contribution—on which the ideal distributional scheme is calibrated.

The Hold-the-Line Strategy

A more single-mindedly stringent anti-inflation policy results from a hold-the-line strategy, a term and technique invoked during the World War II control program in the United States.[5] In this perspective, each and every price and wage increase is categorically prohibited, regardless of whether it would be justified by cost or productivity increases and regardless of its distributional effects. Neither the low-paid worker nor the top executive can receive a salary increase. A hold-the-line policy may be instituted in full cognizance of the inequities and distortions in production it may generate, but it deliberately defines the anti-inflationary police mission as paramount, not to be watered down by accommodation to other values or justice claims. Any price, wage, or rent increase is deemed inflationary. Any price, wage, or rent increase is "bad."

Unlike the other approaches, implementation of the hold-the-line strategy does not require attention to the particular situation of each firm or work group. To the contrary, each company and worker must be treated in a strictly identical manner without regard to the financial or functional differences among them. To grant a price increase to one business firm, on any

---

[3] See, e.g., Robert Ayres, "The 'Social Pact' as Anti-Inflationary Policy: The Argentine Experience Since 1973," 28 *World Politics* 473 (1976).

[4] During World War I, an effort was made to set shoe prices so as to induce producers to shift manufacturing resources from a variety of fashions to a single, simple and therefore cheaper model, dubbed the "liberty shoe." See Robert Cuff, *The War Industries Board: Business-Government Relations During World War I* (Baltimore: Johns Hopkins Press, 1973).

[5] See Harvey Mansfield et al., *A Short History of OPA* (Washington: Government Printing Office, 1949).

grounds, would only increase the costs incurred by its customers, worsening *their* position and encouraging them to seek a compensating price or wage increase. For the same reason, the hold-the-line strategy calls for universal rather than selective coverage. Any sectors of the economy exempted from an absolute freeze can inflict higher costs on the frozen sector, generating cost-income squeezes and demands for compensating price or wage increases. Whatever equity, whatever stability a hold-the-line policy can produce would stem from broad and consistent application of a single uniformly stringent policy.

THE FREEZE ORDER AND POLICY CHOICE

The freeze order of August 15, 1971, appears to have been a clear vote by the president and his economic advisors in favor of a hold-the-line strategy, at least for the first three months of the stabilization program. The order was sweeping in its application. Its essential operative provision, but one sentence long, seemed to prohibit categorically any increase in prices and wages over pre-freeze levels.

> Prices, rents, wages and salaries shall be stabilized . . . at levels not greater than the highest of those pertaining to a substantial volume of actual transactions by each individual, business, firm or other entity of any kind during the thirty-day period ending August 14, 1971, for like or similar commodities or services.

There were a number of reasons why a sweeping and comprehensive hold-the-line strategy might have seemed appropriate. An absolute freeze would help dispel the reigning inflationary psychology. It would be politically popular, signaling an unambiguous and determined attack by the administration on the problem of inflation. An absolute freeze would buy time for the formulation of more sophisticated control policies, responsive to a wider range of values, to be implemented in the next phase of the program.

Nevertheless, a searching examination of ostensibly stringent legislative mandates, such as the freeze order, will often reveal implicit instructions to the implementing agencies to consider competing values in pursuing the police mission. While the first section of the order stated an unqualified prohibition of all price and wage increases, a later section empowered the Cost of Living Council to "make exceptions or grant exemptions" in carrying out the order. Still another section stated, "In all of its actions the Council will be guided by the need to maintain consistency of price and wage policies with fiscal, monetary, international and other economic policies of the United States." These provisions suggest that a freeze agency determined to find warrant in its legal mandate to formulate policies responsive, at least in part, to the values implicit in a "perfect competition" price control model or a redistributive one could have done so.[6]

The most explicit invitation to accommodation, however, was an express provision in the order that it "shall not apply to the prices charged for raw agricultural products." According to Arnold Weber, executive director of CLC, this exemption stemmed from the belief that the farm market was basically uncontrollable. Thousands of producers are involved and thousands of products with fluctuating prices. In prior price control programs, attempts to regulate agricultural prices led farmers to withhold crops from the market or resort to illegal evasion of the ceilings.[7] If the freeze order's exemption of raw agricultural prices was understandable, its implications for the rest of freeze policy were unclear. If farmers could increase prices, should not their customers—wholesalers and processors of agricultural products—be allowed to pass them on?[8] And if raw agricultural products were exempt, should other "natural" products, such as seafood and timber, also be exempted, or other commodities which, like farm products, are subject to a fragmented, volatile, and highly competitive market?

Consequently, despite the initial appearance of clarity and total stringency presented by the order, freeze agency officials were in much the same position as other regulators, confronted with very real alternatives in the formation of policy. Arguments based on the perfect competition strategy and various redistributive notions were very common. As recounted by Arnold Weber,

> Among the Cost of Living Council members there were perceptible differences of opinion concerning the scope and degree of stringency with which the freeze should be administered. . . . Those council members with a less rigorous

---

[6] For an argument and demonstration that regulatory officials, particularly at the outset of programs, have leeway to reinterpret their authorizing legislation in a creative manner, see Alfred Blumrosen, "Administrative Creativity: The First Year of the Equal Employment Opportunity Commission," 38 *George Washington Law Review* 695 (1970).

[7] Arnold Weber, *In Pursuit of Price Stability: The Wage-Price Freeze of 1971* (Washington: Brookings Institution, 1973), pp. 41–42. During the World War II control program, the agricultural sector was troublesome both when regulators tried to control it and when they did not, except for one year-long period when agricultural price controls were combined with special subsidies to farmers. Chester Bowles, *Promises to Keep* (New York: Harper & Row, 1971). See also Mansfield, *Short History of OPA,* pp. 59–63, 255–256 and Marshall Clinard, *The Black Market* (New York: Rinehart, 1952).

[8] If middlemen could not pass along price increases in raw agricultural products, they would be caught in a severe cost-price squeeze, perhaps inducing *them* to curtail purchases or resort to illegal evasion. On the other hand, if middlemen *were* allowed to pass on price increases to the ultimate consumers, wage earners, held by the freeze to a constant wage, would experience a pinch in the most important part of their household budget. Food price stability, it has often been argued, is the key to the political viability of any system of wage control.

approach to the freeze generally favored wider exemptions, some pass-through of costs, and a flexible attitude toward the operation of existing contract provisions that might result in some increases in wages.[9]

The conflict in approaches led General Lincoln, director of OEP, to say in his public appearances that the substantive policy of the freeze was guided by three principles, "consistency, stringency, and reasonableness."[10] Fine principles all, but a seemingly incompatible troika, inasmuch as "stringency" and "reasonableness" pulled in rather different directions. To discover the real thrust of the freeze policy, we must undertake a more detailed analysis of the decisions the agencies actually made, in this chapter at the level of CLC rules, and in later chapters at the level of inquiry-responses in the national office of OEP.

STRINGENT POLICIES AND ACCOMMODATIVE RULES

In the course of the freeze, CLC issued 415 rules, covering everything from custom-made steel forgings to fees for college dormitories. In the opinion of Arnold Weber, CLC's executive director,

> It is accurate to say that, overall, the hard line position prevailed and that marginal issues were generally decided in favor of restraint and "toughness" rather than flexibility.

Weber even concluded, in retrospect, that "an overly rigorous approach" was taken. Any inclination to make adjustments "because of economic or equity requirements" was overwhelmed in the "struggle for consistency," producing a "hard freeze" of highly restrictive policies, causing what Weber thought were unnecessary hardships and inequities.[11]

As indicated in Table 1, the standard indexes of price and wage changes support the view that the freeze was indeed a "hard" one.[12] A substantial portion of the price and wage index increases shown as having occurred during the freeze can be attributed to increases that took effect in the first part of August, before the freeze was instituted. In addition, a special Bureau of Labor Statistics analysis of 98,000 individual prices in the September–November period indicated that 74 percent remained constant, 10 percent

---

[9] Weber, *In Pursuit of Price Stability*, p. 31.

[10] Harry Yoshpe et al., *Stemming Inflation: The Office of Emergency Preparedness and the 90-Day Freeze* (Washington: Government Printing Office, 1972), pp. 75–76.

[11] Weber, *In Pursuit of Price Stability*, pp. 31, 126–127.

[12] Other calculations based on BLS data show the effects of the freeze as somewhat less stringent, with both the Consumer Price Index and Wholesale Price Index increasing by 2 percent in the August–November period. Marvin Kosters, *Controls and Inflation* (Washington: The American Enterprise Institute, 1975), pp. 40–41. Discrepancies may be due to different ways of correcting for the "overlap" of BLS data at the beginning and end of the freeze and in making seasonal adjustments.

Table 1. The Impact of Freeze Policy: Economic Indicators

	Annual Rate of Percentage Increase	
	Six Months Prior to Freeze	*August–November 1971*
Consumer Price Index	4.0	1.6
Wholesale Price Index	4.9	−0.3
Average Hourly Earnings	6.7	2.2

SOURCE: Bureau of Labor Statistics, Weber, *In Pursuit of Price Stability,* p. 102.

declined, and 11 percent increased.[13] Finally, a number of economists calculated the probable course of price movements had the freeze not been imposed; all projections indicate that the freeze had a substantial deflationary effect.[14]

If one takes a closer look at the CLC rules, however, a very different picture seems to emerge. Almost *half* the rules can fairly be classified as accommodative in nature, departures from a wholly stringent hold-the-line strategy; that is, they expressly *permit* wage or price increases of some kind. Table 2 analyzes ninety-two randomly selected rules (a 25 percent sample) issued by CLC's Executive Committee (ExComm) in all areas of substantive policy. As shown in the vertical columns, only 41 percent of ExComm's rules stated flatly that the transactions involved were "frozen," while 38 percent of the rules said that designated kinds of price and wage increases were conditionally, partly, or sometimes allowed, depending on the presence in particular cases of certain facts or established practices. Almost 21% of the rules stated flatly that the transaction in question was not subject to the freeze. Even more revealing is the classification, displayed horizontally, based on analysis of the options presented by the OEP staff to ExComm with respect to each rule decision. In almost 50 percent of the decisions involving clear-cut choices, ExComm selected a more accommodative option rather than the most stringent alternative.[15]

The high incidence of accommodative rule choices, however, does not in itself disprove Arnold Weber's characterization of CLC's policies as favoring a "hard" freeze. The quantitative data clearly indicate that CLC did not apply the freeze order in a *wholly* legalistic fashion or take it as a mandate to

[13] Weber, *In Pursuit of Price Stability,* p. 101.

[14] See Robert Lanzillotti, Mary Hamilton, and Blaine Roberts, *Phase II in Review: The Price Commission Experience* (Washington: Brookings Institution, 1975).

[15] In some cases, early in the freeze, the alternatives considered and rejected by ExComm are not shown in the ExComm minutes. For these cases, I constructed an array of plausible options, based on my knowledge of OEP's general approach to preparation of issue papers (having drafted several myself), and I classified the relative stringency of CLC's choice in light of that array.

Table 2. ExComm Rules

Policy Alternative Chosen	"Frozen"	Objective Result "Depends" "Partly Allowed"	"Not Frozen"	
More accommodative	1	23	16	40 (43.5%)
More stringent	37	4	1	42 (45.7%)
No judgment possible	0	8	2	10 (10.8%)
	38 (41.3%)	35 (38%)	19 (20.7%)	n = 92

suppress every conceivable increase. They suggest, too, that even where a regulatory enactment appears to demand highly stringent policies, pressures for accommodation will not be wholly denied. Nevertheless, Table 2 tells us nothing about the *degree* of accommodativeness implicit in those rules or the overall effect of the accommodative rules on freeze policy.

Some legal rules have broader economic and precedential importance than others. A regulatory agency might be rigidly stringent in a small number of early decisions affecting major firms or industries and accommodative (or only slightly accommodative) in many subsequent cases of only marginal economic impact. Moreover, every agency, even if strongly motivated toward stringency, will be faced with numerous cases that make powerful arguments for accommodative exceptions on four grounds: 1) that the regulatory legislation or the agency's own rules are cast too broadly, covering programmatically unimportant cases; 2) that regulatory rules clash with expectations and commitments based on other, preexisting legal rules; 3) that the rules, literally construed, apply to situations not anticipated by the rule maker, producing socially undesirable results; 4) that the rules impose unequal and unjust burdens. An agency's policy is revealed, therefore, not merely in the *frequency* of its accommodative rules, but in the *character* of its response to these arguments. To determine how deeply CLC's numerous accommodative decisions eroded the philosophy of stringency claimed by Arnold Weber, a more qualitative analysis is required, focusing on the four basic problem areas.

THE PROBLEM OF OVERBREADTH

Legislators, observed H.L.A. Hart, inevitably suffer from relative ignorance of fact and indeterminacy of aim.[16] The language they use to regulate an activity sometimes is too limited; actions they would have wished to prohibit, had they but known of their occurrence, are left beyond the

---

[16] H. L. A. Hart, *The Concept of Law* (Oxford, Eng.: Clarendon Press, 1961), ch. VII.

literal words of their rule. More commonly, however, rules are cast too broadly, covering by their terms activities that are either irrelevant or marginal to the primary evil in the legislator's mind. The *law applier,* therefore, is faced with a choice: should the overinclusive rule be applied literally to the marginally important activity? Or should he "suspend" or modify the rules where coverage is not really necessary to the success of the legislative program?[17] In the case of economic regulation, to assert the broadest possible jurisdiction increases a regulatory agency's capacity to control all potential infringements of police-mission values. Breadth of control, however, entails costs. It intrudes upon the jurisdiction of competing centers of power, both public and private. It diffuses the inevitably limited resources and energies of the agency. To relinquish jurisdiction over a marginally important activity and to exempt firms regulated by the market or other agencies, while ostensibly accommodative in nature, is often a sensible option.

For the freeze agencies, these issues first arose in the form of inquiries that probed the *conceptual boundaries* of the order's prohibition against increases in "prices, wages, salaries, and rents." Property owners wanted to know if the freeze on prices banned increases in their property taxes or municipal charges for sewer service. Unions asked whether the freeze on wages barred increases in employee health insurance and argued the freeze should apply to corporate profits. The hold-the-line strategy, of course, would call for the broadest possible coverage. An increase of any kind of charge or payment would chip away at the uniformity of the freeze and create new cost pressures, generating demands for compensating price and wage increases. CLC, responding to that strategy, construed the order broadly, ruling that even charges such as voluntary association dues and hunting license fees were "prices," that fringe benefits of all kinds were "wages," and that college dormitory charges were "rents," all subject to the freeze.[18] In terms of economic function, of course, those charges were all closely analogous to prices and wages and rents; CLC's judgment that they were "prices," "wages," or "rents" was not an overly strained reading of the executive order. On the other hand, CLC would not take the pursuit of stringency beyond a broad but essentially conventional

---

[17] The institution of prosecutorial discretion is a characteristic way of dealing with the problem of overbreadth in the American legal system and reflects a bias in favor of permitting law appliers to counteract overly broad statutes. See Robert Rabin, "Agency Criminal Referrals in the Federal System: An Empirical Study of Prosecutorial Discretion," 24 *Stanford Law Review* 1036 (1972).

[18] I suspect it would be both unnecessary and annoying to include citations to each and every CLC rule mentioned in the text. The CLC rules are cumulated in Economic Stabilization *Circular 101,* 36 *Federal Register* 18739 (No. 183, September 21, 1971) and *Circular 102,* 36 *Federal Register* 20482 (No. 205, October 22, 1971). All freeze rules, as well as those of subsequent phases of the program, are also compiled and indexed in Commerce Clearing House, *Economic Controls Reports* (New York: Commerce Clearing House, 1971–74).

reading of the words in the order. Some important departures from a totally rigorous hold-the-line strategy ensued. Neither taxes nor corporate profits, neither dividends nor welfare payments, could be considered "prices" or "wages," CLC ruled, and were therefore exempt from the freeze.[19]

The problem of overbreadth was posed more sharply by inquiries concerning transactions that clearly *were* prices or wages, but that traditionally had been controlled by other governmental entities. Did the freeze, for example, prohibit price increases called for in the Department of Defense supply contracts or electric utility rate increases previously authorized by other regulatory agencies? In each case, an argument was made that such increases, having been deemed necessary by more specialized, knowledgeable, and directly responsible agencies, should be allowed to take effect. The governor of Texas, moreover, publicly challenged the legal authority of the agencies to block salary increases for state employees granted by the Texas legislature. Nevertheless, CLC refused to relinquish jurisdiction, on the grounds that price or wage increases allowed by other government bodies would shatter the consistency of the freeze.[20] There was one striking accommodative exception, however—CLC's ruling that the freeze did not apply to interest rates. This was due, Arnold Weber reported,[21] to doubts about CLC's legal authority to control them (although it would not seem implausible to read the executive order's freeze of "all prices" as covering interest rates) and the

---

[19] It is likely, of course, that any attempt by CLC to freeze taxes or welfare payments would have been challenged in court as beyond the authority of the agency, both on grounds of the "plain meaning" of the words of the executive order and in terms of the probable intent of Congress in granting the president power to stabilize prices and wages. To control increases in profits (which could occur, of course, despite the freeze), CLC would have had to compel profit-increasing firms to *reduce* prices, or to tax "excess profits" (as was done during World War II and the Korean War), neither of which the executive order seemed to authorize. An excess profits tax *clearly* would have required congressional authorization, but CLC sought no such authority. The council did call for a *voluntary* freeze on corporate dividend levels, however, illustrating one way around legal restrictions. CLC even enforced those voluntary guidelines by threatening violators with adverse publicity, much to the dismay of legal commentators. See Ernest Gellhorn, "Adverse Publicity by Administrative Agencies," 86 *Harvard Law Review* 1386, 1403–06 (1973). On a few occasions CLC's reading of the conceptual limits of the order seemed somewhat legalistic, as when it ruled that increases in maintenance charges to (or among) condominium owners were not banned by the freeze on rents and that increases in reimbursement rates for physicians under government-paid health plans were beyond the scope of the freeze on prices.

[20] Previous federal wage-price controls had exempted prices charged for government services and government-regulated prices. The Phase II agencies, moderating CLC's position, did so as well. CLC, however, even froze postal rate increases approved by the Postal Rate Commission.

The legal authority of federal price and wage regulators to limit salary increases for state employees was upheld by the Supreme Court against both statutory and commerce clause challenges in *Fry* v. *United States*, 421 U.S. 542 (1975).

[21] Weber, *In Pursuit of Price Stability*, p. 39.

expectation that interest rates would not go up under the conditions prevailing during the freeze period (although the same might have been said of many other products and services). More to the point, I suspect, was CLC's reluctance to intrude upon the jurisdiction of the Federal Reserve Board, whose chairman (Arthur Burns) attended CLC meetings and whose dedication to the anti-inflationary cause was not doubted.

A third set of challenges to the breadth of freeze coverage was posed by inquiries seeking exemptions for wage or price increases claimed to be economically insignificant, or "not really inflationary." Regulatory programs often relinquish coverage of very small business units—such as the "mom and pop" store, and "Mrs. Murphy's boarding house"—on grounds that compliance would be burdensome for such entities, enforcement difficult, and evasion programmatically insignificant.[22] Subsequent phases of the Economic Stabilization Program exempted businesses with fewer than sixty employees from price and wage controls. CLC, however, specifically ruled that the freeze applied even to tiny wage and price increases, opting for the symbolism and consistency of comprehensive coverage. Similarly, CLC ruled that the freeze applied to prices of items such as real estate, used cars, and products traded at auctions and commodity exchanges, despite the claim that those markets were effectively regulated by competitive pressures, that they had been exempted by prior price control programs (as they were destined to be under Phase II), and that like the already exempted raw agricultural products, they were basically uncontrollable.

Three additional exceptions to CLC's determination to control almost everything within the literal scope of the freeze order should be mentioned. First, CLC ruled that the prices of imports and exports were not subject to the freeze; in this area, the goal of suppressing inflation was subordinated to efforts to reduce the country's international trade deficit. (Leaving export prices uncontrolled while freezing domestic prices would encourage exports, it was reasoned. In addition, if imported commodities were exempted and their prices increased due to the devaluation of the dollar, American firms would be doubly encouraged to seek out domestic sources, whose prices would be frozen.) Second, CLC ruled that notwithstanding the freeze, wages below the level set in state minimum wage laws could be increased, apparently on grounds of distributive justice.[23] Third, consulting firms which

---

[22] The Civil Rights Act of 1964, Title VII (Equal Employment Opportunity), for example, applies only to employers with twenty-five or more employees. In the first year after enactment, it applied only to employers with 100 or more workers. 42 U.S.C. Sec. 2000e. Similarly, Title II of the act (Public Accommodations) exempted inns, hotels, and boarding houses in which the owner resides and has five or fewer rooms for rent.

[23] This rule was limited to minimum wage laws of general application and did not authorize increases for specific occupations, such as school teachers. The post-freeze treatment of low-paid workers was considerably more accommodative, exempting those paid less than $2.75 per hour from wage controls.

specialized in the creation of employee pension and profit-sharing plans protested CLC's rule freezing the installation of new plans (as forbidden increases in "wages," which included fringe benefits); the firms contended that such plans actually defer any additional compensation and are "really" anti-inflationary since they force additional savings. CLC finally relented and modified its rule, but less, I suspect, because of the persuasiveness of the reasons advanced by the pension consultants than because of the repeated complaints that they were being driven out of business by the freeze. It is noteworthy, however, that none of the reasons underlying these three exceptions—the priority of public policies other than price stability (such as international trade policy); distributive justice; the noninflationary nature of price or wage increases, or adverse impact on industry—was invoked by CLC to create other exempt areas, although such arguments were often made.

Each major exemption from coverage—agricultural products, interest rates, exports, imports—unleashed a new barrage of inquiries that probed the conceptual boundaries of the exemption itself. If exports were exempt, for example, how about sales of components that would be incorporated in exported products? ("Frozen," said CLC.) The council's stance in these boundary-drawing issues was not uniformly stringent, and the basic clash between the hold-the-line strategy and the theory on which the exemption was based often produced a kind of arbitrary hair-splitting, but the loopholes created were plugged up at some point. CLC ruled, for example, that raw seafood products, like raw agricultural products, were exempt, but also that they became subject to the freeze "when they are shelled, shucked, skinned, or scaled."[24] The concern for stringency blocked most attempts to extend the exemptions by analogy or by economic logic. They were treated as exceptions, not as new policies.

THE PROBLEM OF PRIOR EXPECTATIONS

The right to rely on lawful expectations or agreements is a fundamental principle of justice. It underlies not only the law of contract, but the very idea of the rule of law.[25] Pervasive acceptance of that principle forces any agency that attempts to implement significant changes in the law to deal with a fundamental issue of transition: should the new rules impose penalties

---

[24] Fish merely *frozen* on board ship, however, were not frozen, OEP ruled. Even the bureaucrats thought that was funny; soon OEP lawyers were circulating a fictitious inquiry from an ice company asking whether its products were frozen.

[25] See Lon Fuller, *The Morality of Law* (New Haven: Yale University Press, 1964); Gregory Vlastos, "Justice and Equality" and Paul Freund, "Social Justice and the Law," in *Social Justice*, ed. Richard Brandt (Englewood Cliffs, N.J.: Prentice-Hall, 1962); Bertrand de Jouvenal, *The Ethics of Redistribution* (Cambridge, Eng.: Cambridge Press, 1951).

on those who made plans and solemn agreements or even built their entire careers and businesses in good faith reliance on the old rules? Many regulatory programs make accommodations on this issue. They provide for a transitional grace period or enact "grandfather clauses" exempting firms or businessmen who have long operated in accordance with the prior legal regime.

In a modern economy, changes in prices and wages are regulated by a variety of complex agreements and standardized practices. The freeze order attempted to slice into this web of plans at a single point in time. Almost 25 percent of the inquiries answered by OEP's national office during the freeze concerned the legal status of prices and wages in the process of changing on or about the freeze date, August 15, or changes that had been agreed upon prior to the freeze. In late July, for example, a major steel company, having just concluded an agreement calling for substantial wage increases, announced price increases effective August 10. By August 15 the company had taken orders at the new price, but most of these orders had not been shipped. Could the company charge the increased prices for shipments made after the freeze date? Tenants had signed leases and made deposits on August 1, providing for occupancy on September 1 at a rent higher than that paid by the previous occupant. Did the freeze prevent the agreed-upon rental increase from taking effect? Collective bargaining agreements in operation long before the freeze called for wage increases that would fall due during the freeze. Were they blocked? Workers had relied on the promised increase in income to make new commitments, such as buying a new car, just as landlords had relied on the promise of higher rents to repaint and repair.

The freeze order forbade increases in prices, wages, and rents over the level "pertaining to a substantial volume of actual transactions . . . during the thirty-day period ending August 14, 1971." But what was a "transaction"—the signing of the contract, the placing of an order? Or was more required, such as actual payment at the new rate or actual provision of the goods or services involved? For CLC, the choice was a crucial one. From the standpoint of a hold-the-line strategy, the stability of the freeze would be threatened if the price and wage increases triggered by preexisting agreements, practices, or statutory arrangements could take effect. The rule CLC adopted was consciously stringent, running counter to everyday understanding of what "transaction" might mean. The transaction occurs, it was ruled, only when the seller actually *delivers* the product or service in question. The price at which the product was delivered prior to the freeze or the rent at which the apartment was occupied prior to the freeze was the ceiling, even if a contract had been made, an order taken, or even a deposit paid on the premise of a higher price. Similarly, a planned or contractually agreed-upon wage increase could not take effect unless work had actually been performed at the higher rate and the higher rate paid or accrued prior to August 15.

Designed to reinforce the credibility and stability of the freeze, the stringent transaction rule touched a raw nerve. It produced fervent opposition, legal attacks on the freeze administration, and some pockets of noncompliance. Millions of public school teachers, denied salary increases scheduled to take effect in early September, were outraged. This letter from a Pennsylvania teacher was typical.

> I now ask you? Can the President of the United States, by a mere order, abrogate the terms of a contract? Especially if there are rights and privileges that have accrued under that contract? As a teacher, I teach the ideals of democracy, and the built-in safeguards against the misuse of power. Should I just ignore them? Or would you prefer that I not mention them, and have our future leaders take our country back into another Dark Ages?

The Amalgamated Meat Cutters Union raised the same question in a lawsuit against CLC. In 1970 it had negotiated an agreement with the major meatpacking companies calling for a September 6, 1971, wage increase. The union claimed that CLC's transaction rule, which blocked that increase, was an unconstitutional impairment of its contractual rights and that the Economic Stabilization Act itself was unconstitutional. The three-judge federal court rejected both claims.[26]

CLC continued to adhere to the transaction rule in a somewhat legalistic manner, even where it produced rather severe inequities. Many football teams, both college and professional, had increased season ticket prices for the fall season and had actually received payment for a substantial number of tickets before the freeze. CLC and OEP ordered them to roll back their prices to the previous year's level, since the "product" (the football games) had not been "delivered" and hence no "actual transaction" had occurred prior to the freeze. This too led to several lawsuits, but again the courts upheld CLC's legal power to block the increase.[27] In the case of the school teachers, CLC ruled early in the freeze that if *any* teachers under a system-wide contract had worked and accrued pay at a higher rate prior to August 15, the new contract was "in effect" and the general increase could be implemented. However, after the transaction rule had been formulated—and CLC came to realize how many teachers might get raises under the "any teacher" rule—the council

---

[26] *Amalgamated Meat Cutters* v. *Connally,* 337 F. Supp. 737 (D.D.C., 1971). The opinion was written by Judge Harold Leventhal, who had been head of the price control agency during the Korean War. The opinion is also notable for upholding the ostensibly standardless Economic Stabilization Act as a valid delegation of legislative power.

[27] See *University of California* v. *CLC,* 343 F. Supp. 606 (C.D. Cal., 1972), *reversed,* 472 F. 2nd 1063 (Temp. Emerg. Ct. App. 1972).

reversed itself and ruled that planned salary increases could be implemented only for those individual teachers who had worked (provided services) and accrued pay at the higher rate prior to the freeze.[28] The reversal prompted great confusion, disregard of the freeze by many school districts, and a ruling by a United States District Court in Louisiana that the second CLC rule was contrary to the executive order. The court decision came late in the freeze and was believed by agency officials to be erroneous; pending appeal, they adhered to their stringent interpretation of their stringent transaction rule.[29]

Two relaxations of the transaction rule actually demonstrate the intensity of CLC's commitment to stringency. First, a number of municipalities sought permission to charge higher sewer, water, or garbage collection fees that had been announced and enacted into law prior to the freeze, but not scheduled to take effect until September. They argued that the increased revenues were needed to meet finance charges on new sewage and waste treatment plants, constructed in anticipation of the fee increase. In some cases, the increases were required by state laws or bond agreements that conditioned the financing on the fee increase. CLC refused to modify the transaction rule so as to allow such rate increases. Its only concession was to grant hardship exceptions in the case of two small towns already in default and virtually bankrupt. The second modification arose from CLC's decision in the first days of the freeze that *previously scheduled* and announced tuition increases were not frozen. CLC's motive had been to provide financial relief for hard-pressed private schools and colleges. A few days later, however, as they were formulating the transaction rule, agency officials realized it was logically inconsistent with the earlier and more accommodative tuition rule. Their impulse was to restore consistency, but in the direction of the hold-the-line strategy. In a revised rule, CLC announced that schools could increase tuitions only if *payments* at the higher rate had actually been received prior to August 15. This was still at odds with the transaction rule, which

---

[28] After promulgating the first teacher's salary rule (if any worked, all get the raise), CLC learned a bit more about the actual teacher compensation practices in the thousands of school districts in the nation. In most school districts, teachers were scheduled to receive a salary increase after summer vacation in September, but a few teachers in the district came in early—before the August 15 freeze date—and worked and were paid at the new, higher rate. Under the CLC rule, these "golden sheep," as they came to be called, "qualified" all their fellow teachers for pay raises. Moreover, this meant, according to some estimates, that 75 percent of the nation's teachers would receive pay raises *during the freeze*. CLC's reversion to the teacher-by-teacher standard was an effort to shut the gate.

[29] According to OEP's official history of the freeze, "noncompliance on teachers' salaries was widespread and enduring." Yoshpe, *Stemming Inflation*, p. 129. The federal court order against the agencies was in *U.S. v. Jefferson Parish Schoolboard*, 333 F. Supp. 418 (D.C. La. 1971).

required *delivery of services* at the new rate prior to August 15 in order to validate a price increase. Inquirers' lawyers, such as those representing the professional football teams, were quick to point out the inconsistency. Agency officials eventually admitted the conflict in principle, but stated that the accommodative tuition rule was a special case, not a beachhead for the idea that prior expectations or financial hardship would justify accommodation in other spheres of activity.[30]

UNANTICIPATED CIRCUMSTANCES

Legal rules are formulated on assumptions about the "typical" range of behavior subject to regulation. Where the social arena affected by a rule, such as the freeze order, is diverse and fluid, the enforcement agency is constantly confronted with the problem of whether to make exceptions for situations that fall within the literal language of the general rule, but were not anticipated when the rule was formulated. A basic assumption of the hold-the-line strategy was that the status quo of August 15, 1971, was a tolerable one for most economic actors. Businesses could tolerate a freeze on prices, because labor costs and the prices they paid for supplies were also frozen. Households could tolerate a freeze on wages and salaries because the prices of the things they bought would be frozen. In terms of economic theory, the underlying assumption was that each economic entity was in or close to equilibrium, or at least that whatever disequilibrium existed could be tolerated for a three-month freeze.

The validity of that assumption, however, depends upon another—that the regulated economy is a closed system, that no *new* cost increases would be introduced during the freeze. Unfortunately for the agencies, the system was not and could not be entirely closed. One opening was temporal. As of the chosen starting date, August 15, 1971, many businesses had just sustained an increase in material or labor costs, but had not yet reestablished their previous position by passing on these increases in the form of higher prices. The freeze on their prices drove them into further disadvantage day-by-day, as they continued to make purchases or pay wages at higher rates. For example, the major steel companies announced increased prices in early August on some products and completed transactions at the higher price just before the freeze. Purchasers of those products—forgers, steel warehouses, jobbers, other fabricators—did not have time to increase *their* prices and thus were faced with mounting average costs-of-materials throughout the freeze.

---

[30] In subsequent phases of the stabilization program, the stringency of the transaction rule was moderated. Congress, amending the Economic Stabilization Act, provided that contractual wage increases blocked by the freeze should be paid retroactively. The Price Commission's regulations allowed most pre-freeze long-term contracts with escalator clauses to take effect.

Low-margin fabricators claimed that unless they were allowed to increase their prices correspondingly, they would soon have to close down operations and lay off workers.

Other violations of the assumption of equilibrium stemmed from areas exempt from the freeze, such as raw agricultural products and imports. The result of price increases in those sectors was an unanticipated cost-price squeeze for firms subject to the freeze. An increase in the price of peanuts (exempt agricultural products), for example, led the Peanut Butter Manufacturers and Nut Salters Association to complain that unless peanut *processors* could pass on the increased prices to their customers, they would have to stop buying peanuts. That result would not only deplete supplies of peanut butter and candy—a predicament about which reasonable men and their children might differ—but would obligate the federal government to pay increased price-support payments to peanut growers for the unbought crop. Other sources of disequilibrium were government-mandated cost increases. Coal mining companies incurred higher costs during the freeze due to compliance with new coal mine safety regulations. Electric utilities were forced by anti-pollution rules to shift from coal to higher-priced fuel oil. In all these and many similar cases, a stringent application of the freeze seemed particularly unfair and potentially disruptive.

Here then was a critical choice: could unanticipated cost increases incurred during the freeze be passed on in the form of higher prices? More broadly, the question was whether the hold-the-line strategy or the perfect competition strategy would be the ultimate guide to policy, for if the steel fabricators and peanut processors and coal mine owners were allowed to pass on their higher costs, would their customers when they received higher prices be given a pass-through as well? CLC's basic decision was that no cost pass-through would be permitted. The literal provisions of the freeze order would apply. The steel fabricators, the peanut butter processors, and others would have to "live with it." Devising rules for the pass-through of costs was a problem reserved for the subsequent phases of the Economic Stabilization Program.[31]

A few accommodative exceptions were made, however, with respect to unanticipated cost-price squeezes. CLC ruled that price increases for raw agricultural products could be passed on, dollar-for-dollar, provided the products were not "processed." If a middleman or a retailer paid ten cents

---

[31] The Price Commission in Phase II, pursuing a "perfect competition strategy," permitted businesses which sustained cost increases to pass them on in the form of higher prices. Moreover, those costs could be passed on not merely dollar-for-dollar, but the seller was allowed to add his customary percentage markup. The Price Commission rules, at bottom, sought only to keep businesses from raising prices so far as to increase their profit margins as a percentage of sales. See Lanzillotti et al., *Phase II in Review*.

more for a bunch of spinach and sold it as is, he could increase his price ten cents (but could not add his customary mark-up to the increase). The same was true for imported commodities, CLC ruled; as long as the imported merchandise was not transformed or incorporated into a domestically made product, a price increase on the import could be passed on dollar-for-dollar.[32] For CLC to have denied the pass-through in these areas would have undercut the policy underlying the two exemptions—the presumed competitiveness and concern for continuity of supply in agriculture, and deterrence of imports. On the other hand, by ruling that agricultural products *lost* their exemption when "processed" and imports when "transformed or incorporated"—decisions which were arbitrary from the standpoint of those competing policies and the "perfect competition" strategy—CLC demonstrated its fundamental concern for stringency.[33]

CLC's "lean" toward stringency was also exhibited in its treatment of applications for exceptions in individual cases on grounds of hardship, usually the result of an unanticipated cost-price squeeze. Claims that the freeze would soon force a firm into bankruptcy did not, CLC held, warrant permission to raise prices. Detailed proof of immediate and unavoidable harm, due solely to the effects of the freeze, was required. Out of some 5,500 individual

---

[32] The "processing" and "transformation" rules were not wholly lacking in rationality. If one were to predict the class of cases in which price increases in raw agricultural products would create the most severe cost-price squeezes, the best guess is that wholesalers, who simply resell the product untransformed, usually at a minimal markup, would likely be hurt worse by a freeze on their prices than processors who mix it with labor and other materials so that the raw agricultural product constitutes a smaller percentage of their total cost.

[33] A similar set of exceptions involved agreements with flexible pricing formulas: store rentals based on the monthly volume of sales; insurance rates that vary with periodic assessments of "loss experience" by the insurance company; "net leases" obligating tenants to pay increases in taxes and maintenance costs; "fuel adjustment clauses" requiring utility rates to meet changing fuel costs. Which is frozen, the price actually paid in the pre-freeze base period or the *formula?* If the latter, then prices to customers could actually go up during the freeze. CLC allowed such formulas to operate when they were designed to match compensation to greater services, but not to offset higher costs due to other factors. A worker could earn a higher weekly pay during the freeze by working more hours or selling more computers, and magazines could increase advertising rates pursuant to a preexisting formula linking rates to the number of customers reached. But a worker could not receive higher pay pursuant to a contract linking wages to increases in the Consumer Price Index, and fuel adjustment clauses for utilities were not allowed to operate—the services provided did not change. However, CLC allowed landlords to pass through tax and cost increases under "net leases," and insurers were allowed to increase rates to reflect higher loss experience. These pass-throughs can easily be justified in terms of the perfect competition theory: the landlord under a net lease and the insurer (at least according to the statistics supplied CLC) can ill-afford to absorb such increases; but neither can a utility easily absorb substantial increases in fuel prices or a worker increases in his cost of living. The "net lease" and the "loss experience" rules are anomalous, then, simply because they are two of the very few CLC rules that reflect the perfect competition strategy and set of values.

case applications, CLC granted only five exceptions: two for municipalities already in default on bonds that required increases in municipal fees and three for groups of public employees who would have been left totally without health insurance if the rule forbidding their employer to add new fringe benefits had not been waived.[34] This record contrasted sharply with the more liberal issuance of individual case exceptions during subsequent phases of the control program, where the general rules themselves were much more accommodative.[35]

THE PROBLEM OF DISTRIBUTIVE JUSTICE

Every regulatory program affects the distribution of income and wealth generated by the market practices and market structure that preceded it. Every regulatory agency is confronted with arguments based on the distributional impact of its choices between stringency and accommodation. Conceivably, these arguments can be ignored. The agency may define its role purely technically and legalistically, but the ideal of legality pushes the agency to take responsibility for at least the more extreme distributive consequences of its policies.

Issues of distributive justice are particularly salient in a program that directly regulates prices and wages for an entire nation. As the economist Henry Wallich pointed out,

> Inflation, bad as it is, performs a social function. It resolves the conflict among competing groups—labor, capital, the farmer, the poor—over the distribution of the national income. When these contenders are not satisfied with the way the market slices up the pie, inflation usually takes over as an allocator. Now [under the Phase IV price freeze announced June 13, 1973] inflation has played out that role. Its successor is confrontation.[36]

An uncontrolled market gives everyone at least a chance to "catch up" with losses in purchasing power due to price and wage increases grabbed by others. An arbitrary halt, such as a freeze, leaves everyone acutely aware of how far he has been left behind and suspicious that the government has called upon him (or his class) to make special sacrifices, letting more fortunate or less deserving groups off lightly. As a wage earner from Pennsylvania wrote to the chairman of CLC,

---

[34] The employer in each case had canceled the old employee health insurance policy when the new, improved one was signed. Yoshpe, *Stemming Inflation,* ch. V.

[35] In Phase II, the Price Commission granted ninety-six price and rent exceptions in its first four months of operation. CLC, *Economic Stabilization Program Quarterly Report, January 1–March 31, 1972.*

[36] Henry Wallich, "Inflation vs. Confrontation," *Newsweek,* July 9, 1973, p. 77.

> Since I now live under a dictatorship and my leaders are forcing un-American policies on the citizens with the big freeze, I have a question or two . . . why aren't taxes frozen? or business profits? Giving all the benefits to the businesses so I could work steady at starvation wages did not help me . . . Mr. Connally in my opinion you are a mangy stinking coyote.

The hold-the-line strategy thus seemed to lock all distributive inequalities into place. It called for official indifference to the issues of distributive justice raised in requests for accommodation. Some of these requests, such as that of the wage earner quoted, essentially called for an incomes policy: if wages were to be frozen, profits and taxes should be too; if profits could go up, wages should be allowed to rise, at least proportionally. Other claims were based on the idea of distribution according to merit. The wife of a Texas construction worker, told that her husband's expected wage increase was frozen, wrote OEP to ask whether he could get his raise, adding

> My husband has served our country in Vietnam, we pay our taxes, we vote as intelligently as possible, we obey the laws of our country and we consider ourselves responsible citizens.

A small businessman—like others who felt that they personally, by reason of their industriousness, frugality, and restraint, had not contributed to inflation—wrote to the president asking for permission for a price increase.

> I agree you had to act the way you did. But the honest and fair man, who is not looking for big profits and exploiting his fellow men like me is terrible hurt.

Even more prevalent were pleas for accommodation based on a theory of distribution, or redistribution, according to need. As in Anatole France's ironic jibe about the "majestic equality" of the law, the freeze denied wage increases to the rich as well as the poor and forbade the rich firm as well as the poor one to increase its prices.[37] No inquiry received as much intensive, high-level attention in the freeze agencies as a letter from Ralph Nader suggesting blanket relief from wage restrictions for low-income families. CLC ultimately rejected the Nader suggestion and made no rule changes allowing rent or price increases for unprofitable landlords and businessmen.

---

[37] "The Law in its majestic equality forbids the rich as well as the poor to sleep under bridges, to beg in the streets, and to steal bread." This applies to laws of formally equal application that purport to treat all persons (or firms) the same, despite their individual differences. But laws are not necessarily cast in that way. The infinite complexity of the Internal Revenue Code is at least partly a reflection of the effort to equalize the application of a law in terms of ability to pay. See, however, Louis Eisenstein, *The Ideologies of Taxation* (New York: Ronald Press, 1961).

CLC's ideal was consistency, and to CLC consistency meant formal equality of treatment, "to each the same," regardless of differences in economic importance, or merit, or need. While agency officials were chary of any proposed rule that might appear to favor business interests, it was never suggested that large corporations should be treated more stringently than small businesses or wage earners. In short, there was little support for contentions that the freeze should be used for redistributive purposes. The OEP issue paper dealing with the Nader request argued, inter alia,

> The freeze is not intended to be a social welfare program. There is no way to correct social injustice through administrative regulation of a program of this sort. . . .
>
> Public support for the wage-price freeze would be significantly reduced among the sizeable part of the populace that does not want to redistribute income to the poor. . . .
>
> It would be difficult to allow wages to increase without allowing the pass-through to prices.

A few CLC rules reflected sensitivity to distributional concerns. As noted earlier, wages could be increased to the level required by state minimum wage laws, even where those laws called for an increase in the minimum during the freeze. Increases in welfare and Social Security benefits were ruled exempt from the freeze, as were previously planned increases in pension benefits for retired workers; in each case, the argument was partly that the payments in question were not wages or prices, but the issue papers suggesting the exemptions also justified them on distributive justice grounds. Nevertheless, concessions of this nature were not nearly as great during the freeze as in subsequent phases of the stabilization program.[38] The principle of merit was reflected in CLC's rule that military personnel on combat duty were exempt from the wage freeze, but that was a rare exception. Ordinary salary increases based on merit alone were prohibited, as were price or rent increases for firms or landlords who had previously exercised restraint.

Consequently, while CLC, like most agencies, never explicitly endorsed any single principle of distributive justice to the exclusion of others, the dominant tendency was to adhere to the principle of formal equality implicit in the stringent hold-the-line strategy. The few exceptions made, although suggestive of sensitivity to competing notions of distributive justice, were not accompanied by explicit endorsements of those principles, thereby discouraging their application to a broader range of issues.

---

[38] In Phase II, as noted, workers with hourly incomes below $2.75 were exempted from wage controls. The Price Commission wrote special, looser regulations for businesses operating at a loss or at a very low profit margin.

CONCLUSION: THE THRUST OF FREEZE POLICY

While many of CLC's rules appear to have been accommodative in nature, a more meaningful assessment of the substantive thrust of its policies stems from analysis of how CLC dealt with four major problems that often pull regulatory agencies toward accommodative postures: 1) whether to limit jurisdiction only to the most important or easily regulated sectors, 2) whether to grant concessions based on legitimate expectations rooted in the preexisting legal order, 3) whether and how far to make accommodations to avoid hardships and side-effects not anticipated by the original regulatory enactment, and 4) whether to adjust policies in accordance with theories of distributive justice. In all these areas, the general tenor of the freeze policy was, on balance, quite stringent, a judgment strengthened by comparison of CLC's policies in each of these areas with the policies implemented by subsequent phases of the Economic Stabilization Program.

There were some significant accommodative departures from the simple hold-the-line strategy. The exemption of raw agricultural products was explicitly mandated by the executive order and that of taxes by clear implication, but CLC was clearly making exceptions to the literal terms of the order when it exempted interest rates, imports and exports, raw seafood and newly cut timber, when it allowed some wage and price adjustment formulas to operate, and when it permitted wage increases for servicemen in Vietnam. These exceptions suggest that CLC members were not zealots or ideologues with respect to their police mission or legalistic in the sense of feeling obligated to apply the freeze order literally, regardless of the consequences. In some instances, at least, they were willing to make accommodations on the basis of other values and public policy goals if the reasons to do so were strong and the concessions did not seem to jeopardize the overall success of the freeze, conceived in terms of a hold-the-line strategy.

Nevertheless, on the most economically important and difficult questions—coverage of state government employees, the pass-through of most cost increases, the fulfillment of agreements, statutes, and regulations calling for price, wage, or rent increases—the hold-the-line strategy, the most stringent and categorical of anti-inflation strategies, prevailed. The concessions to competing values were treated as necessary but basically undesirable exceptions, not as endorsements of a perfect competition or redistributive philosophy.

A good number of CLC's numerous accommodative rules, in fact, were concerned with defining, and hence limiting, the major exceptions. Each accommodative rule—for instance, that raw agricultural products were exempt or that prices or wages could be increased if warranted by substantial changes in a product or job—stimulated a flurry of definitional problems; many CLC rules thus dealt with whether certain kinds of processing removed a product from the "raw agricultural product" category or whether a particular change made a job or a product "new."[39] Even the clarification of a stringent rule requires promulgation of some accommodative rulings; a legal line is best drawn by providing examples that fall on both sides. In fact, it was *because* CLC's basic rules were primarily stringent that so many transaction-specific ones were accommodative. Lower-level officials were able to decide most applications for accommodative rulings on their own simply by applying stringent CLC rules. As in other hierarchies, the issues that reached the policy makers tended to be those which made a particularly strong argument for incremental accommodative adjustments.[40] If the trunk of the tree leaned in a stringent direction, a number of accommodative branches dealing with narrow, industry-specific problems could be added without producing much net movement toward price and wage increases for the economy as a whole. Or, to shift metaphors, CLC was like a football team that started by kicking the ball deep into its opponent's territory and then yielded a number of short gains but not very much total yardage.

CLC must be judged, of course, not merely in terms of how fiercely it held the line, but whether the accommodative exceptions it made were fair and intellectually justified, or conversely, whether it legalistically ignored equally compelling cases for accommodation. The council issued so many rules so quickly and with so little effort to articulate a set of principles concerning when the hold-the-line strategy could be relaxed that some failures in this regard were virtually inevitable. CLC sometimes issued an accommodative exception in one situation, but legalistically adhered to a stringent rule in another situation that seemed very much like the first. This was not only unfair to those involved, but produced confusion for citizens and businesses and even lower-level agency officials.

---

[39] CLC allowed increases in prices for products that were "new," in the sense of being "substantially different" from their predecessors and, for rental property to which "substantial capital improvements" had been made, and wage increases for persons who obtained or were promoted to a "bona fide" new job. One consequence, however, was upward movement in prices for the new line of fall fashions, new model automobiles with demonstrated additional features, and "new" cuts of meat devised by butchers. See Weber, *In Pursuit of Price Stability,* pp. 73–74, 101. The "new product" problem plagues all price control programs. See Mansfield, *Short History of the OPA,* pp. 74–79.

[40] For example, OEP's Policy Analysis Office, which was responsible for referring to CLC the policy questions that came up through the inquiry-response system, decided most of the requests that came along on its own. A sample of the cases in its files revealed that officials gave a stringent response to 74 percent of the inquiries seeking an accommodative answer. By contrast, in cases it sent on to ExComm, about 50 percent resulted in stringent rules. And that was not because ExComm was more lenient in attitude than Policy Analysis. In nineteen sampled ExComm cases, they rejected the ruling recommended by Policy Analysis. In fourteen of those nineteen disagreements, ExComm chose a *more stringent* position than the Policy Analysis recommendation.

Reading through the entire body of CLC rules, however, the departures from intellectual consistency are remarkably few, especially in view of the pace and style of the CLC and ExComm deliberations. The OEP issue papers which posed the rule-making problems reflect a preoccupation with the problem of consistency, especially the recurrent argument, "If we make an exception for X, wouldn't we have to for Y and Z?" Sometimes, of course, the bureaucratic position, "If we make an exception for you, we'd have to do it for everybody," is a legalistic cop-out, but sometimes, where an accommodative exception for one would have immediate adverse consequences for others or might reasonably be expected to jeopardize compliance by others, the consistency argument is quite rational and even fair. Some policies require toughness and consistency in rule application if they are to succeed, and the hold-the-line anti-inflation policy seems to fall in that category. That, of course, does not settle the basic substantive question of whether the hold-the-line policy itself, which consciously tolerates the imposition of hardship and unfairness on some in order to stop inflation and thus benefit the many, was itself justifiable under the circumstances.[41]

---

[41] See the discussion of this issue in Chapter 10.

CHAPTER 4

Sources of Stringency

What impels a regulatory agency to adhere to a stringent policy in the face of demands for accommodation to other values? The freeze agencies steadfastly resisted many of the same arguments that produced more accommodative policies in subsequent phases of the Economic Stabilization Program. One might think, "Well, naturally the freeze was stringent. That's what a short-term freeze is!" What *is* there about a freeze, however, as a type of regulatory activity, that makes one expect its administrators to adhere to a stringent position? CLC officials, in their own minds, faced very real choices between a hard or a soft freeze. They did issue a number of accommodative rulings. Freezes during World War II, the Korean War, and the subsequent Phase IV freeze of June 13, 1973, were all implemented in a more accommodative manner than the one under discussion here. It would seem instructive, therefore, to examine why regulatory officials in this instance held concessions to persuasive accommodative arguments within narrow bounds. The answers may illuminate sources of stringency in the regulatory process in general.

EXPLANATIONS OF REGULATORY POLICY

Explanations of regulatory policy usually focus on one of the following factors: the ideology or philosophy of regulatory officials; the legal and political mandate of the regulatory program; the social and political organization of the regulatory process; and the economic effects of the regulatory program.

Ideology of the Regulators

Accommodative regulatory policies are often explained by reference to regulatory officials' personal concern for the stability and growth of the regulated industry or of particular firms in it. Such accommodative philosophies are often attributed to the recruitment of regulators from the controlled industry or from a general business or corporate law background. An industry orientation, it is argued, is often created or reinforced by continuing association with officers of regulated firms and by the prospect of later employment in those firms.[1] By implication, then, greater stringency would result from the recruitment of regulatory officials from groups ideologically committed to the police mission of the program at hand or sympathetic in general to regulatory restrictions on business.

Legal and Political Mandate

The legislation that authorizes and guides a regulatory program has often been stressed as a primary determinant of a regulatory agency's sense of mission and policy-making style. Many analysts attribute accommodative policies to ambiguity or vagueness in the legal mandates of regulatory agencies, reflecting a legislative irresolution about the goals of the regulatory program. Some writers attribute the statutory weakness to the political influence of business at the legislative level; a good deal of regulatory legislation has been designed as much to prevent "disruptive" competition as to protect the public.[2] Other analysts point to a general reluctance of legislatures to make firm choices between regulatory effectiveness and values of economic continuity.[3] In any case, authorizing statutes are often devoid of explicit rules or guides to decision of the hard issues. They merely transfer the problem of choice, and hence of contending with conflicting political interests, to the regulatory body. Consequently, the theory goes, the agency is cast adrift without firm political support for stringent enforcement of the police mission or decisions that would threaten the status quo. It falls back on ad hoc and directionless "balancing" of conflicting arguments on a case-

---

[1] See E. Pendleton Herring, *Public Administration and the Public Interest* (New York: McGraw-Hill, 1936); Robert Fellmeth, *The Interstate Commerce Omission* (New York: Grossman Publishers, 1970), ch. 1; Robert Cuff, *The War Industries Board* (Baltimore: Johns Hopkins Press, 1973). By contrast, it has been alleged that the staffs of agencies formed in the late 1960s and 1970s, such as the Environmental Protection Agency and the Occupational Safety and Health Administration, are dominated by "Naderites," persons ideologically hostile to business and to arguments based on the economic costs of stringent regulation. See Irving Kristol, "A Regulated Society?" 1 *Regulation* (July–Aug. 1977) p. 12.

[2] Gabriel Kolko, *Railroads and Regulation* (Princeton, N.J.: Princeton University Press, 1965); James Weinstein, *The Corporate Ideal in the Liberal State* (Boston: Beacon Press, 1968).

[3] See Theodore Lowi, *The End of Liberalism* (New York: W. W. Norton & Co., 1969); Marver Bernstein, *Regulating Business by Independent Commission* (Princeton, N.J.: Princeton

by-case basis or endorsements of bargains struck by competing interests, both of which produce a drift toward accommodation. Conversely, under this theory, a forceful political mandate and articulation of specific, stringent rules in the authorizing legislation should result in more consistently stringent regulatory policy.

Social and Political Organization

The social and political relationships in which regulatory agencies are typically enmeshed have been held responsible for tendencies toward accommodation. Some theorists argue that after the initial legislation has been passed, public and legislative interest in regulatory issues tends to decline dramatically. The performance of an individual regulatory agency is rarely a salient political issue.[4] Particular regulatory decisions are seldom scrutinized and evaluated in the press or in the electoral arena. Agencies usually are not subjected to objective measures of performance.[5] As one consequence of public inattention, it is claimed, regulators are free to choose policies that maximize their own security, or create the appearance of most "success" with the least work, or incur the least resistance and political opposition.[6] This also means, some analysts assert, that the substantive direction of agency policy is molded by the interactions between the agency and relevant interest groups and the relative power of those groups to "cause trouble" for the agency. Those who stand to benefit from stringent regulation, such as consumers, are often scattered or weakly organized, only marginally or sporadically interested, and unable to provide the agency with reliable information. The regulated industry, in contrast, is typically highly organized, intensely interested, and in constant contact with the agency. Representatives of the regulated firms are continuously in a position to present their problems, data, and perspectives to the regulators and to mount political and legal attacks against stringent regulatory policies.[7] The agency often needs their

University Press, 1955); Henry Friendly, *The Federal Administrative Agencies: The Need for Better Definition of Standards* (Cambridge, Mass.: Harvard University Press, 1962).

[4] See Murray Edelman, *The Symbolic Uses of Politics* (Urbana: University of Illinois Press, 1964); Bernstein, *Regulating Business*.

[5] Anthony Downs, *Inside Bureaucracy* (Boston: Little, Brown, 1967).

[6] Richard Posner, "The Behavior of Regulatory Agencies," 1 *Journal of Legal Studies* 305 (1972); Stephen Breyer and Paul MacAvoy, *Energy Regulation by the Federal Power Commission* (Washington: Brookings Institution, 1974); George Stigler, *The Citizen and the State* (Chicago: University of Chicago Press, 1975); Roger Noll, *Reforming Regulation* (Washington: Brookings Institution, 1971).

[7] David Truman, *The Governmental Process* (New York: Alfred A. Knopf, 1953); Avery Leiserson, *Administrative Regulation* (Chicago: University of Chicago Press, 1942); James Turner, *The Chemical Feast* (New York: Grossman Publishers, 1970) (The Food and Drug Administration).

On the other hand, see David Seidman, "The Politics and Economics of Pharmaceutical cooperation to implement policies and must bargain to get it.[8] Thus the agency is either pressured or persuaded, the theory goes, into acceding to the positions preferred by the regulated firms. Initial zeal is gradually replaced by heartfelt concern for maintaining the status quo.[9] By implication, then, a regulatory program which experiences high public visibility, which is subject to objective measures of performance, which is confronted with a more balanced pressure group structure, and which has multiple sources of intelligence and advice, is more likely to maintain a relatively stringent stance.

Economic Effects

Economic analysis of regulatory policy focuses on the market structure of the regulated industry, and the effects of regulation on the costs and competitive position of regulated firms. Compliance with regulatory directives and restrictions, economic theory suggests, imposes additional costs on the regulated firms. To achieve regulatory goals, therefore, the agency will have to protect those firms from competition with firms not under regulatory control, to grant rate increases to cover the costs of meeting regulatory standards, or to moderate the rigor of regulation, so as to ensure the continuity and stability of the regulated activity or product.[10] More generally, the implied thesis of this kind of analysis is that regulators will seek to avoid disruption of production and employment in the regulated sector. Consequently, if enforcement of stringent regulations threatens the profitability of the most important regulated firms, policies will be modified in an accommodative direction. The converse of this thesis would be that the more "slack" there is in the regulated firms, that is, the greater their capacity to

---

Regulation," in *Public Law and Public Policy,* John Gardiner, ed. (New York: Praeger, 1977) for a description of the FDA's sensitivity to Congressional pressures for stringent regulation. Paul Sabatier, "Social Movements and Regulatory Agencies: Toward a More Adequate—and Less Pessimistic—Theory of Clientele Capture," 6 *Policy Science* 301 (1975), describes an air pollution control agency's efforts to organize pro-regulation pressure groups.

[8] See Philip Selznick, *TVA and the Grass Roots* (New York: Harper & Row–Torchbooks, 1966); Leon Mayhew, *Law and Equal Opportunity* (Cambridge, Mass.: Harvard University Press, 1968); Philippe Nonet, *Administrative Justice* (New York: Russell Sage Foundation, 1969).

[9] See Bernstein, *Regulating Business;* Samuel Huntington, "The Marasmus of the ICC," 61 *Yale Law Journal* 467 (1952); Downs, *Inside Bureaucracy.*

[10] This is not to say that regulatory agencies will always pursue policies that maximize economic efficiency. A major complaint of economists is that they do not, that regulatory agencies, in seeking to "manage" the industry, shield regulated firms from the rigors of competition, promoting inefficient investment practices, delaying technological innovation, and producing higher prices than competition would yield. See Stigler, *Citizen and the State;* Richard Caves, *Air Transport and Its Regulators* (Cambridge, Mass.: Harvard University Press, 1962); Martin Levine, "Is Regulation Necessary? California Air Transportation and National Regulatory Policy," 74 *Yale Law Journal* 1416 (1965); Paul MacAvoy, ed., *The Crisis of the Regulatory Commissions* (New York: W. W. Norton & Co., 1970); Robert S. Smith, *The Occupational Safety and Health Act* (Washington: American Enterprise Institute, 1976).

absorb the costs of compliance with regulations without significant impairment of profitability or quality of service, then the more stringent we might expect regulatory policy to be.[11]

THE SALIENCE OF ECONOMIC EFFECTS

The explanatory factors in regulatory policy making just reviewed are not mutually exclusive. Each directs our attention to variables that undoubtedly influence an agency's relative stress on stringency or accommodation, but all are not necessarily of equal importance. The freeze experience provides some clues to their relative weight. It suggests that the outer limits of regulatory stringency are likely to be set by the economic impact of stringent regulations, and hence at bottom, by the primacy of values of economic continuity. If there is no "slack" in the regulated firms with which to absorb the costs of compliance with stringent regulations, significant accommodative modifications are likely *regardless* of the ideology of the regulators, their legal mandate, or the social organization of the regulatory process. Where the economic impact of the regulation allows the regulated firms and the agency more room to maneuver, the other three factors rise to greater significance.

With respect to the factors of ideology, legal mandate, and social organization, the freeze agencies were in an excellent position to maintain a stringent stance. 1) *Ideology.* Agency officials, as we will explore more fully later, defined their role in terms of effective implementation of their police mission, rather than in terms of responsibility for long-term economic planning, growth, or efficiency. They were not deeply committed in an ideological sense to price and wage controls, but neither were they hostile to them. By and large, they were government economists, civil servants, and lawyers, not recruited from the business community. They saw their job as a technical, not a political, one and were determined to do it efficiently. 2) *Legal Mandate.* The legal and political mandate they received was unusually clear and strong. The executive order that created the program was not a vague statement of conflicting goals and considerations but an explicit *rule.* There were vocal expressions of support for the anti-inflationary mission from all sectors of business and society. 3) *Social Organization.* Intense coverage by national and local news media kept the program highly visible. The clarity of the idea of a freeze, together with the monthly Bureau of Labor Statistics indexes, provided external and objective measures of agency performance. The constellation of groups affected included a healthy balance of forces—unusually active consumer groups, congressmen, labor unions, and a broad range of competing business interests, each on the alert for any regulatory concessions

---

[11] For the concept of "slack" as applied to individual firms, see Richard Cyert and James March, *A Behavioral Theory of the Firm* (Englewood Cliffs, N.J.: Prentice-Hall, 1963).

to another group. Interference, pressure, and second-guessing of freeze agency decisions by the president and Congress, on behalf of special interests, were almost nonexistent.

It is striking, however, that most of these same factors were operating in much the same way throughout the subsequent phases of the Economic Stabilization Program, during which the stringency of the initial freeze was progressively moderated until the program was finally abandoned. Most interesting of all was the Phase IV freeze instituted in June 1973. In that case, the authorizing executive order was similar to that of the Phase I freeze. The duration of restrictions called for was even shorter (sixty days). The national desire for a halt in inflation was, if anything, more intense. Nevertheless, the Phase IV freeze was characterized by widespread evasion, withholding of products from the market, and shortages of certain foods, fuel, and other commodities. It conjured up a storm of criticism, to which CLC officials yielded by moderating some policies and lifting portions of the freeze before the scheduled termination date. In the sixty days of the freeze, CLC granted 100 exceptions, compared to the five allowed during Phase I.[12] Price indexes continued to climb, and, unlike Phase I, the later freeze was generally judged, even by the Nixon administration, to have been a failure.[13]

The difference between the two freezes is not hard to identify. The Phase I freeze was instituted in a slack economy. In the late summer and fall of 1971, unemployment was high. Industrial production was just beginning to pick up after a recession. Many industries still experienced slow demand and a considerable amount of idle operating capacity. The inflation was fueled by "cost-push" factors and an inflationary psychology, rather than by serious shortages on the supply side. In contrast, beginning with Phase III of the program and continuing through the Phase IV freeze in June 1973, the economy was booming and capacity utilization was high. Grains, livestock, copper, steel, petroleum, lumber, paper, and many other products were in short supply. Under Phase III, prices had been increasing rapidly (more rapidly, in fact, than during the period before the Phase I freeze), especially in the uncontrolled sectors: raw agricultural products and imported commodities, such as petroleum and copper. The announcement of the Phase IV

---

[12] See CLC, *Economic Stabilization Program Quarterly Report, July 1–September 30, 1973* (Washington: Government Printing Office).

[13] President Nixon stated, in curtailing the Phase IV freeze, "The freeze is holding down production and creating shortages which threaten to get worse, and cause still higher prices. . . ." "Statement of the President," in CLC, *Phase IV Announcement* (Washington: Government Printing Office, 1973). The accelerated Phase IV, CLC noted, "took careful note of freeze lessons and distortions as it balanced price objectives with the need to maximize supplies."

freeze, in consequence, resulted in severe cost-price squeezes on many industries. Firms withheld products from the market or sought to sell only in the uncontrolled export market. Some factories closed for want of supplies.[14] Under these circumstances, the administration quickly retreated from a stringent policy rather than risking further disruption of the economy.

These developments suggest strongly that when vigorous enforcement of a stringently defined regulatory mission actually disrupts (or clearly threatens to disrupt) continued production or provision of valued goods and services, the agency's policy will move toward accommodation, no matter how strong its sense of mission, how explicit its rules or how strong its support from pro-regulation interest groups.[15] Businesses and unions often protest any stringent regulations, of course, and claim intolerable hardship, but the more severe the incursion *actually is,* the more intense their protest is likely to be and the more concrete and persuasive the evidence they can produce. Regulatory officials are likely to weigh specific, focused hardships caused by economic disruption more highly than the diffuse, long-run benefits provided by stringent regulation. To do otherwise, in the pragmatic American legal and political culture, would generally be regarded as arbitrary.

There are exceptions, of course. Clear and present danger to human life often sustains stringent protective regulations even when the result is economic disruption. Regulatory officials may eventually shut down coal mines that fail to meet safety requirements and forbid the sale of chickens fed with carcinogenic chemicals, even when it means financial hardship for producers and their employees.[16] Government subsidies for the regulated firms or wartime appeals for continued production and the toleration of shortages may also sustain stringent regulations that severely impair profits. In most regulatory programs, however, these offsetting capabilities are not available, the risk to human life is more remote, and the benefits of stringent regulation are more intangible than unemployment and shortages.

---

[14] Poultry and egg producers, for example, their prices frozen, were locked into a loss position by high feed prices and cut back production, some of them by means of highly publicized destruction of chicks and eggs. Operators of feedlots for beef cattle, dairymen, grain millers, meatpackers, textile producers, and metal fabricators were caught in similar squeezes. When they cut back production, shortages and some shutdowns by their customer firms resulted. CLC, *Economic Stabilization Program Quarterly Report, July 1–September 30, 1973,* pp. 27–30; *New York Times,* July 19, 1973, p. 25.

[15] Another example: the winter of 1973–74 saw the relaxation of stringent air pollution regulations concerning fuel burned by electric utilities—restrictions zealously monitored by environmental protection groups and agencies—in the face of an oil shortage generated by the Arab boycott that threatened to disrupt the continuity of electrical production.

[16] See *New York Times,* March 31, 1974, p. 49, and "Costly Clean Air Move, *San Francisco Chronicle,* December 30, 1974 (Environmental Protection Agency rule and court order results in shutdown of furnaces at U.S. Steel's Gary, Indiana works, the nation's largest, and in the layoff of 4,000 employees).

Even regulatory systems oriented toward stringency are organized to be especially alert to the overly disruptive effects of their regulations, for if left uncorrected they breed evasion or defiance. During the freeze, OEP field offices were instructed to transmit daily reports to the OEP national office noting any "problem areas." Top officials in CLC and OEP met virtually every day with delegations from industry, unions, school boards, and other groups who claimed to be hurt by the freeze. The entire inquiry-response system was structured to bring problem cases to the attention of the policy makers. One can only conclude that a major reason that freeze policies remained so stringent was that these feedback processes brought relatively few cases of unavoidable and intolerable freeze-induced hardship to CLC's attention, and this was because the freeze, imposed upon a slack economy, in fact caused relatively little severe disruption.[17]

The relatively mild economic impact of the Phase I freeze is not sufficient, however, to explain the stringency of CLC's stand. Even where the disruptive effects of stringent police-mission enforcement are in fact relatively minor, there will be claims that they are or will be major. The facts of the matter are often tremendously complex and difficult to ascertain or predict accurately. Judgments about what risks should be tolerated and what future adaptations industry might make to avert them are always problematic. In such a context, the ideology of the regulators, their legal mandate, and the political and social organization of interested groups are likely to determine an agency's reaction to factual and evaluative uncertainty. In the case of the freeze agencies, the additional impetus toward stringency was provided primarily by the nature of their legal mandate and the public's real and predicted reactions to the freeze.

THE LEGAL MANDATE AND STRINGENCY

The authority and responsibility delegated to CLC—to govern prices and wages and rents in a gigantic economy—was vast, even frightening. The decisions it would have to make, directly affecting peoples' struggle for financial advantage and security, were politically sensitive and highly visible. The problems it faced were novel; there was no accepted body of theory concerning how the balance between price stability and other values should be struck. Searching for some intellectual anchor, agency officials often looked directly to the words of their legal mandate for guidance. The freeze order and the conception of the freeze it suggested were often referred to in the issue papers presented to ExComm and CLC. Several features of the order

---

[17] Some economic hardship did result from the freeze. There were thousands of exemption applications, and a thick black book of "problem areas" was compiled by OEP. Still, very few were as substantial and dramatic as the Phase IV freeze disruptions.

were important in this regard, and they encouraged a lean toward stringency in dealing with policy problems.

First, the freeze order stated an explicit and stringent rule rather than a series of conflicting considerations and goals. True, it provided that exceptions could be granted to correct inequities, and it exempted raw agricultural products and urged CLC to maintain harmony with other national policies. Those provisions, as noted earlier, provided an opening for accommodative rulings. Even an explicit rule does not foreclose choice, but such a rule makes it easier to avoid choice, to resolve difficult choices quickly, and to terminate a deadlocked discussion by reference to the terms of the rule. The explicitness of the operative section of the freeze order also made it feasible for agency officials to conceive of their job as legal interpretation and implementation of *predetermined* policy, as opposed to open-ended economic policy formulation. They could make decisions by deduction from the preformulated intent expressed in the order, rather than by full-scale inquiry into what would serve the public interest in each particular case. Their authority could be seen as limited to making only those exceptions that would promote effective implementation of the preformed policy of stringency.

Second, the general theory of the freeze, which the officials drew from the political background of the executive order, was suggestive of an uncomplicated, stringent stance. The president's economic advisers, CLC officials knew, saw the current inflation as buoyed primarily by an inflationary psychology. The freeze, accordingly, was conceived as an instrument to administer shock therapy to the economy, to change expectations of continuing wage and price increases by means of dramatic and forceful government intervention. Under this conception, an emphasis on sophisticated fine tuning of the economy was hardly called for.[18]

Third, the short duration of their mandate encouraged agency officials to view their role narrowly and to avoid responsibility for the effort of balancing conflicting values, gathering data, and formulating principles of justifiable accommodation—all on the grounds that the agencies had no legal authority to control economic activities after November 13, 1971, or to make accommodative rules that would limit the options of those responsible for post-freeze policy. The crucial aspect of the short duration of the freeze, therefore, was not its temporariness per se, but the division of labor it suggested: responsibility for more sophisticated policy formulation was reserved for the administrators of Phase II; the freeze agency officials, on the other hand, had the simpler job of "holding the line." The temporal limitation of authority was analogous to the functional limitation of jurisdiction so common in other government bureaus. It provided an excuse to limit the intellectual task of

---

[18] See Arnold Weber, *In Pursuit of Price Stability* (Washington: Brookings Institution, 1973), pp. 36, 51.

regulation by saying that responsibility for longer-range problems was the job of another department or agency.

Finally, a simplistic view of the agencies' mission was suggested most powerfully by the graphic metaphor used by the president in characterizing the program—a *freeze.* This term, which was quickly adopted by agency officials and the news media, evoked an image of rigidity. To agency officials, what a *freeze* meant was initially assumed to be relatively unproblematic; they seemed to be continually amazed that so many different policy problems persisted in arising. They would not have disagreed with a woman from Buffalo, complaining of some price changes, who wrote to OEP as follows,

> I wish you'd take time out to explain to a retarded citizen your definition of—price freeze! I'll tell you mine. A price freeze means to me that food, gas, and other consumer products stay stable—their prices DO NOT fluctuate. . . .

This argument, together with the limited duration of the program, was repeatedly used by agency officials to rationalize stringent resistance to inquirers' justice-claims. "I'm sorry, but that's what a freeze *is,*" they would say, or, "You can't give in all the time and still have a freeze," or "A freeze means there are going to be some inequities." Indeed, for agency officials to have systematically attempted to relieve inequities or follow something more akin to a perfect competition strategy, they would have had to abandon the notion that they were administering a "freeze." They would have had to relabel the program.

SOCIAL ORGANIZATION AND STRINGENCY

An initially stringent regulatory mandate and clear sense of mission have been known to erode under the pressures and conflicts of implementation. Patterns of interaction between the agency and the regulated firms can easily subvert an initial tough-minded policy. In the case of the freeze, however, the social organization of the regulated public supported a continuing inclination toward stringency. It did so first of all by generating a special kind of compliance problem and, second, by enhancing the visibility of regulatory policy making.

The Problem of Compliance

Agency officials were haunted by the specter of noncompliance. Despite their vast legal powers and indications of popular support for the freeze, the atmosphere in the upper levels of OEP and CLC was one of almost tangible anxiety. Officials scoured daily newspapers and field office reports for indications of illegal price or wage increases, criticisms of freeze administration, or other signs of public disaffection. CLC and OEP leaders pressured IRS officials to investigate reported violations immediately and to "get a compliance case" that could be prosecuted in court and publicized for its deterrent value.[19]

This concern was linked to the social organization of the regulated public and the presumably fragile structure of compliance. The regulated arena was vast and diverse, populated by millions of business firms, landlords, and individuals with fixed plans and expectations for price and wage increases. While they might all desire a sudden halt in the inflationary spiral as an abstract, collective goal, it was not in the interest of any individual firm or household to give up *its* price or wage increase.[20] And it was certainly not in firm A's interest to keep its prices steady if its suppliers violated the freeze or for union B to accept a wage freeze if other unions did not or if rents on its members' apartments were increased. To agency officials, therefore, it seemed that compliance was at best *conditional*. Evasion and defiance could quickly snowball, they thought, if regulated entities began to perceive the freeze as anything short of universally effective. They would have agreed with Chester Bowles, head of OPA during World War II, who said that 20 percent of the population would automatically comply with any regulation, 5 percent would attempt to evade it, and the remaining 75 percent would go along with it as long as the 5 percent were caught and punished.[21] Moreover, any noncompliance would be highly visible, both to individual consumers and to readers of the Bureau of Labor Statistics monthly reports. Here was a situation in which a clear and relatively objective measure of regulatory performance existed, and the agency could easily be labeled a failure.[22]

At the outset of the freeze, general expressions of support were common, but countless letters from the public also indicated that support was linked to parity of treatment. The most prevalent type of complaint received by the agencies referred to rules that seemed to accord other firms or groups favored

---

[19] See Harry Yoshpe et al., *Stemming Inflation: The Office of Emergency Preparedness and the 90-Day Freeze* (Washington: Government Printing Office, 1972), pp. 117–125.

[20] This is the dilemma presented by any attempt to provide *indivisible* "public goods," as analyzed by Mancur Olson, Jr., *The Logic of Collective Action* (New York: Schocken Books, 1968). Logically, any individual firm would benefit from a halt in inflation regardless of whether it cheated or not, provided all the others complied.

[21] Chester Bowles, *Promises to Keep* (New York: Harper & Row, 1971), p. 25.

[22] By contrast, the perception of instances of false or misleading advertising in a community is not widely defined as an overall "failure" of the Federal Trade Commission or consumer protection laws, just as persistence of crime is usually not defined as "failure" of the police department or criminal law. Such agencies are generally evaluated by whether they are doing "the best they can" given current levels of staffing or whether they deliberately avert their eyes from offenses they have the power to prevent.

treatment. The support of the AFL-CIO, its president (George Meany) indicated, depended on whether the freeze was enforced evenhandedly against business as well as labor.[23] The public remained suspicious throughout that the freeze "wasn't working." A special survey conducted by the Census Bureau in late September indicated that only 60 percent of a national sample of individuals felt that the freeze had stopped wage increases, while a mere 33 percent thought it had stopped price increases.[24] Freeze officials' apprehensions about the public's attitude and willingness to comply were apparently not irrational.

The resulting watchword in the inquiry-response system was "consistency." Consistency of treatment, avoidance of even the appearance of favoritism, was urged upon CLC by virtually every staff issue paper. And the appearance of consistency was most easily achieved by adherence to a policy of stringency. A rule that allowed prices or wages to rise, even for a justifiable reason, was suspect from an enforcement standpoint, for it might give the worker or the businessman the impression that the freeze was beginning to thaw, that everyone else was cheating, or that the agencies were showing favoritism. Conversely, a consistently stringent policy enabled agency officials to deny accommodative rulings to particular firms with the statement that they were being treated no worse than anyone else, or that "If we gave in to you, we'd have to do the same for everybody."

In addition, because of its breadth of coverage and pocketbook significance to all groups in society, the freeze evoked pressure on the agencies from a broad variety of organized groups. While agency officials met with representatives of many organizations, they had no opportunity to become sympathetic specialists in the problems of any one industry. Moreover, representatives of the regulated entities, while seeking accommodative rulings for themselves, exerted cross-checking pressures. If a concession was made to one union, others could be expected to knock on OEP's door the next day to complain (or ask for similar benefits). Businesses were alert to, and argued against, concessions to their competitors or suppliers.[25] The broad distribu-

---

[23] *Newsweek,* August 30, 1971; Yoshpe, *Stemming Inflation,* pp. 144–165. Significantly, neither major unions nor major corporations exerted substantial pressures for special treatment or for more generally accommodative policies, either directly on the agencies or through the White House or Congress. Of course, many corporations and unions sought accommodative rulings by substantive legal arguments addressed to specific problems.

[24] Yoshpe, *Stemming Inflation,* pp. 120–121.

[25] There were some exceptions. Employers sometimes *supported* unions' demands for implementation of wage increases ostensibly blocked by the freeze; this was consistent with the recurrent position of industrial management that looser wage controls are preferable to labor strife and resultant disruption. See Arnold Weber, "Making Wage Controls Work," 30 *The Public Interest* 28, 34 (Winter 1973). Some employers undoubtedly colluded with individual

tion of regulated entities meant that the agencies did not have to seek support from any *single* economic group or co-opt its representatives. To the contrary, formal equality of treatment, most easily symbolized by completely stringent rules, was assumed to be a quid pro quo that had to be paid to win compliance.

Visibility

Another striking feature of the relationship between the agencies and the regulated public was the intense and prominent coverage of agency rulings by the mass media, particularly major newspapers, news magazines, business publications, and national television and radio networks. This front page coverage was in part the product of government initiative. The president himself announced the new law on television, and cabinet officers held news conferences on the subject the next day. However, governmental efforts to obtain publicity and, more importantly, the *continuing* media coverage the freeze received were a result of the freeze law's breadth of jurisdiction, its continuing relevance to a wide variety of important interests, its novelty, and its stimulation of widespread demands for more detailed and precise explication of the law. At the outset, television news programs featured regular "question and answer" sessions based on CLC rulings. Newspapers printed the CLC rules issued each day. Reporters sought interviews with agency officials and assessments of the stabilization program by business and labor leaders, politicians, economists, and the man-on-the-street. Reporters also stood ready to uncover examples of indecision, favoritism, or ineffectiveness on the part of the freeze agencies. If the freeze was newsworthy, its failings were too.

The media seemed especially alert to instances of inconsistency and unwarranted leniency. The *New York Times* editorialized, "If the national freeze on wages and prices is to be effective in curbing inflation, it must be enforced both . . . vigorously and broadly." It urged CLC to deny a rate increase for school bus companies in New York City, arguing that "Steel and auto companies, which had already begun paying their workers higher wages, have been precluded from effecting a price boost and the private school bus companies are on even weaker ground in seeking to effect theirs."[26] When OEP submitted an issue paper on the case to CLC, that editorial was attached. Similarly, the *Washington Post* reported and criticized an OEP deci-

---

employees to avoid freeze restrictions in order to retain a valued worker. Similarly, purchasers of materials in short supply undoubtedly absorbed without public complaint price increases that violated the freeze. In this regard, the general availability of materials during the freeze—as contrasted with the situation during Phase IV—contributed to the willingness of businessmen to support strict enforcement and, hence, to a stringent agency philosophy.

[26] *New York Times,* Sept. 13, 1971.

sion that resulted in a salary increase for teachers in a Maryland county;[27] the editorial became the subject of avid discussion in OEP's General Counsel's Office. Citizen allegations of freeze violations by retailers or landlords were reported in many local newspapers, and some papers undertook their own investigations of compliance with the freeze. In reaction, agency leaders actually changed their enforcement strategy to intensify their image of stringency, seeking to prosecute violators in court rather than quietly pressuring them to roll back their prices.

For agency officials, the intense news coverage also created a heightened sense of the significance of the program, producing an atmosphere of crisis and high purpose. The media held up a mirror to the agencies, magnified and accelerated the feedback they received, and emphasized that their decisions were having an important impact on real people. With today's decisions displayed on tomorrow's front pages, the small initial cadre of CLC and OEP officials quickly became especially conscious of their power and responsibility. They worked extremely hard, into the nights and over weekends. The sense of urgency and intellectual challenge immediately enveloped new recruits as they were sent to CLC and OEP from bureaucratic jobs in other agencies. It generated a strong sense of solidarity and commitment to the "success" of the freeze enterprise.

More importantly, "success" was defined in terms of police-mission effectiveness. Handed a great deal of power, galvanized to a high level of energy and effort, pushed by the media for "success," agency officials were attracted to simple and dramatic goals rather than complex ones, forceful regulation rather than passive moderation. For hardworking officials who a month earlier had only inchoate feelings about inflation and government controls, the success of the freeze in stopping inflation became a vital mission. Stringency became the emotionally preferred position. Special pleaders for accommodation were morally suspect. An unwarranted relaxation of the freeze was a worse "mistake" than an instance of unnecessarily harsh stringency.

EXTENT OF REGULATORY CONTROL

Additional insight into the sources of regulatory stringency is provided by comparing the agencies to the Price Commission, which regulated prices and rents during the second phase of the Economic Stabilization Program. The Price Commission, too, was deeply concerned about voluntary compliance. The Consumer Price Index and the Wholesale Price Index continued to function as external and objective measures of the agency's success or failure.

---

[27] *Washington Post,* October 7, 1971.

The commission was subject to broad and diverse pressures for stringency, and it was fearful of making accommodations to one firm or industry that might be taken as a mark of favoritism or weakness. News media coverage continued at an intense level and affected the internal life of the agency. Staff motivation and belief in the importance of their enterprise was very high. There was considerable slack in the economy during most of Phase II. Unlike the freeze agencies, however, the Price Commission did not issue very stringent rules. By and large, they adopted a perfect competition theory of control. Prices were allowed to increase in accordance with demonstrated cost increases and historically established markups or percentage profit margins.[28] Despite pressures for greater stringency—pressures exerted by the news media, organized labor, consumer groups, staff members, and a substantial minority of the commission itself—the Commission adhered to its middle-of-the-road balancing of anti-inflationary goals with concern for economic recovery and continuity.

The Price Commission's more accommodative stance reemphasizes the importance of an agency's legal mandate in determining its policies. The commission was *not* given an explicit rule to implement. The executive order establishing Phase II merely created the commission and told it to deal with the problem of inflation. Price Commission members, accordingly, felt and talked more as economic planners responsible for the health of the economy in general than did rule makers in CLC's Executive Committee during the freeze. Unlike ExComm members, the commission members could not conceive of themselves as the enforcers of a preexisting law or policy from which they could deduce more specific rules. Unlike CLC, which could mentally assign responsibility for long-range problems to their successor agencies, there was no other agency the commission could rely on to deal with unintended adverse effects of stringent regulations. Its members and staff had no idea how long their tenure would last. They took the attitude that even if their tenure might be short, they should proceed as if it were indefinite in duration.

But there was one additional source of the Price Commission's accommodative policies: it regulated only prices. Wages and salaries were under the jurisdiction of the Pay Board. That body issued regulations allowing wages and salaries to increase at a 5.5 to 6 percent annual rate, and it granted liberal exceptions to that standard in individual cases, allowing implementation of larger increases called for in preexisting collective bargaining agreements and in industries in which workers were deemed to deserve "catch-up" increases. Moreover, exemptions from Price Commission regula-

---

[28] See Robert Lanzillotti, Mary Hamilton, and Blaine Roberts, *Phase II in Review: The Price Commission Experience* (Washington: Brookings Institution, 1975); C. Jackson Grayson and Louis Neeb, *Confessions of a Price Controller* (Homewood, Ill.: Dow Jones–Irwin, 1974).

tions were under the jurisdiction of the Cost of Living Council, which exempted raw agricultural and seafood products, exports and imports, all prices charged by small firms, and prices and fees charged by government bodies (such as the Post Office). Consequently, the regulatory powers of the commission were more restricted than those of the freeze agencies. They could not control as broad a range of costs incurred by the firms whose prices they regulated. If wages or other exempt costs could increase substantially, it was much harder to hold a stringent line on price increases.

This suggests that a major source of stringency in CLC's freeze policy—as it might be in other agencies—was the relative completeness of legal control the agencies enjoyed. They could be confident that there would be relatively few disequilibrating inputs into the regulated market. If they could prevent most firms' suppliers and workers from increasing operating costs, they could forcefully deny all price increases; if they could be confident, due to the breadth of control, that consumer prices would not increase, they could feel more comfortable about denying all wage and salary increases.[29] The more factors of production, the more variables a regulatory agency can control, it would seem, the greater its ability to pursue stringent policies. It should not be surprising then, that regulatory agencies characteristically seek ever-broader regulatory powers and more expansive jurisdictional coverage.[30]

CONCLUSION

The freeze experience, particularly in the context of the Economic Stabilization Program as a whole, provides several insights into the conditions under which an agency will adhere to a more stringent and uncompromising approach in defining its regulatory policy. A crucial factor, in the case of the freeze agencies, was the existence of economic "slack" in the regulated market, the capacity of the regulated firms to absorb the costs of complying with

---

[29] The agencies, operating in a slack economy, could also be reasonably confident that there would be no sharp increases in exempt areas, such as raw agricultural products and interest rates, during the freeze period, or so the economists told them. While increases in the prices of imported commodities might have been expected, these are a relatively small component in the United States economy.

[30] See Louis Jaffe, "The Effective Limits of the Administrative Process," 67 *Harvard Law Review* 1105 (1954); James Q. Wilson, "The Rise of the Bureaucratic State," 41 *The Public Interest* 77, 97 (1976). The Price Commission's most controversial steps, in fact, involved efforts to affect transactions outside its formal jurisdiction. In an effort to deter the Pay Board from making exceptions, the commission ruled that businesses could not pass on, in higher prices, wage increases in excess of the Pay Board's basic 5.5 percent annual standard. To exert control on the exempt raw agricultural sector, it called upon the administration to curtail price supports, increase acreage, and eliminate import quotas on meat. To deal with the diversion of supplies through exports—which were exempt from price controls—the commission pushed the administration to adopt export controls for some commodities.

stringent regulations without severe impairment of profitability. As comparison with the Phase IV freeze revealed, the main reason the Phase I agencies adhered to a stringent stance was that under the prevailing economic conditions, stringent policies did not cause very much severe disruption of economic activity.

A drift toward accommodative policies is possible, however, even in a relatively "slack" economic environment. The mere threat of economic disruption is often sufficient to produce accommodation, especially in view of the regulated firms' political and legal advantages and their control of information concerning the likely costs and consequences of regulatory restrictions. CLC's resistance to that tendency was abetted by four additional factors.

The first was the nature of its legal mandate. By its terms, the freeze order was both explicit and stringent. It articulated a basic standard—the price or wage in effect before the freeze—and no standard for accommodative departures. The temporal limitation of the agencies' jurisdiction seemed to absolve them of responsibility for the economic consequences of strict regulation. The rhetoric that accompanied the law—the metaphor of a "freeze"—helped to create in the minds of the public and administrators alike a simple and extremely rigid image of the program's purpose and an objective standard for measuring its success or failure.

Second, the freeze order gave the agencies extensive regulatory powers, the ability to control and prevent almost all cost increases for regulated firms. With such extensive powers, the agencies would rarely have to make accommodations to compensate for cost increases introduced by other regulatory agencies and external economic forces or to help regulated firms compete with unregulated competitors.

The third factor was the diverse structure of political support and pressure associated with the freeze. The freeze was a law that demanded sacrifices from all economic sectors and social groups; such sacrifices are justifiable only if the law actually works, that is, if it is effectively and uniformly enforced. To retain political support and voluntary compliance, therefore, the agencies were motivated not to make accommodations to powerful complainants but to see to it that the law was applied consistently and stringently to everyone. The diversity and attentiveness of the affected groups helped in this regard. The beneficiaries of stringent regulation were located in all economic sectors, including (or perhaps especially) corporate business, while the interests of dispersed groups, such as consumers, were well-represented by other highly organized entities, such as unions and retail merchants' associations, both of which opposed accommodations to producers.

Finally, the agencies were under intense scrutiny by the mass media. This visibility and subjection to outside criteria of performance seemed to enhance agency officials' dedication to the "success" of their mission and their tendency to define it in dramatic, police-mission terms. Indeed, if it is true, as some would argue, that the executive order was implemented in an overly stringent and uncompromising fashion, it was due primarily to the intense atmosphere and the commitment to "success" that was abetted by the media coverage, along with the politically powerful but simplistic image of a "freeze." On the other hand, in an agency such as CLC—without effective legal controls on its procedures, without mechanisms for public participation and consultation—the knowledge that every ruling would receive wide publicity was an important deterrent to secret and inconsistent accommodative decisions.

Part II:
Rule Application
in a Bureaucracy

CHAPTER 5

Rules and the Problem of Legality

The larger a regulatory agency's case load grows, the more it must delegate and disperse decision-making authority and the more elusive the ideal of legality seems to become. As more decisions are made by inspectors in remote field sites or bureaucrats on the lower floors of large office buildings, there is a greater risk that the basic policies formulated by agency leaders will be eroded by selective and accommodative settlements or applied in an overly rigid and harsh manner. The problem of legality is to establish procedures and attitudes that will prevent inconsistent and arbitrary decisions, but that will also promote the rational adaptation of regulatory policies to the requirements of specific cases.[1]

The freeze agencies' response to this problem, we saw earlier, was to create a regime of changeable rules. The numerous rules promulgated by CLC, it was assumed, would state the authoritative policy for most kinds of transactions. By following the rules, the thousands of individual decisions by OEP and IRS inquiry-response officials could be kept reasonably consistent with each other and with CLC's intentions. In the relatively few cases where the applicable rule was unclear, or when the case was thought complex or novel, the issue was to be referred to CLC for the formulation of a new rule or an amendment to an old one. A growing body of increasingly specific rules could thus provide a desirable blend of consistency and flexibility, stringency and accommodation in the decision of individual cases.

[1] See Philip Selznick, *Law, Society and Industrial Justice* (New York: Russell Sage Foundation, 1969), ch. 1, esp. pp. 11–18, "The Ideal of Legality."

Whether this method of decision can, in fact, solve the problem of legality, however, has been a subject of some debate. One view is that an emphasis on rules causes lower officials to concentrate on rule following as an end in itself, thereby increasing bureaucratic arbitrariness and inflexibility and impeding the fulfillment of official policies. A contrasting view is that rules are made to be broken or manipulated by lower officials or that they are inherently incapable of controlling concrete decisions. One might wonder, therefore, how the regime of rules actually worked in the freeze agencies and how it affected the implementation of CLC's policies. This chapter begins that inquiry by discussing the nature of decision according to rule.

FORMAL-RATIONAL RULE APPLICATION
AND LEGAL REALISM

The simplest and perhaps still the most prevalent conception of rule application parallels Max Weber's construct of *formal-rational* legal thought.[2] In the formal-rational conception, judicial or bureaucratic decisions are made by deducing the "correct" result from preexisting rules. Such rules take the logical form, "If factual conditions x, y, and z are present, legal status A applies, and legal consequence A1 shall be imposed." For example, a motor vehicle code might read, "*Section 5.* Any person who drives a motor vehicle through a red light is guilty of a violation and shall be fined $25.00." A complete system of such rules, whether for a legal system as a whole or a particular bureaucracy, presumably establishes an exhaustive set of classifying and dispositional categories for all factual situations encountered in that system. Each case can therefore be authoritatively decided by an impersonal syllogistic process: the decision maker 1) ascertains the facts in the case presented, 2) finds the rule that refers to or covers those facts, and 3) applies the rule (or follows its dispositional portion) to impose the correct outcome. The idea of formal-rational rule application thus approximates the ideal of formal justice, i.e., unbiased, universalistic, prompt, and predictable decision making.

Many linguistic and legal philosophers have argued, however, that the formal-rational conception of rule application is illusory. The abstract and generally stated terms used in rules, they hold, have no logically necessary application to any particular instance. Thus a decision maker, no matter how long and hard he stares at Section 5 of the motor vehicle code, cannot deduce from the rule itself whether it "applies" and compels the imposition of a fine in the case of a motorist who proceeds through a malfunctioning traffic light

---

[2] Max Rheinstein, ed., *Max Weber on Law in Economy and Society* (New York: Simon and Schuster, 1967).

that is stuck on red, or an ambulance rushing a patient to the hospital, or, indeed, an ordinary citizen rushing through a light to make an urgent appointment. The words of the rule call into mind simplified conventional pictures; but when we are confronted with any concrete case, in all its factual detail, the words cannot tell us whether particular elements in that case render it *different* from the spare picture drawn in the rule and thus render the rule inapplicable. Conversely, the rule cannot tell us whether factual details present in the particular case are irrelevant, do *not* make the case "different," and hence warrant the application of the rule. The decision as to whether a rule "applies" must rest on considerations extraneous to the rule.[3]

The American legal realists of the 1920s and 1930s joined the assault on the formal-rational conception. Since general rules do not or cannot decide concrete cases, they argued, judges do not "find" the law in preexisting rules, precedents, or eternal legal principles. "The common law," Oliver Wendell Holmes had said years earlier, "is not a brooding omnipresence in the sky."[4] Judges actually decide particular cases, the realists asserted, on the basis of their own political preferences and conceptions of justice, rationalizing them after the fact by citation of those precedents or rules that appear to support their own views.[5] Similarly, students of public administration, such as Herbert Simon, have questioned the prevalent idea of a division between policy making and administration, in which the administrators simply "apply" the policies (typically embodied in statutes, rules, or regulations) made by their superiors. The ambiguity of abstractly stated policies, together with the variety and uncertainty of actual fact situations, it is argued, make the ideal of deductive implementation of preexisting policy an impossibility. Every decision is a policy decision.[6]

From this perspective, the freeze agencies' reliance upon a system of rules to control the decision of inquiries seems to have been a delusion. Nevertheless, these officials, like those in other government agencies who take the trouble to issue rules, were not deluded. OEP officials, wondering how to answer an inquiry, could often be seen poring through their manual of Stabilization Program Guidelines, and they could be heard to tell an inquirer from time to time, "I'd like to help you out, but the CLC rule here says you're

---

[3] See the materials collected in William Bishin and Christopher Stone, *Law, Language and Ethics* (Mineola, N.Y.: Foundation Press, 1971), chs. 8 and 12. The red light example is suggested by Erving Goffman, *Relations in Public* (New York: Harper & Row, 1971), p. 102.

[4] *Southern Pacific Co.* v. *Jensen,* 244 U.S. 205, 222 (1901).

[5] See Bruce Ackerman, *"Law and the Modern Mind* by Jerome Frank," *Daedalus* (Winter 1974), pp. 119–130; G. Edward White, "From Sociological Jurisprudence to Realism," 58 *Virginia Law Review* 999 (1972); William Twining, *Karl Llewellyn and the Realist Movement* (London: Weidenfeld & Nicholson, 1973).

[6] Herbert Simon, *Administrative Behavior,* 2nd ed. (New York: Macmillan, 1957).

frozen."[7] To all appearances, they actually "applied" rules to decide cases. The legal realists' critique of the formal-rational conception, in fact, captures only part of reality. Baseball umpire Bill Klem, a legal realist with a chest protector, was noted for chastising over-assertive players with the observation, "They ain't strikes, they ain't balls, they ain't nothin' until I call 'em." However, like law professors Harold Berman and William Greiner, we might ask, "How does he know what to call 'em?"[8] And so even if the legal realists were logically correct in asserting "rules do not decide cases—men do," we must still ask, "What do men in fact do when they purport to apply rules?"

THE SOCIAL CONSTRUCTION OF RULE MEANINGS

Emile Durkheim's observation that "everything in the contract is not contractual" refers to the network of unstated norms and expectations that people implicitly rely on in making specific legal agreements.[9] They assume that the words in their contract will be interpreted in conventional ways and that the courts stand ready to enforce their agreements (or excuse nonperformance) under generally known principles and conditions, even if those conditions are not exhaustively spelled out in the contract. The cultural and institutional context, in other words, supplies predictable meaning to the contract in most cases and governs its interpretation and application.

Other sociologists have elaborated Durkheim's insight. While words in themselves may be ambiguous guides to desired behavior, people working in specific institutional contexts learn to *assign* mutually understood meanings to the words they use in order to achieve their purposes. They do so through social interaction: discussion, explanation, criticism, authoritative definition, and example. Conventions develop concerning the purpose and meaning of the words used and how ambiguities or omissions are to be resolved; these conventions are taught to newcomers to the institution and influence their modes of thought and behavior.[10]

Some post-realist legal philosophers, writing in an entirely different tradi-

---

[7] See Robert Cover, *Justice Accused: Anti-Slavery and the Judicial Process* (New Haven, Conn.: Yale University Press, 1975) ch. 7, for a sophisticated discussion of "the judicial 'can't,' " that is, judges' protestations of inability to grant remedies which their personal moral convictions would support.

[8] Harold Berman and William Greiner, *The Nature and Functions of Law*, 2nd ed. (Brooklyn, N.Y.: Foundation Press, 1966), p. 24.

[9] Emile Durkheim, *The Division of Labor in Society* (New York: The Free Press, 1964 [1893]), p. 211.

[10] Peter Berger and Thomas Luckmann, *The Social Construction of Reality* (New York: Doubleday–Anchor Books, 1966); C. Wright Mills, "Language, Logic and Culture," 4 *American Sociological Review*, 670 (1939).

tion, seem to corroborate the idea that relatively fixed rule meanings can be socially constructed. Judges assign meaning to rules and precedents, they suggest, by referring to general standards, principles, and techniques of interpretation, all of which are regarded as obligatory aspects of the judicial role. These standards and techniques are learned by lawyers and judges through training in a specific institutional tradition and reinforced by the continuing process of legal argument.[11] So, too, at least one author has suggested that the "bureaucratic role" established in modern regulatory agencies includes a series of internalized "decisional referents," developed in the course of specific regulatory tasks and used to interpret inconclusive regulations and statutes.[12] In this view, the use of rules is not an abstract, logical operation but a social process, in which participants draw on a learned repertoire of conventions to produce shared understandings of what the rules mean and of how and when they should be applied.

The culture of rule interpretation in the American legal system, according to many commentators, emphasizes the belief that rules are not Delphic statements, but purposive directions given by specific authorities.[13] American judges, lawyers, and administrators are repeatedly told that statutory rules must be interpreted so as to further the policies or goals that apparently motivated the lawmakers.[14] Thus a police department may develop a tacit understanding that the purpose of Section 5 of the motor vehicle code is to maintain an orderly flow of traffic and to protect human life and that it does not further that purpose to give tickets to drivers who proceed cautiously through a light that is stuck on red or to ambulances rushing to a hospital. The rule, the policemen implicitly agree, does not "apply" in such cases because it does not make sense, in terms of the public policy "behind the rules," to apply it. Intra-agency conceptions of organizational purpose are used to determine which specific circumstances should be treated as irrelevant to the applicability of the rule (such as the driver's race or his lateness for an appointment) and which ones make the case so "different" as to compel a judgment that the rule should not be applied. The "meaning" of a rule is

---

[11] Lon Fuller, "Positivism and Fidelity to Law—a Reply to Professor Hart," 71 *Harvard Law Review* 630 (1958); Ronald Dworkin, "The Model of Rules," 35 *University of Chicago Law Review* 14 (1967); Graham Hughes, "Rules, Policy and Decision Making," 77 *Yale Law Journal* 411 (1968). See also Karl Llewellyn's later work, *The Common Law Tradition—Deciding Appeals* (Boston: Little, Brown, 1960).

[12] Daniel Gifford, "Decisions, Decisional Referents, and Administrative Justice," 37 *Law and Contemporary Problems* 3 (1972).

[13] See Fuller, "Positivism and Fidelity"; Hughes, "Rules, Policy and Decision Making"; Morton Horwitz, "The Emergence of an Instrumental Conception of American Law," in *Law in American History*, eds. Donald Fleming and Bernard Bailyn (Boston: Little, Brown, 1971).

[14] See, e.g., Felix Frankfurter, "Some Reflections on the Reading of Statutes," 47 *Columbia Law Review* 527 (1947).

thus determined by cumulative judgments concerning the desirability of applying it in particular cases.

A key role in the development of such intra-agency understandings is played by officials regarded as authorities on matters of organizational policy or rule interpretation. When they review the decisions of subordinates and justify or criticize them by reference to a rule, they indicate the kinds of situations in which it is appropriate to apply that rule. Each review tends to become a precedent within the system; officials attend to these precedents to avoid criticism and because they often believe that they *should* learn to apply the rules "correctly."

Not only do officials develop conventional interpretations of specific rules, they also generate norms about how rules should be interpreted in hard cases, where conventional rule meanings or the outcomes they call for are perceived as inappropriate. We see such norms of interpretation most clearly in the judicial setting, where they are formally articulated. Judges refer to canons of statutory construction to guide their inquiries into the purpose and coverage of legislative rules. Judicial maxims of equity reflect the idea that rules should be interpreted so as to avoid producing results that are unnecessarily harsh or contrary to other public policies. Judges employ "if in doubt" rules for hard cases, such as the presumption of constitutionality or the maxim of strict construction of criminal statutes. Such presumptions and canons of interpretation are not absolutes, but they guide and constrain judgment by enumerating authoritative criteria to be considered in deciding hard cases and advising the judges to "lean" toward certain outcomes.[15] We can expect regulatory bureaucracies, too, to develop philosophies of decision making, presumptions, and norms of rule interpretation, thereby creating a "lean" in favor of a particular balance of stringency and accommodation. Moreover, for reasons of efficiency alone, we can expect them to develop methods of internal review and communication concerning cases perceived as novel or hard, so that today's authoritative decision of a hard case becomes a precedent, transforming similar situations encountered subsequently into easy cases, i.e., matters of routine rule application.

THE CULTURE OF RULE APPLICATION: VARIANT PATTERNS

Once we focus on the *culture* of rule application, on the notion that the use of rules stems from a process of social communication and learning, then it seems likely that the use of rules will vary from setting to setting, depending on the specific norms of rule application and communication that prevail in

---

[15] See Dworkin, "The Model of Rules," and Hughes, "Rules, Policy, and Decision Making."

the bureaucracy in question or in each portion of it at a particular time. Indeed, we can easily identify a variety of subcultures or modes of rule application.

The Judicial Mode

The preferred pattern of rule application in American regulatory agencies is what we might call the *judicial mode,* for it has been most frequently articulated by analysts of judicial decision making. The judicial mode calls for a two-step method of rule application. The decision maker is expected first to "look backward" to preexisting rules (as conventionally interpreted in the system) to find the one applicable to the case at hand. Secondly, the decision maker should "look forward" to assess the *consequences* of applying the literally applicable rule or of each arguably applicable rule. He must ensure that the result of applying the literally applicable rule "makes sense" in terms of existing public policy and conventional notions of fairness. As Justice Cardozo wrote, "The first thing the appellate court judge does is to compare the case before him with the precedents"; but a judge "worthy of his office" must also be alert to whether "there is something wrong with the results," because "the rules and principles of case law have never been treated as final truths but as working hypotheses."[16] Where the results of literal rule application are substantively questionable, the decision maker must consider reinterpreting the rule, or, if he is so authorized, creating a new rule to cover the case at hand and similar cases that may arise in the future. "We want the just act to be defined not simply by correct application of a rule, whatever that rule may be, but further by correct application of a just rule."[17] That is not to say that a rule *must* be abandoned whenever the result in a single case seems unfair; the issue is whether a better, more specific *rule* can be devised, taking into account the costs of abandoning or carving out an exception to the old one.[18]

The key to this difficult process is a continuing effort within a legal institution to develop common conceptions of that institution's proper pur-

---

[16] Benjamin Cardozo, *The Nature of the Judicial Process* (New Haven, Conn.: Yale University Press, 1921), pp. 19–25; see also Richard Wasserstrom, *The Judicial Decision* (Stanford, Calif.: Stanford University Press, 1961).

[17] Ch. Perelman, *Justice* (New York: Random House, 1967), p. 33.

[18] One of the costs of abandoning the old rule, of course, is the disruption of arrangements and practices built in reliance upon it, and uncertainty generated whenever rules change too rapidly. The doctrine of stare decisis, conceived as a rebuttable presumption against change, is one expression of this concern. See Martin Shapiro, "Stability and Change in Judicial Decision-Making: Incrementalism or Stare Decisis," 2 *Law in Transition Quarterly* 134 (1964). It is expressed also in the emphasis on linking new rule interpretations or exceptions to general principles applicable to all similar cases (as opposed to ad hoc reactions to particular cases). See Herbert Wechsler, "Toward Neutral Principles of Constitutional Law," 73 *Harvard Law Review* 1 (1959).

poses and values and to interpret and change the rules so as to produce results consonant with those purposes. One can observe settings, the most salient examples being appellate courts, in which powerful norms and institutionalized practices push officials toward adherence to the judicial mode. On the other hand, one can observe courts and bureaucratic offices in which decision makers slip into other modes of rule application and in which the intra-organizational culture of decision supports such "deviant" modes.

Legalism

Observers of bureaucracies in action have often noted their tendency to transform compliance with written rules from a means of implementing organizational purposes into an end in itself. This phenomenon has been called *legalism,* the mechanical application of rules without regard to their purpose, without regard for the fairness or substantive desirability of the results produced by applying the rules.[19] A legalistic mode of decision suggests a milieu in which the decision maker is allowed or encouraged to focus wholly on the conventional definitions of rule meanings and to ignore extenuating circumstances that would provide valid occasions, in terms of existing organizational policies or values, for suspending or reformulating the rules. The extreme case would be the policeman who tickets and the judge who fines a driver who carefully goes through a light that is stuck on red.

It should be clear, however, that following rules is not necessarily mechanical legalism. A decision maker who adheres to the letter of the rule is acting in the judicial mode if he has considered the outcome it produces and judges it substantively defensible. The judicial mode—in its more conservative form—even tolerates results which seem unjust in the particular case if the decision maker lacks legal authority to change the rule or if *general reasons* for making exceptions cannot be found. Thus, it is not necessarily legalistic to apply Section 5 of the traffic code to a driver who ran a red light because he was unavoidably late for an important appointment, even if he was cautious and actually endangered no one. One might well conclude that to allow traffic officers to suspend the rule in such a case would invite corruption or encourage motorists to make their own judgments, undermining the safety goals sought by the democratically-elected lawmakers who enacted the prophylactic red light rule.[20]

---

[19] See Robert K. Merton, "Bureaucratic Structure and Personality," in *Reader in Bureaucracy,* eds. Robert K. Merton, et al. (New York: Free Press, 1952); Peter Blau, *The Dynamics of Bureaucracy* (Chicago: University of Chicago Press, 1955), p. 234; Lawrence M. Friedman, "On Legalistic Reasoning: A Footnote to Weber," 1966 *Wisconsin Law Review* 148 (1966).

[20] So too, a court may rule that a police interrogator's failure to warn a suspect of his right to silence and counsel according to the rule in *Miranda* v. *Arizona,* 384 U.S. 436 (1966)

This example suggests that there is a gray area between the judicial mode and mechanical legalism in which decision makers interpret rules in light of their purposes and consequences, but place great value on adherence to a system of general rules and separation of law-making from law-applying powers. No extenuating circumstances based on competing values or visions of justice are recognized unless there is explicit warrant in the *officially formulated* body of rules or principles to do so. This style of decision is called legalism by some writers,[21] although it falls short of the more mechanical, insensitive, consequence-obtuse mode of decision I have called legalism. It could just as easily be seen as a style within the judicial mode analogous to the philosophy of judicial restraint, based upon a high regard for consistency and reflecting a reluctance to accord bureaucrats, policemen or even judges much power to remake public policy on their own initiative.

Unauthorized Discretion

There is a contrasting pattern of decision in which officials frequently appear to ignore the rules, even as conventionally interpreted, and focus entirely on producing the results in each case that *they* think best or will best fulfill their agency's purposes. Sociologists have described law enforcement agencies where work group norms or subcultural stereotypes lead officials to disregard ostensibly applicable rules that would block certain desired outcomes.[22] Officials in such settings often seem to cite rules in a selective, post hoc fashion in order to provide an official-sounding cover for the decisions they reach on other grounds. An extreme case would be the policeman who tickets drivers who have broken no legal rule at all but who he thinks are a threat to public safety or the policeman who violates constitutional rules of search and seizure in order to apprehend drivers who the policeman thinks have broken the law in other contexts. Another example would be the welfare department official who circumvents the rules prescribing maximum welfare payments for different classes of recipients in order to provide a recipient with what he—the official—believes is a minimal amount of money to live

---

requires the exclusion from evidence of his confession, even if there is no sign that the confession had been coerced and the consequence is the dismissal of charges against an obviously guilty criminal, on the grounds that the overriding goal of controlling police behavior would be jeopardized if exceptions were to be made.

[21] See Judith Shklar, *Legalism* (Cambridge, Mass.: Harvard University Press, 1964); James Q. Wilson, *Varieties of Police Behavior* (Cambridge, Mass.: Harvard University Press, 1968), ch. VI, "The Legalistic Style"; Martin Levin, "Urban Politics and Judicial Behavior," 1 *Journal of Legal Studies* 193 (1972) ("legalistic" sentencing style).

[22] See Jerome Skolnick, *Justice Without Trial* (New York: John Wiley & Sons, 1967); Egon Bittner, "The Police on Skid-Row: A Study of Peace-Keeping," 32 *American Sociological Review* 699 (1967); Irving Piliavin and Scott Briar, "Police Encounters with Juveniles," 70 *American Journal of Sociology* 206 (1964).

on decently.[23] One possible result of unauthorized discretion in large systems is nonuniform patterns of decision and unequal treatment, as each separate official seeks to define organizational policy. Another is a tendency toward decisions that emphasize the achievement of certain organizational goals, but downgrade competing values reflected in the rules and in the notion of rule of law.

There are occasions, of course, when ignoring the rules will seem just fine to the observer, probably because he does not like the policies exemplified by the rules. It is still unauthorized discretion, however. There is a gray area, however, in which a lower-level decision maker, who is ordinarily attentive to the authoritative rules and is not officially *authorized* to modify them, makes an exception to or reformulates a rule that would produce undesirable consequences—undesirable in terms of official organizational purposes or recognized public policies. This pattern often occurs when the prescribed mechanisms for rule alteration are not easily invoked.[24] It differs from pure unauthorized discretion in that the substance of the decision reflects a blend of values implicit in the stated purposes of the organization or system, rather than the decision maker's personal and perhaps more idiosyncratic view of proper policy. It might be considered a judicial activist version of the judicial mode, reflecting somewhat less concern for maintaining the integrity of existing rules as a source of stability, more willingness to make exceptions and rely on implicit rather than explicitly stated official purposes, and more trust in the judgment of the decision maker.

Retreatism

The judicial mode represents an effort to combine allegiance to official policies or ends, broadly conceived, and to officially prescribed means of implementing and balancing those policies—the rules. Legalism—stated most starkly—reflects an emphasis on official means without adequate attention to their original ends. Unauthorized discretion is an emphasis on certain substantive ends, but without regard to the instructions or competing values expressed in the rules. If we display these dimensions in dichotomized form, as in Figure 2, we find a space for a decisional subculture which allows or encourages disregard of official purposes and official rules. Following Robert

---

[23] See Victor A. Thompson, *Without Sympathy or Enthusiasm: The Problem of Administrative Compassion* (University, Ala.: University of Alabama Press, 1975), p. 11.

[24] An excellent example, involving the adaptation of bureaucratic rules by local offices in a state employment office, is described by Peter Blau in *Dynamics of Bureaucracy,* ch. 2. Mortimer Kadish and Sanford Kadish, *Discretion to Disobey: A Study of Lawful Departures from Legal Rules* (Stanford, Calif.: Stanford University Press, 1973), provide an elaborate and persuasive argument justifying disregard of rules by lower-level officials, under some circumstances, in terms of the values of the judicial mode.

Figure 2. Modes of Rule Application

		Emphasis on Realization of Organizational Ends	
		+	−
Emphasis on Adherence to Rules	+	Judicial Mode	Legalism
	−	Unauthorized Discretion	Retreatism

Merton, we can label this mode of decision *retreatism.* [25] Retreatism is characterized by avoidance of decisions, refusal to take responsibility for any definitive rule application, or cynical manipulation of the rules for the purely personal gain or convenience of the official. Patterns of retreatism in legal and bureaucratic systems range from more respectable ones, such as encouraging informal settlement of cases without the necessity of any official rule application, to such techniques as procrastination, buck-passing, decision based on bribes or favors, or utter indifference and carelessness in the disposition of cases.

The notion of respectable retreatism, such as the encouragement of private settlements, also suggests the existence of a gray area between retreatism and the judicial mode, in which a legal institution avoids or delays decision for explicit reasons of policy or quality control. Courts, for example, refuse to decide cases where no justiciable controversy exists or where an administrative decision appealed from is not "ripe" for review. It is often wise to postpone a decision if the facts involved have not been determined or if further inquiry into the likely consequences of alternative decisions seems

---

[25] Robert K. Merton, *Social Theory and Social Structure* (New York: The Free Press, 1957), ch. 4. Merton wrote that individuals, when confronted by a perceived disjunction between culturally prescribed goals and institutionally prescribed means, employ various modes of adaptation. These include 1) *deviant innovation*—circumventing the prescribed means to achieve the desired goals (equivalent to Unauthorized Discretion in Figure 2); 2) *ritualism*—mechanical adherence to prescribed means, but ignoring the goals (e.g., legalism); and 3) *retreatism*—a withdrawal from concern with either. The judicial mode, as outlined, is the equivalent to Merton's *conformism.*

Merton's typology includes an additional mode of adaptation: *rebellion*—the affirmative rejection of officially prescribed ends and means and the substitution of a radically different set of goals and values. Bureaucrats can rarely get away with using their positions *consistently* to pursue public policies strikingly different from those prescribed by legislatures and their superiors. But organizational subcultures favoring rebellious policies may develop and exist for a time, producing rebellious outcomes in particular cases. The plight of northern antislavery judges expected to enforce the Fugitive Slave Law epitomizes the kind of situation in which a rebellious response to official rules occasionally is precipitated. See Robert Cover, *Justice Accused.*

desirable. Such doctrines of restraint or judiciousness, however, can also become manipulable shields behind which a legal institution avoids the risk of decision. And sometimes, with a little active effort or encouragement to uncover the necessary facts, a responsible decision *could* be made or a decision could be framed to encompass fact situations as they later develop.

CONCLUSION

This chapter began by asking whether a regime of written rules can hope to solve the problem of legality, to impose consistency on a multitude of individual decisions by scores of bureaucrats, and to adapt regulatory policy in a rational way to the requirements of specific cases. In theory, I have argued, it can. Through discussion, example, and the accumulation of precedent, administrators can develop common understandings of the purpose and meaning of rules. By adhering to the norms of rule application called for by the judicial mode, they can adapt the body of rules, and hence official policy, to diverse and changing circumstances. There is nothing *inherent* in a decision system that relies upon rules that frustrates rational and consistent policy implementation.

To outline that capacity, however, does not tell us how often the judicial mode is actually followed in the real world or what are the conditions that encourage its use. It is but one of several ways of using rules and a particularly demanding one. Some students of organizational behavior, in fact, have argued that bureaucratic organization in itself—its fine division of labor, impersonality, and emphasis on hierarchy—impels individual bureaucrats to concentrate on seeking personal satisfactions rather than organizational goals. In consequence, their decision making is characterized by dedication to routine, defensiveness, and secrecy.[26] This, in turn, would seem to promote legalistic or retreatist patterns of decision. Another common observation is that the fragmentation of authority and function in bureaucracy leads to formulation of distinct, conflicting departmental subgoals, rather than overall organizational goals and purposes; the consequence, in terms of rule application, would be the unauthorized exercise of discretion. Some scholars, however, contend that members of organizations can and often do become imbued with a relatively unified sense of purpose;[27] hence they should

---

[26] See, e.g., Michel Crozier, *The Bureaucratic Phenomenon* (Chicago: University of Chicago Press, 1964); Robert Presthus, *The Organizational Society* (New York: Random House–Vintage Books, 1962).

[27] See, e.g., Philip Selznick, *Leadership in Administration* (Evanston, Ill.: Row, Peterson, 1957). See also William K. Muir, Jr., *Police: Streetcorner Politicians* (Chicago: University of Chicago Press, 1977). Muir constructs a typology of styles of police conduct that parallels in many respects the typology of modes of rule application offered here, and argues that police organizations can train many officers to avoid the pitfalls of excessive coercion (legalism), sympathetic non-enforcement (unauthorized discretion), and conflict-avoidance (retreatism).

be capable of conforming with the judicial mode of rule application.

My assumption, based on the observation of rule application in OEP, is that most agencies incorporate a mixture of these modes of decision. Individual officials and entire offices may shift from the judicial mode to other forms of decision and back again, as organizational and external conditions change and as different kinds of cases and parties appear on the scene. The problem is to identify *predominant patterns* of decision making in particular organizations and to discern the conditions and types of cases that produce those patterns.

It is difficult, perhaps impossible, to detect and classify every decision in an agency in terms of the typology of styles suggested here. Many decisions are made hurriedly, leaving no trace of the motivations and thought processes of the deciding official. Whether a particular decision represents legalistic rule application or one which is substantively defensible in terms of the judicial mode is often a matter of debate. Nevertheless, it would seem possible to distinguish flagrant cases of legalism, retreatism, or unauthorized discretion. One can identify which kinds of decisions are praised and which ones are criticized in an office or in the agency as a whole. By focusing on the mechanisms of social control, the ways in which a bureaucracy identifies and detects error, we can infer which modes of decision are encouraged and how often "mistakes" occur and begin to look for both their causes and their substantive consequences.[28] To that task we now turn, examining rule application in the inquiry-response process in OEP.

---

[28] A focus on the role of *control agents* in defining normatively approved and deviant behavior has been stressed by proponents of the "labeling" approach. See Howard Becker, *Outsiders* (New York: Free Press, 1963); Kai Erikson, *Wayward Puritans* (New York: John Wiley & Sons, 1966).

CHAPTER 6

The Judicial Mode of Rule Application in OEP

The national office of OEP was the headquarters of the freeze agencies' inquiry-response system. By their decisions in over 10,000 inquiries and by the example they set for the field offices, OEP National officials determined whether CLC's policy of stringency would be enforced strictly or applied in a more accommodative manner, whether the regime of rules would be a mechanism of sensible and fair policy implementation or an instrument of arbitrary control. This chapter describes and analyzes the *preferred* method of rule application in OEP National.

The General Counsel's Office (GC) in OEP National served as the "court of appeals" of the inquiry-response system. Inquiries thought to raise difficult problems of rule interpretation were referred to GC by OEP's regional offices and other offices in OEP National. As delegations from trade and professional associations, unions, and corporations descended on OEP in Washington to plead for reinterpretations of CLC rules, GC lawyers were assigned to hear their arguments. Most of the cases that flowed into GC were essentially petitions for price or wage increases. While CLC policy as a whole was a bulwark against this current, for almost every case in GC there was a CLC rule that by some analogy, however strained, suggested that an accommodative ruling was permissible. The very arrival of an inquiry in the GC office, in fact, meant that someone in the inquiry-response system had concluded that the increase was not clearly prohibited.

How did GC officials—not all of whom, incidentally, were attorneys—

resolve these hard cases?[1] Not every case, of course, was decided in the same manner, and every case was in some respect unique. Nevertheless, an illustrative case, one which was not atypical and which therefore reveals much about the style of rule application in OEP, was that of the school bus contractors.

It is a case I can report in detail because I participated in its decision; the account that follows is an edited version of my field notes, written the same night. Here too, I cannot represent that every other agency official would have thought about the case or handled it exactly as I did. But the method of decision described was the "approved method," a method which I, as a newcomer to a government office, learned from my colleagues and observed among OEP lawyers and nonlawyers alike.

THE SCHOOL BUS CONTRACTORS' CASE

On September 8, 1971, Mr. Reynolds, an officer of the School Bus Contractors Association of America, was ushered into GC by Doug Johnston, the head of OEP's Correspondence Section. Johnston urged that Reynolds be given a quick answer to his inquiry, which appeared to raise a question of rule interpretation. I was asked to deal with the matter. Reynolds explained that in the spring and early summer of 1971, well before the August 15 freeze, many private school bus companies had contracted with school boards to provide service for the 1971–72 school year at rates higher than those charged during the 1970–71 year. I told Reynolds that they would appear to be frozen at last year's rates: the basic CLC rule was that the price of pre-freeze "transactions" established the ceiling price for any commodity or service. Another important rule (in *Circular* 7) stated that in contracts for services, "the transaction takes place when the service is performed," as opposed to the time of payment or the time of the making of the contract.

Mr. Reynolds acknowledged that, but pointed out that many bus contractors, before the freeze, had undertaken various actions to prepare for the new school year, such as scheduling routes and determining loading zones, making test drives, hiring and training drivers, and buying and repairing equipment. Those actions, he argued, were the

---

[1] GC was unable to recruit "expendable" attorneys from other federal bureaus as rapidly as needed, and a number of nonlawyer civil servants were added. One, John Simpson, a United States Army major, became the General Counsel's right-hand man and played an important role in the decision of many hard cases. To my initial surprise, in my daily encounters with these men and with other nonlawyers in the inquiry-response process, I could detect no essential difference between their approach to rule interpretation and that of the attorneys.

necessary first step in performance of the new contract, and they had been completed before the freeze. Since these contractual services had been performed before the freeze, couldn't the contracted-for rate increases be charged? Besides, Reynolds said, the bus companies had relied upon getting those rate increases when they had given raises to drivers and purchased new buses. If they couldn't get those rates, many could not break even and could not provide the bus service. Reynolds also urged OEP to provide them an immediate answer, because the new school term was already beginning in thousands of districts across the country. I told him we'd have an answer for him by the next day.

Jim McAleer, an OEP lawyer who shared an office with me, overheard my conversation with Mr. Reynolds. After Reynolds left, McAleer suggested that the higher rate was not allowable. The preparatory services, he argued, were not "performance" within the meaning of the *Circular* 7 rule; only actual busing of students was the service contracted for, and only that would qualify under the rule. Jerry Tankel, another attorney, listened to McAleer's discussion with me and entered his disagreement; he thought the preliminary actions *did* constitute performance of a service. If a school district canceled the contract at this point, he argued, the bus company would be entitled to some compensation under ordinary contract law for what it had done. Tankel also pointed out that under one CLC rule, a teacher was entitled to receive a planned September raise if, before the freeze, he or she had come into school and begun work under the new contract, even if it was only preparatory administrative work.

Left alone for a moment, I reread *Circular* 7 and other CLC rules. I decided that they were certainly not clear about what "performance" meant, or whether the preparatory actions were "performance" as used in *Circular* 7. I also thought it was not an issue worth sending to CLC for further definition; I felt that CLC would not approve a price increase but would define performance more narrowly to mean actual transportation of school children. They would reject a broad definition of performance, I thought, because it would open the door to price increases under a lot of contracts in other areas and because it was not clear that the resulting disruption and hardship would be as unavoidable or as great as Reynolds claimed.

I consulted with Elmer Bennett (OEP's general counsel) and John Simpson, his assistant. They agreed. I drafted a letter to Reynolds for Bennett's signature, declaring that no increased contractual rate could be charged unless actual transportation of school children had been performed before August 15 at the higher rate. The letter cited *Circular* 7 and stated, "Preliminary and preparatory work under the contract

. . . does not . . . constitute delivery or furnishing of service within the meaning of the above provisions."

THE NORMS OF RULE INTERPRETATION

Implicit in this account are several basic norms of decision making. Most fundamental are those that might easily be taken for granted or noticed only when breached—the familiar bureaucratic norms of *impersonality* (no attorney talked about Mr. Reynolds as an individual, his politics or character or motives) and *fidelity to legally constituted authority* (the discussion was about what response would be justified by CLC's rules, not about the OEP lawyers' own views of desirable school bus rates).

Attention to these norms was reflected in the whole approach to the decision: its focus on impersonal, generally stated rules and its orientation toward CLC policy as a source of proper decision. Despite the fact that the ostensibly applicable rule did not seem dispositive, the attorneys repeatedly read and referred to CLC rules. They sought to lend further definition to the rule in question, and the ultimate response to Reynolds was supported by reference to that new definition. The decision process, in sum, was defined and conducted as a matter of rule interpretation. The obvious polestar in this process was CLC. Any decision in accordance with CLC policy, as OEP officials saw it, was legally right, and any decision at variance from that policy was wrong. CLC rules, taken as a whole, were seen as guides or clues to that policy. If a rule did not at first seem dispositive, it was assumed that CLC policy could be divined and used to clarify the meaning of the rule.

The first implicit rule of rule interpretation in GC, therefore, was to predict how CLC would decide the case if it were referred to the council. This is reminiscent of Holmes' famous definition: "The prophecies of what the courts will do in fact, and nothing more pretentious, are what I mean by the law."[2] In GC, those "prophecies" were actually arrived at by three overlapping processes: 1) conceptual analysis (an effort to categorize the facts at hand by reference to concepts in the CLC rules); 2) normative or consequence-oriented analysis (a judgment as to what the answer "should be" in terms of the aims and values of freeze policy as revealed in the entire body of rules); and 3) intra-office consultations aimed at achieving consensus on the correct interpretation.

Conceptual Analysis

One of my first steps as a decision maker in the School Bus Contractors' Case was to ask whether the facts at hand (the bus companies' preparatory

---

[2] Oliver Wendell Holmes, "The Path of the Law," 10 *Harvard Law Review* 457, 460 (1897).

actions) matched the concept (performance) in the ostensibly applicable CLC rule (*Circular* 7). That, too, was the purpose of the McAleer–Tankel discussion. Matching the facts of individual cases with legal concepts or categories is always a crucial decision in rule-based systems.[3] Lawyers, for example, often argue about whether a transaction is a "rental" or a "bailment," an "operating expense" or a "capital improvement." They do so because those concepts are embedded in prescriptive rules; specific legal outcomes flow automatically from the act of classification. Similarly, OEP officials applying CLC rules would argue whether a municipal license fee was "really" a price (and hence frozen) or a tax (and hence exempt).

In OEP, if the facts of a situation seemed to fit clearly within an existing rule, the matter would usually end there, regardless of the decision maker's personal sympathies. For example, had the bus companies *not* undertaken any preparatory action—that is, had they done nothing that was arguably "performance"—the case would have been an easy one for OEP officials, even though the result might have been financial hardship for some bus companies. *Circular* 7 would have been read as a clear indication of CLC's views on the matter and therefore dispositive. Or, had there existed at the time (as there did later in the freeze) a CLC rule stating explicitly that preparatory work in service contracts did *not* constitute delivery of the service, the answer would have been "clearly frozen."[4] Regardless of OEP officials' personal views of the desirability of the freeze as a whole or of particular CLC rules, there was little or no informal support for decisions that departed from clearly applicable CLC policy.

In the School Bus Contractors' Case, however, where the applicability of the concept "performance" *was* questionable, efforts at further definition followed. One resource was conventional usage. McAleer, for example, argued that performance in *Circular* 7, as in ordinary business terminology and contract law, meant "provision of the bargained-for quid pro quo," in this case, transportation of students. References to ordinary usage would often be persuasive, at least if no plausible competing definition came to mind, for then it seemed likely that CLC had used the term in the conventional manner; but here Tankel argued that there *were* other conventional uses of the term, that preliminary services were treated as compensable contract performance in some legal contexts.

---

[3] See Vernon Dibble, "What Is and What Ought to Be: A Comparison of Certain Characteristics of the Ideological and Legal Styles of Thought," 79 *American Journal of Sociology* 511 (1973).

[4] About a week after the School Bus Contractors' decision, CLC issued a rule echoing GC's letter to Reynolds. A few days later, at a meeting with a group of school superintendants from around the country, one asked the very same question Reynolds had posed. I did not even hesitate before answering that bus companies that had performed preliminary scheduling runs were frozen.

Another source of definitions for rule concepts was the body of related freeze decisions, definitions implied by CLC rules dealing with other topics. Thus Tankel pointed out that under one CLC rule, when a teacher had done preparatory administrative work, his or her contract was deemed "in effect" prior to the freeze. Tankel's unstated premise was that similar cases should be treated alike; to maintain consistency with the teacher rule, "performance" in *Circular* 7 should be read to include preparatory action. Again, such analogies would often be dispositive, because maintaining *consistency of treatment* was a highly salient canon of rule interpretation in OEP, but the problem, of course, was to decide what features rendered the two situations truly analogous. In this case, the different situations did not "feel" sufficiently alike to convince me that the analogy held. On subsequent analysis, I can see why. I assumed (perhaps erroneously) that in the case envisaged by the CLC rule, the teacher's contract specifically required and provided pay for preparatory administrative duties; the school bus contractor's preparatory work, on the other hand, was not specifically called for by the contract, he was not directly paid for it, and it provided no immediate benefits to the school district. (A teacher would *not* be entitled to receive pay at the higher contract rate, under CLC rules, simply because she had begun preparations before August 15 for teaching in the fall, as by reading books at home or preparing her own course outlines.) These distinctions seemed important because they represented a different balance of equities and expectations, factors that might induce CLC to favor different, more stringent treatment for the school bus contractors. Consequently, this form of conceptual analysis, too, left the "correct" decision doubtful in the School Bus Contractors' Case.

Analysis of Consequences

A second (or simultaneous) approach to determining CLC's preference in the hard case was to inquire into the purposes that presumably lay behind the ambiguous rule and adopt the interpretation that best furthered that purpose. CLC did not make this task an easy one: it wrote no opinions explaining its rules and left no recorded legislative history. Nevertheless, by reexamining CLC's transaction rules concerning executory contracts, I concluded that overall they seemed to reflect a stringent, anti-inflationary purpose. These rules almost invariably prevented price increases during the freeze even if contracted for earlier, even if it meant contravening the ordinary law of contract and the parties' reasonable expectations. This argued for a restrictive definition of "performance," but there was always room for doubt. Under the norms of interpretation fostered in OEP, CLC's policy preferences were discerned from the body of rules *as a whole,* and some specific rules reflected CLC's willingness to modify stringent policies that would produce manifest unfairness or economic disruption. Because of CLC's policy of selective accommodation, every case was potentially a candidate for an accommodative rule interpretation. Was this such a case? How could one tell?

The requisite inquiry was to assess, at least in an intuitive manner, the likely consequences of alternative decisions and their relative impact on inflation control and economic continuity. In this case I asked myself, more or less explicitly, how many bus companies in how many districts would actually default if denied their contractual increases, and what would happen if they did? Would they ultimately work out some kind of arrangement with the school district for the duration of the freeze, or would children have to walk to school? On the other hand, if the increases were allowed, what were the inflationary consequences? What would the financial impact on the school districts be? Would the ruling get a lot of publicity and lead people to believe the freeze was thawing? Would it be seen as establishing a principle that would permit increases in "preliminary performance" situations in other industries?

Ideally, an agency would deal with such questions by investigation, such as commissioning a study of the economic consequences, or by holding a hearing at which opposing interests would present proofs, cross-examination, and arguments concerning the likely effects of alternative rule interpretations. Neither hearings nor investigations were conducted in OEP, however, on the grounds that "there isn't time." (Reynolds had urged, with some justification, a prompt decision, and I promised him an answer by the next day.) Rather, like decision makers in many legal institutions, OEP officials tried to simplify the problem of assessing consequences. In effect, they allocated the burden of producing evidence to the inquirer. They employed a *presumption in favor of stringency*. That meant that unless the party seeking a price or wage increase produced clear and convincing proof that an accommodative interpretation was both necessary and legally warranted, a stringent interpretation would be favored.

The presumption in favor of stringency was not articulated in official OEP documents. As a newcomer to the agency, I only gradually sensed its existence, inferring it from the general tenor of case discussion in various offices. New recruits sometimes asked impatiently, "What's the philosophy here, to be lenient or strict?" Older hands said, "It's not that simple. It's a matter of judgment." There was such a thing as *good* judgment, however. It meant that in doubtful cases, one should "lean" toward stringency unless the case for the accommodative ruling was clear—that is, unless a specific, accommodative CLC rule was unambiguously analogous or it appeared that a stringent interpretation almost certainly would create unavoidable disruption or hardship. The lean toward stringency was in accord, of course, with the basic thrust of CLC policy, despite the profusion of specific accommodative rules, but it was also supported by OEP officials' belief in consistency. They assumed that an accommodative interpretation would stand as a precedent, binding them to decide similar cases that arose in the future in the same way. An accommodative decision, therefore, was an open-ended risk: it could lead to accommodative decisions in an unpredictable number of unforeseeable similar cases, creating still more pleas for further accommodative rulings. A stringent interpretation, on the average, was "safer." Just as the presumption of innocence in criminal procedure reflects the idea that convicting the innocent is a worse mistake than freeing the guilty, OEP officials presumed that an overly accommodative decision, in the context of the freeze, was a worse mistake than an overly stringent one.

That did not mean that arguments for accommodation should be ignored. They were seriously considered and often prevailed. The presumption in favor of stringency was rebuttable, just as the presumption of innocence does not preclude a finding of guilt if the evidence is very strong. In the School Bus Contractors' Case, therefore, I was attentive to Mr. Reynolds' claims about the adverse consequences of the stringent ruling. Nevertheless, the presumption, as applied to this case, seemed strong to me: I thought that an accommodative decision would, in principle, open up a rather wide door to price increases in many other situations involving preliminary actions under executory contracts and might well stimulate protests from school districts and teachers' associations. Nor did Reynolds' arguments offset these considerations, at least in my eyes. His claims of hardship to the bus companies were neither documented nor otherwise substantiated. I was not sufficiently persuaded that freezing the bus companies for three months would seriously and inevitably disrupt the school systems of the nation. An interpretation denying the increase thus seemed more in accord with CLC policy, the decision they would most likely reach if the case had been presented to them.

Consultation

The capstone of the process of rule interpretation in the School Bus Contractors' Case was a search for consensus. If an individual OEP official had doubts about the correct decision on a case, he or she was expected to consult with colleagues in the same office. If disagreement or uncertainty persisted, the practice in GC was to argue the case to the head of each subsection, or the deputy general counsel, or if necessary to the general counsel. In this case, the "clincher" was General Counsel Elmer Bennett's agreement that a stringent interpretation was best and that CLC would probably decide it the same way.

Consultation also transformed the individual decision into a precedent, part of the collective memory of the office, indicative of the proper decision in similar cases that might arise in the future. The awareness—or as-sumption—that the decision would set a precedent affected the style of the consultation and thereby of the whole decision-making process. Consultation was oriented toward finding *general* reasons for the decision, so that it would be one the decision makers could "live with" in the future. This was rein-forced by the norm that inquiry-responses should take the form of a generally stated rule—"preliminary and preparatory work does not constitute perform-ance of services within the meaning of *Circular 7.*" For that reason, too, consultation often focused on the precise wording of an answer. The accepta-bility of an interpretative decision met its most rigorous test when the official attempted to draft such a subrule, and its wording was discussed with his superiors. When OEP officials consulted, much of it was in silence, as one read the work of the other and pencilled in more precise or qualifying language.

THE LIMITS OF THE JUDICIAL MODE

The process of rule interpretation employed in the School Bus Contractors' Case approximated the judicial mode of rule application. It involved fidelity to official purposes as expressed in preexisting authoritative rules. It also emphasized the necessity of interpreting or reformulating those rules in light of their consequences. It insisted, moreover, that such adjustments and respecifications be done in a consistent, principled manner.

The case also suggests, however, that the judicial mode of rule application does not in itself guarantee accurate policy implementation or fairness or procedural due process. For example, if I doubted Mr. Reynolds' claims, why should he not have had the opportunity to prove them? Or why should OEP not have had to investigate the situation and produce some supporting findings of fact before deciding, in effect, that no intolerable hardship would result from its decision? The presumption in favor of stringency, in fact, divested agency officials of responsibility for a thoroughgoing inquiry into the consequences of decision. The freeze agencies made no provision for hearings or adversarial argument at which such proofs might be produced.

This was arguably unfair to inquirers in many cases. It certainly jeopar-dized the reliability of OEP officials' assessment of consequences, and hence it jeopardized the accuracy with which policy was adapted to the situation. The fact-finding procedures necessary for full inquiry into consequences, however, entail costs as well. Policy ends may be served better by rapid and intuitive judgment, even with a risk of error, than by time-consuming hearings and investigations, and perfect justice delayed may be worse than rough justice now. To forego extensive searches for information, to rely upon presumptions that shift the burden of persuasion to those who seek a change in the status quo, is neither uncommon nor, in the opinion of some analysts, an irrational method of decision making.[5]

The judicial style of courtroom adjudication, emphasizing adversarial procedures and rules of evidence—whatever its advantages—is only one mode of fact-finding. It is not synonymous with the judicial mode of rule application, which is concerned with the adaptation of rules in light of their consequences, but which is neutral with respect to the methods by which those facts are ascertained or estimated. OEP's inquiry-response system employed a highly informal method of fact-finding and put the burden of proof or persuasion on the applicant. However, OEP officials *were* expected to attend to any adverse consequences pointed out by the inquirer and to evaluate them as best they could in the time allotted. If their investigation was limited, it was not a denial of the desirability of consequence-oriented rule application but an attempt to adapt it to the felt necessity to decide inquiries quickly, even at the risk of injustice in some cases.

The judicial mode of rule application and the presumption in favor of stringency also served to protect a basically harsh and absolutist substantive policy from continued modification on the basis of individual justice-claims. Mr. Reynolds' type of claim—based on the injustice of defeating financial expectations grounded in prior agreements (and hence causing undeserved losses) and on the threat of disruption of services or production—was extremely common in the freeze agencies. By placing the burden of persuasion on inquirers and excusing freeze officials from conducting investigations, the presumption reined in, without totally stifling, the impulses of officials to respond to claims for individualized justice and values of economic continuity. It was an intuitive way of identifying only the most *obviously* unjust or disruptive consequences of the freeze while dismissing the less severe ones. The emphasis on linking decisions to *generally stated* rules or rule interpretations did the same thing, by magnifying the burden of persuasion borne by the accommodation-seeking inquirer. Mr. Reynolds, for example, first had to convince OEP that a ruling allowing the bus companies to increase their rates was fair or necessary and not too destructive of the anti-inflationary policy.[6] Secondly, Reynolds also had to convince the GC lawyers, in effect, that a general rule defining "performance" to include "preliminary and preparatory actions under a contract" was permissible or desirable; that it would

---

[5] See David Braybrooke and Charles Lindblom, *A Strategy of Decision* (New York: Free Press, 1963).

[6] He might have argued, for example, that a price increase by school bus companies, unlike an increase by most other businesses, would not result in a cost-price squeeze for customer firms or price increases for households; it would be borne entirely by school districts, which presumably had already budgeted for it and were also saving on teachers' salaries.

not open up "too wide a door" and allow inflationary increases for other, perhaps less deserving, companies; and that it would not provoke a barrage of complaints from teachers or other workers or businesses ("If we're frozen, why aren't the bus companies?") and create the impression that the freeze was thawing or being unfairly administered. In sum, under the branch of the judicial mode which emphasizes the legitimacy of change only at the level of rules and on the basis of general principles, substantively harsh consequences in one case are not necessarily enough to warrant an exception to a rule, and existing policies are given an extra measure of protection. In employing the judicial mode in that manner, OEP both defended and mirrored CLC's hold-the-line vision of the freeze, a vision that tolerated hardships and disruptions in some cases for fear of creating an impression of favoritism or weakness and thereby provoking noncompliance and "failure" in the war on inflation.

This analysis perhaps overemphasizes the strength of the lean toward stringency in the norms of rule interpretation in OEP. There were many accommodative rules to which an inquiry could be analogized more easily than the school bus contractors' situation. GC actually issued accommodative rulings in almost *one-half* of the inquiries it answered.[7] It referred scores of cases to Policy Analysis and ExComm with the suggestion that a new and perhaps more accommodative rule should be considered. The presumption against stringency obviously could be rebutted. Nevertheless, for that to happen—in the absence of systematic procedures for proof and argument concerning the desirability of exceptions—much depended on the quality of interaction between inquirer and official, on the inquirer's ability to catch the official's imagination and empathy, on the official's ability to decide whether further information was required, and on his capacity to distinguish the deserving argument for accommodative rule adjustments from those in which the applicant was only crying wolf. In that respect, the inquiry-response system, despite its effort to control discretion by means of rules, moved closer to the expert model of decision making. One obvious risk, therefore, was a failure in the intuition or judgment of officials. The advantage in obtaining an accommodative ruling might easily flow to inquirers who were most persistent and articulate and well-prepared in presenting their cases, unless the officials were capable of discerning and compensating for differences in presentational skill.[8] There was also a risk of legalism: unless officials were truly attentive to pleas for accommodation, unless they took seriously the right to rebut the presumption, the presumption in favor

---

[7] See Chapter 9.
[8] See Chapter 9 for empirical evidence relating to this issue.

of stringency could become an insensitive barrier which *no* claim of disruption or hardship could pierce. The extent to which attention to consequences remained a salient concern in all cases depended upon the entire atmosphere of decision in the agencies and the pressures which it applied to individual officials.

CHAPTER 7

Supports for the Judicial Mode

What impelled OEP decision makers involved in the School Bus Contractors' Case, or indeed in any case, to adhere to the norms of the judicial mode of rule application? A simple answer would be that they had internalized those norms in the course of their general or legal education or during their socialization as bureaucrats. And surely it is true that most of us—government official, lawyer, and layman alike—think that government decisions should have legal justification and believe that rules should be interpreted to produce reasonable and consistent results; but everyday experience also teaches that adherence to these norms is by no means universal. Popular stereotypes of bureaucratic indifference and arbitrariness are not wholly without foundation. The problem is whether bureaucrats will remain *motivated* to act in accordance with the norms of the judicial mode, to overcome inclinations toward indifference, and to decide cases with "a sense of trusteeship" and the "pride of the craftsman."[1] This chapter describes the intra-agency attitudes and practices that supported that kind of motivation in the OEP national office and the external conditions that tended to sustain that effort.

INTRA-AGENCY PRESSURES FOR CONSISTENCY

An important prerequisite for a system of rule-oriented decision making is pressure to take rules seriously. In OEP National, such pressure derived

---

[1] Lon Fuller, *The Morality of Law* (New Haven, Conn.: Yale University Press, 1964).

from both formal and informal social controls. The most important formal mechanism was a system of *multiple reviews* within each inquiry-response office. In GC, for example, each answer drafted by an attorney was reviewed first by the head of his section (Wages or Prices and Rents), then by the deputy general counsel, and finally by the general counsel, who doggedly read and signed every letter. These reviews, above all, institutionalized the practice of *rule citation.* Any draft answer that failed to quote or enclose a relevant CLC rule as authority was sent back to its author with notations as to which rule should be cited.

Multiple reviews, in which the answers prepared by many officials were funneled through a few superiors, also increased the chances for consistency, while forcefully reminding each official that his answers would be evaluated by his superiors in those terms. A review that stresses consistency, interestingly enough, generates pressure for close attention to the "meaning" of rules and hence is a hedge against the most blatant kind of legalism; for in order to apply a rule consistently to a series of slightly different cases, there must be a common understanding of the policy preferences which the rule attempts to communicate. By carefully editing the phrasing of each draft answer and sending the edited version back to the original draftsman, superiors in each office helped to develop those common understandings of CLC policy. They instinctively resisted administrative pressures to curtail these multiple reviews in order to speed up response time. *"Every* letter is important," protested Deputy General Counsel Dick Murray, when it was suggested that some could be sent out without his review. "They've just got to be accurate. We have to watch every comma."

Recurrent *informal consultation* and debate about specific inquiries, as in the School Bus Contractors' Case, also focused attention on consistency and accuracy in rule application. Overcrowding facilitated discussion. Inquiry-response officials were clustered several to an office. Conversation about cases and recently issued CLC rules began easily. An argument between two officials soon attracted the attention of others. The official who took either an overly legalistic position or one without support in CLC rules was exposed to collegial criticism. Officials who excelled in discussion, who successfully challenged the rule interpretations proposed by colleagues and superiors, were generally admired, both for their ability and for "caring." In turn, they were consulted more often by others.[2]

One consequence was a high level of case discussion. The ordinary workday discourse among OEP National officials was filled with references to

---

[2] Peter Blau, "The Research Process in the Study of *The Dynamics of Bureaucracy,"* in *Sociologists at Work,* ed. Philip Hammond (New York: Doubleday–Anchor Books, 1967), describes a similar relationship between frequency of consultation and social status in a law enforcement office.

"right" and "wrong" answers, comparisons of different CLC rules, and expressions of concern about inconsistency. At bottom, this concern was rooted in the impulse to avoid the *injustice* of treating similar cases differently. "I feel sorry for the poor teacher we tell one thing to, and then CLC says something else, and we don't even know if the first teacher hears about the CLC ruling"—that was the comment of a Correspondence Section worker during a casual lunchtime conversation. That kind of concern was reinforced by the flurries of corrective activity that occurred in an office whenever it was discovered that an inconsistent answer had been sent out.

The concern for consistency was also reinforced by interoffice pressures. CLC staff members denounced OEP's general counsel from time to time for "reaching," i.e., deciding as a "matter of interpretation" cases that the CLC people thought should have been forwarded to CLC as a "policy question." GC officials in turn sought to prevent the exercise of unauthorized discretion by other OEP offices, frequently cautioning them to refer hard cases to GC. The other side of the coin was that OEP personnel often expressed discomfort or criticized CLC if they faced a situation for which no clear rule had been issued or if CLC rules seemed inconsistent. "People have got to know," said an OEP official urging CLC to issue a new rule. "We can't just decide these things arbitrarily." Similarly, lower inquiry-response offices repeatedly urged OEP's general counsel to compile GC's interpretive rulings and disseminate them throughout the system. For an agency official, authoritative rules seemed to ease the burden of choice and confirm his personal sense of legitimacy. It was not *he* who was telling the landlord he could not raise his rent; the rule was. And as long as the rule was consistently applied, the landlord had no grounds to blame the official. He was being treated no differently from anybody else in the same situation.[3]

INTRA-AGENCY PRESSURES FOR SUBSTANTIVE FAIRNESS

Review procedures and discussion, particularly when they failed to produce an immediate consensus, had a natural tendency to push the search for the "right" answer beyond conceptual analysis into consideration of the consequences of alternative decisions. The following case, recorded in my field notes, provides an example.

---

[3] See Torstein Eckhoff, "The Mediator, the Judge and the Administrator in Conflict-Resolution," in *The Sociology of Law,* ed. Vilhelm Aubert (Baltimore: Penguin Books, 1969), for a similar view of the role of rules in bolstering authority and demonstrating impartiality. Robert Presthus, *The Organizational Society* (New York: Random House–Vintage Books, 1962), argues that "bureaucratic man" has been socialized to feel anxiety when deprived of authoritative directions or rules; but this varies, I would expect, depending upon the configuration of internal and external pressures for consistency in different agencies.

Pruitt–Igoe

The basic rule for apartments is that the rent for each housing unit is frozen at the level charged for that unit during the pre-freeze base period. But *Circular 2* adds: "State-aided and Federal low-rent housing programs mandate that rents rise according to the income of the individual. . . . Increases in rentals tied to family incomes at rates established prior to August 15, 1971, will be permitted as long as rates per given amount of family income are not raised."

This concession from a "hard line" definition of the freeze prompted new inquiries and two new CLC rulings to limit its application: 1) where a government agency prior to August 15 authorized a rent increase but not effective until during the freeze, the increase cannot take effect, *Circular 101,* Sec. 601 (8); 2) where an agency planned to switch during the freeze from a fixed-dollar rent schedule to a percentage-of-income schedule, it can be done, but "the rent may be no higher than the dollar amount in the base period for any individual unit," *Circular 3.*

An inquiry from Missouri came to OEP. Under Missouri law, rents in public housing must equal 20 percent of tenants' income. Nevertheless, the housing authority in St. Louis had been charging flat rates, often less than 20 percent. Finally, under great budgetary pressure, it planned to enforce the 20 percent rule during September and October 1971. Mike Wade, an official from HUD in OEP's Operations Center, drafted an answer saying the rents were frozen. A GC lawyer, Harry Graham, reviewed Wade's answer; in his redraft, the increase *was* allowable. I had been assigned to do a final check on all answers to OEP's regional offices; noting the conflict between Wade and Graham in this case, I questioned Graham about his answer.

Graham argued that *Circular 2* controlled; the housing authority was merely enforcing a rental formula established by law prior to the freeze. Moreover, he said, that provision indicated the freeze should not frustrate the policy of state housing law. I suggested the formula was not really in effect prior to the freeze, that *Circular 3* barred any change of formula during the freeze that would increase rents, and that many freeze rulings (e.g., *Circular 101,* above) overrode state legal policies. Harry replied that I was just trying to protect the tenants, but that this was shortsighted: according to the information in the inquiry, the project in question *(Pruitt–Igoe)* was falling apart and needed higher rents to maintain decent housing.

Since we disagreed, Harry and I argued our cases to Dick Murray, deputy general counsel. "We are not supposed to stop people from living up to their legal obligations," said Graham. He argued it was morally wrong (as well as bad economics) for the freeze to lock the housing authority into continued violation of the law. "Don't talk to me about morality," Murray interrupted. "One of my professors in law school said, 'If you want to talk about morality, go to a clergyman. If you want to talk about law, come to me!' " But nevertheless, by the time I returned to the debate, after having been called away on another matter, Murray had decided, with Graham, that *Circular 2* was controlling and that the increase was permissible. I sent Graham's answer to the Operations Center for transmittal back to the regional office.

But before it was sent out, Mike Wade, told of the change in his answer, came back up to GC to challenge it; he felt strongly that GC's answer was wrong. He also seemed to have a personal, status-maintaining stake in fighting the lawyers on this. He got into an argument with Graham. Wade talked about the burdens of poverty, Graham about welfare chiselers. (The longer and more intense a discussion, the more it tends to focus on social impact and political evaluation, exposing the underlying policy question at stake.) Wade got some additional support from other officials listening in and Dick Murray was asked to reconsider. He did and changed his mind (without giving Graham, much less the housing authority, a hearing). The teletype went out saying the rents were frozen, pursuant to *Circulars 3* and *101*.

The prevalence of such arguments concerning the substantive fairness of particular rulings created an environment in which an official who encountered a rule that he thought unfair was able (and sometimes encouraged) to challenge it on moral grounds, as in the following incident.

September 26. Vacation Pay

Fransen and Brock, who are responsible for publishing CLC rules in the manual, came into GC. Their work is fundamentally mechanical or ministerial. Yet they came down two floors to talk to a lawyer about a recent CLC rule. It appeared to say that where a worker becomes eligible for a two-week paid vacation for the first time *during the freeze* (because his employment anniversary date came then), he cannot get the pay (because it would be an increase in compensation, which includes fringe benefits, during the freeze).

Fransen and Brock wanted to know if the ruling meant what it seemed to. I told them, "Yes. The guy can't get his vacation pay." "That's wrong!" said Brock, "A guy has worked all year. He's earned that vacation." He wanted me to do something. "*I* can't change it," I replied, "That's the rule." Brock kept insisting indignantly that it was wrong, that it should be changed.

I showed him the issue paper submitted to CLC. It indicated that the alternative of allowing the additional benefit had been suggested and that CLC had considered and rejected the kind of argument made by Brock (that the vacation pay be considered as *accrued* during the period *before* the freeze, hence allowable). Finally, I advised Brock to ask the OEP Policy Analysis Office to prepare a paper asking CLC to reconsider.

CLC's Executive Committee (ExComm) later reversed its ruling on this point, perhaps due to Brock's follow-up or perhaps because similar protests came up through the inquiry-response system at the initiative of companies, workers, and other freeze officials. The route to ExComm's ear, at least for OEP officials who were determined to get there, was relatively short. The OEP Policy Analysis Office was shorthanded and rather disorganized. I quickly learned that if GC lawyers encountered a significant policy question in an inquiry, it could be transmitted to ExComm within a day or two if I stayed late and prepared an issue paper on the subject myself and presented it to Policy Analysis the next day, causing them no extra work. Just as important, ExComm, eager to elaborate freeze law as fully and quickly as possible, was not unresponsive to new issue papers, even those which challenged a prior rule. They did not reverse themselves often, but they did on enough occasions that Brock's kind of protest was not clearly fruitless, and rules that seemed to produce unfair results were not taken as unalterable.

Attention to the substantive fairness of rule application was also encouraged by the relative openness of the inquiry-response system to justice-claims advanced by inquirers. A steady stream of corporation officers, trade association representatives, and presidents of professional organizations met in person with high OEP officials and described the adverse impact of specific CLC rules on their industry. Written inquiries were stated in letters, briefs, and petitions in a form of the inquirer's own choosing, facilitating the presentation of information about the impact of the freeze and emotional pleas for fairness. Consequently, while agency officials were insulated from direct face-to-face contact with most inquirers, on numerous occasions they were exposed in person or in writing to the feelings and troubles of the people they ruled and reminded that their decisions had fateful consequences.

The most common justice-claim by inquirers was simply that the agency should *justify* its answer. This encouraged officials to be alert to the consequences of decision, for the demand for justification included the demand that the decision should be substantively reasonable. "The law should make sense, damn it, and this thing just doesn't make any sense!" shouted an attorney for the New Orleans school board, contesting OEP General Counsel Bennett's interpretation and application of CLC rules to a teacher's salary problem. These demands support Selznick's contention that the idea of legitimacy in our legal culture has increasingly come to require not merely formal legal justification (the decision is in accordance with a valid rule, promulgated by lawfully appointed or elected officials) but "legitimacy in depth" (the decision, or at least the rule itself, must be substantively justified). The culture of decision making in OEP certainly supported that belief.[4]

Controlling Equitable Modification

If inquirers' justice-claims and internal discussion generated concern for the substantive fairness of decisions, they also created a risk that lower-level inquiry-response officials, unlike Mr. Brock, would skip the referral to CLC and respond to perceived unfairness by disregarding or willfully reinterpreting "bad" CLC rules. The problem was to encourage imaginative rule interpretation to fulfill official purposes without permitting the wholesale exercise of unauthorized discretion. Perhaps the most important inducement to maintaining that delicate balance in OEP was the example provided by formal authorities—the quality of leadership, office by office. The intra-office review system emphasized the role of leadership. It ensured that all draft answers would be funneled through the head of each inquiry-review office, such as the chief of the Correspondence Section, the general counsel, the head of the Inquiry-Review Section of the Operations Center. These officials "signed off" each letter, or sent it back to the draftsman for correction, or decided if it raised enough of a new policy issue to refer it to a higher office. Their consent was necessary for any attempt to sidestep or ignore CLC rules that seemed to produce an unduly harsh result. Their attitudes and intellectual style, as reflected in their comments and examples, instructed subordinate inquiry-response officials just how literally the rules were supposed to be applied.

Intra-office pressures tended to push heads of sections toward a judicial activist posture. They were regularly confronted by their immediate subordinates' requests to get around CLC rules that seemed unreasonable or crudely drafted. As *the authority* on freeze policy in their own offices, the heads of sections quickly developed their own sense of what needed to be done and the impulse to do it without consulting higher offices in the hierarchy. On the other hand, their position vis-à-vis other offices and the outside world pulled these officials toward concern for the integrity of the rule system as a whole and consistency of decision. They were responsible for the output of their particular office. If inconsistent rulings were detected, they were the ones informed and criticized for it. Unlike their subordinates,

---

[4] Philip Selznick, *Law, Society and Industrial Justice* (New York: Russell Sage Foundation, 1969).

they met regularly with outsiders and officials from other agency offices and developed more of a sense for how the whole operation cohered and their office's place in it. The trade-off between these two sets of pressures was the practice of *equitable modification* of CLC rules—adjusting, defining, "filling in the gaps," manipulating the rules to achieve the results they thought best—but all within a relatively narrow compass.

These bounds can best be conveyed to the reader—as they were to inquiry-response officials—by reference to a series of examples, taken from my field notes.

September 22. Probationary Wage Increases

Ordinary raises based either on merit or longevity are, of course, prohibited. But a CLC rule says that wage increases for employees hired at a low, probationary wage may be instituted (up to the normal wage for the job) during the freeze, if the probationary period is "three months" or less.[5] We received a case today in which the firm's probationary period is "ninety working days." The Operations Center official (on loan from the Department of Labor) who first dealt with the inquiry said, "OK, the workers in this case can get the increase." The GC lawyers reviewing it said, "No. Ninety working days exceeds three months." But another lawyer argued they should get the increase: the workers were low paid, and it was inequitable to hold them at the low beginners' rate. He argued we could *interpret* "three months" to mean ninety working days.

The dispute went to Dick Murray. He agreed with the liberal, accommodative interpretation and rejected the strict one. The answer went out allowing the increase.

The limits of this kind of equitable discretion, however, were demonstrated a few days later.

September 25. Eligibility Date

A CLC rule deals with situations where employee eligibility to join fringe benefit plans (e.g., pension or health insurance plans) comes up only on certain dates during the year. What if the eligibility date comes during the freeze? To allow the employee to enter the plan would result in an increase in benefits during the freeze. CLC had relented some-

---

[5] CLC's reason for the three-month limitation, no doubt, was to prevent employers from evading the rule by representing that wages increased pursuant to ordinary periodic merit increase or longevity increase plans were actually upgradings after a probationary period. After learning from the Labor Department that most bona fide "learner's programs" provided for a three-month probationary period, CLC imposed that period as a limitation.

what, ruling that where eligibility comes up only *once a year* or longer, and that date occurs during the freeze, the employee may join and receive new benefits.

A case came in today involving a benefit plan where the eligibility date comes up *twice* a year, in September and in March. One lawyer argued we can interpret the CLC rule to cover any long wait for benefit, such as six months. Murray said, "No." I pointed out we extended "three months" to "ninety working days" a couple of days ago. Dick said this was different.

Why was it different? First, to support equitable modification, OEP officials generally insisted that there had to be language in the rule to hang the interpretation on. "Three months" was roughly equivalent in meaning and effect to "ninety working days"—the latter phrase could be considered merely a more precise statement of CLC's real intent, but no plausible reading of the "once a year" phrase could justify reading it to mean "twice a year." Second, the decision had to be one that CLC could, with reasonable certainty, be expected to approve. It had to be in line with CLC's general policy, as perceived in the body of its rulings. In the Eligibility Date Case, the additional step was substantial and in an accommodative direction; there were no grounds for being sure CLC would have approved it. An intra-office consensus on both criteria, including the assent of higher authorities within the office, was needed to support accommodative modifications.

The practice of equitable modification, checked by sensitivity to the subtle limits imposed by plausible readings of the language of rules, made it possible for OEP officials to manipulate a complex set of rules—without ignoring them—in order to achieve results that seemed sensible. It was analogous to the way a good tax lawyer will counsel creative use of loopholes in the rules to *avoid* taxes, but will stop short of counseling tax *evasion,* that is, violating the plain meaning of tax laws. This concern for formal rule compliance, even while the rules are being manipulated and adapted to achieve certain ends, often seems hypocritical to critics of legal institutions; but, like legal fictions,[6] it serves an important stabilizing function. Let me offer one further, if somewhat extended, illustration.

October 1. Girl Scouts

The Girl Scouts of America got a letter from GC two days ago ruling that an increase in their annual dues from $1 to $2, announced in 1969 but scheduled to take effect in September of this year (1971) was in violation of the freeze. They had already begun to collect the $2,

---

[6] See Lon Fuller, *Legal Fictions* (Stanford, Calif.: Stanford University Press, 1967).

however (on advice of counsel), and they had intimated to New York OEP officials that it would not look good for the government to sue the Girl Scouts. An appointment with GC was arranged, and I was asked to meet the officials from the Girl Scouts.

They first presented a variety of legal arguments, e.g., their dues were not a fee for service but charitable donations, and hence exempt. I said CLC rules specifically covered dues and made no exceptions for tax-exempt organizations. Their big plea, however, was based on their financial deficit, on the fact that they had made major and irrevocable commitments for use of the anticipated income, on the fact that this was their first dues increase in twenty-five years, and the argument that "the president hadn't meant to cripple an important and vital youth movement." They had me leaning their way. I read them a loophole in the dues rule that permitted pro rata "special assessments" on association members specifically to meet the cost of increased services. They said they could not recast their dues in that way. I suggested they postpone collections of the additional dollar until after the freeze (Phase II permitting), but they said dues collections had to be in the early fall. I said that if that was the case, there was nothing I could do; they were in violation and should stop collecting the extra dollar.

October 12. Return of the Girl Scouts

Mr. Hurd of the Atlanta OEP office called. He had been receiving complaints that Girl Scouts in South Carolina were collecting $2 dues. He sent them a telegram demanding a rollback and refund. He wanted a quick answer on how to proceed if they failed to comply.

Meanwhile, General Lincoln (director of OEP) had received a memo from a White House staff member concerning the Girl Scouts. It said, "It could be a political embarrassment if this six-million member pillar-of-the-community organization were forced into insolvency by the President's economic program." I was asked to brief Lincoln about the matter. Even he seemed to want to avoid enforcing the rule, less, I gathered, because of the White House memo than because he felt a freeze in this case would be silly. But the violation and other indications that the national Girl Scout leadership was stalling required some response, he thought. Lincoln suggested a letter to the Girl Scouts emphasizing the illegality of their position, but suggesting ways of easing their financial problem. Bennett, the general counsel, suggested making a formal exception to the rule, and we took that tack: CLC was asked to exempt dues of tax-exempt organizations, provided they were less than $5 annually. *"De minimis non curat lex,"* said Bennett's memo.[7]

---

[7] "The law does not concern itself about trifles."

I talked to Hurd in Atlanta. He thought making an exception was "impractical, untactful, and just wrong." How about all the organizations that had complied with the freeze?

October 13. Girl Scouts

ExComm, apparently agreeing with Hurd's position, refused to enact a *de minimis* rule. Weber (CLC's Executive Director) reportedly said he didn't care about the White House position and that the Girl Scouts should be pressured into compliance.

The two Girl Scout leaders (Mrs. McNeil and Miss Wood) met today with General Lincoln, and I sat in. They dressed in their green uniforms and full scouting regalia. (They were in mufti when they came to GC last week.) Lincoln and his aide Lee Butler were sympathetic, but seemed to feel obligated to take the tough line called for by CLC. In asking for a dues rollback, they pointed out, they were not singling out the Girl Scouts; professional football teams had been ordered to roll back season ticket prices. Mrs. McNeil protested putting the Scouts in the same category as a football team. "The freeze scruffs up some strange bedfellows, ma'am," said Lee Butler.

But while maintaining orthodoxy at the level of formal rule, Lincoln, Butler, and I tried to work out a formula, permitted by the rules, that would make the rollback very gentle. The Scouts would have to order the dues held to $1, but it would be permissible to inform those who had not yet joined that a voluntary contribution of another dollar was OK. Restitution would have to be made to those who had already paid $2, but this could be done by granting them credits against next year's membership, and the credit should be 20 cents (an amount we calculated by prorating the extra dollar over the whole year and requiring the rollback only for the ninety-day freeze period). We insisted, however, that they send us a copy of their letter to the state and local Girl Scout Councils calling for this mode of compliance.

In one sense, OEP's insistence on this form of compliance with the letter of the rule, while somehow "interpreting" those rules to allow a fairly accommodative result, seems a bit two-faced. In another sense, however, this is the very essence of the judicial mode: maintenance of continuity of form so as to justify stringent treatment in the plain case, at which the rule was primarily aimed, yet applying it flexibly in the unanticipated and programmatically insignificant case. When OEP leaders followed that pattern, they provided an important example to other inquiry-response officials, indicating that linguistically plausible, accommodative rule interpretations were desirable.

EXTERNAL SUPPORTS FOR THE JUDICIAL MODE

The internal social control system in OEP was certainly not unusual in supporting the judicial mode of rule application. What was striking about it was the intensity of that normative climate, the frequency and spontaneity with which the concern for correct and sensible rule application was articulated and acted upon. How does such a motivational system emerge in a legal agency? What maintains it?

In the case of OEP, the leadership of the agency endorsed the judicial mode but was not particularly inspiring or articulate about it. There was no careful recruitment or indoctrination of personnel. There was a great deal of employee turnover; work groups were hastily assembled and reassembled in an ad hoc manner and were not cohesively organized. The freeze was not part of a morally intense political movement to which agency workers were deeply committed from the start. Working in an agency which administered a ninety-day freeze was obviously a temporary assignment with little opportunity for advancement or other personal benefit. Most of the traditional explanations of high motivation, therefore, were not present.[8]

Rather, the pressure for commitment and responsible decision making seemed to stem from the developing nature of the regulatory program—the kinds of problems generated by the freeze order and the interaction it engendered between the agencies and their social environment. Since these were discussed at some length earlier, they need only be recapitulated briefly here.

Of primary importance was the significance and nature of the *problem of compliance* created by the freeze law. The freeze order demanded sacrifice of immediate income gains from a very large population. Universal compliance was perceived as conditional: unions, corporations, and landlords would comply only if the freeze was enforced consistently and fairly. To forestall evasion and to ensure that the freeze would work, it seemed essential that every decision should be backed by consistently applied, generally stated legal rules—the symbol of equal treatment—and also that every decision should appear to be substantively defensible, something the regulated party could accept as reasonable. In sum, anxiety about retention of broad public support bred concern for adhering to fundamental norms of legitimate governmental behavior.[9]

---

[8] See, e.g., the literature reviewed in Amitai Etzioni, *A Comparative Analysis of Complex Organizations* (New York: Free Press, 1961); James March and Herbert Simon, *Organizations* (New York: John Wiley & Sons, 1958); Victor Thompson, *Without Sympathy or Enthusiasm* (University, Ala.: University of Alabama Press, 1975).

[9] See Robert Cover, *Justice Accused: Antislavery and The Judicial Process* (New Haven, Conn.: Yale University Press, 1975), p. 214. Cover notes that "the presence or threat of resistance and disobedience" tended to push judges beyond a merely formal application of the law. "The judge, in confronting the resister, had to be prepared not only to enunciate the law, but also to justify it."

A second major factor was the unusual visibility of the agencies, a product of the intense coverage and dissemination of their rulings by national and local news media, trade publications, labor unions, and the like. As noted earlier, this visibility and the rapid feedback it produced increased the self-consciousness of agency officials, their sense of the importance of their mission, and their responsibility for making it work. It also increased the likelihood that instances of favoritism, inconsistency, or senseless rigidity on the part of individual officials would be picked up and reported. Indeed, this occurred from time to time: the *New York Times* and the *Washington Post,* for example, ran articles on inconsistent agency decisions. With a large and attentive public of newsmen, congressmen, unions, and businessmen continually monitoring the agencies' output and sending in new requests for price or wage increases based on alleged inconsistencies in prior rulings, OEP officials were more likely than most to regard their jobs as important and to be sensitive to the fairness and consistency of their decisions. There is no stronger inducement to a high level of motivation, wrote Chester Barnard, than "the feeling of enlarged participation in the course of events."[10]

A significant omission from this discussion, thus far, is the most important *formal* mechanism for control of the quality of regulatory decision—judicial review. During the freeze, numerous lawsuits challenged the legality of specific agency rules or decisions or of the program as a whole; similar defenses were raised in a few enforcement actions brought by the Justice Department on behalf of the agencies, but only two court decisions went against the agencies' position. One might attribute that to the short span of the freeze and the slow pace of court cases. Surely, one might think, sooner or later a court would have ordered the agencies to institute more deliberate, participatory fact-finding procedures or formal methods of making and justifying their rules and regulations. That may be so, although the legal status of informal interpretive "guidelines" (as the CLC rules were labeled) and of advisory opinion letters (as the inquiry-responses could be characterized) is far from settled administrative law and so are the procedural requirements imposed upon them.[11] It does seem important, however, that there was in fact no significant interference by the courts with the over four hundred rules and thousands of individual rulings issued by the administrative agencies which were regulating the central economic decisions of millions of corporations and business firms across the whole nation. There was a vast imbalance between the volume and pace of administrative legal decision on the one hand and judicial review on the other. There was nothing unique about the freeze experience in that respect. Judicial review was also infrequent and had

---

[10] Chester Barnard, *The Functions of the Executive* (Cambridge, Mass.: Harvard University Press, 1938), p. 147.

[11] See Ernest Gellhorn, "The Legal Effect of Anti-Inflation Advice from Government Agencies," 17 *Practicing Lawyer* 13 (December 1971).

little effect on agency procedures and rule application in the longer-term Phase II of the stabilization program.

One consequence of the relative infrequency of judicial review, in relation to internal decision making, is that it was not a salient factor in the minds of agency officials, and its availability exercised little *direct* influence on their mode of decision making.[12] As a day-to-day inducement to legal craftsmanship and sensitivity, the close attention of news media was distinctly more important. The potential reaction of courts was a concern of the freeze agency and Justice Department attorneys who worked on the cases filed in court, but litigation was a separate, specialized department. Most officials in the inquiry-response system went about their business without much thought as to whether this or that decision would hold up in court. They worried more about whether a decision was in accord with CLC policy, or how their immediate superiors would react, or how the decision would look to the public. Even the judicial rebuffs to agency decisions on teachers' salaries did not send shock waves through the agencies. Some top officials and lawyers in CLC and OEP were concerned about the court rulings; they initiated an appeal and formulated new rules designed to meet, at least part way, the court's objections, but most of the inquiry-response process went on unruffled. The revised rules on teachers' salaries were received and inserted in manuals and were followed, but they were indistinguishable from the new rules that came down from CLC every day. A rule changed at the behest of the court had no greater significance than a rule changed at the behest of an inquirer.

Confrontation with the courts does affect top officials and others who are specifically engaged in litigation. I was struck by the realization, when working on the teachers' salaries litigation in New Orleans, that we were about to encounter a "real" judge—until then it was agency officials who had been the sole judges on questions of freeze law. Such encounters can also evoke a new perspective: until then, OEP officials had built up their own dogma, ways of interpreting their rules, standard justifications, and definitions of their program. A federal district court judge, however, deciding his first and probably last case on the subject, would approach the freeze law without these inbred notions. He would be attracted to common-sense rule interpretation, more interested in substantive fairness than in maintaining the continuity of agency policy. Whatever potential judicial review thus had for breaking through ingrown agency doctrines and assumptions, it was limited to this one issue, and the lawyers who confronted the court had little

---

[12] Of course, the institution of judicial review undoubtedly was *indirectly* significant in helping to generate the culture of rule interpretation and norms of fairness that pervade the governmental establishment and the press, and its *availability* is surely an important protection against blatant unfairness and irrationality on the part of administrative agencies.

chance of infusing the agency as a whole with that fresh perspective. For most officials, judicial reversals would remain a remote and relatively insignificant contingency.[13]

SUMMARY

What encourages legal decision makers to adhere to the judicial mode of rule application, to decide in accordance with authoritative rules interpreted in light of their purposes, but also to remain alert to the consequences of rule application and the need for exceptions or reformulation of the rules? The OEP experience provides several clues. One is the importance of a supportive informal culture of rule interpretation and informal control mechanisms that continuously invoke the norms of the judicial mode. Several specific mechanisms appeared especially important in this regard: regular, open discussion of cases among colleagues, encouraged by the clustering of officials in the same room and by processes of multiple review; prompt access to rule makers by officials who wished to seek amendments to existing rules and responsiveness of rule makers to such challenges; a system of case presentation that enabled citizens to discuss the impact of existing rules and demand that officials provide substantive justification for their decisions; a tolerance for controlled equitable modification of rules on the part of leaders in rule-applying offices.

Perhaps the most important support for the judicial mode in OEP, however, was the overall environment of decision: the spontaneity with which the informal controls operated and the commitment to doing a good job that motivated most inquiry-response officials. That attitude, it appears, was the product of the nature of the regulatory program, the fact that it seemed both important and difficult to enforce it successfully, and that success was seemingly conditioned on the consistency and reasonableness of agency decision making.

---

[13] For other observations supportive of this point, see Howard Westwood, "The Davis Treatise: Meaning to the Practitioner," 43 *Minnesota Law Review* 607 (1959) and Joel Handler, "Controlling Official Behavior in Welfare Administration," 54 *California Law Review* 478, 491 (1966).

CHAPTER 8

Inducements to Deviant Modes of Rule Application

Even when an administrative agency, such as OEP, works hard to achieve the ideals of the judicial mode of rule application, it rarely can maintain that standard uniformly. Deliberation and attention to principle are not the only values at stake in an active, goal-oriented agency. Competing norms and operational imperatives tend to produce deviations from the judicial mode. Two specific inducements to deviant forms of decision making in the OEP national office were of particular importance—time pressure and bureaucratic organization.[1]

TIME PRESSURE

Confronted by an army of inquirers insisting that uncertainty about the requirements of the freeze be resolved immediately, agency leadership, by example and directive, placed great emphasis on rapidity of response. Delay, it was feared, would increase the risk of noncompliance by alienating inquirers or simply leaving them in the dark with respect to their obligations. Moreover, OEP officials felt that citizens had a basic right to a prompt answer. The meat packing house faced with higher cattle prices (because the price of cattle was not frozen) *deserved* to know, and to know quickly, whether those costs could be passed on. When a certain OEP official repeatedly

---

[1] The term *deviance* is used in relation to the norms of the judicial mode of rule application. Since those norms were supported by OEP officials, *deviance* refers to conduct defined as "wrong" by most participants in the system, even though it was sometimes tolerated.

engaged in long and ponderous deliberations concerning inquiries, colleagues became infuriated and accused him of indifference to the needs of the people "out there" anxious for guidance. Officials often sincerely apologized to inquirers whose letters had not been answered promptly.

Organizational pressures to speed response time by increasing "production" were soon exerted. The OEP Operations Center, which had telex links to OEP regional offices, IRS, and state attorney generals' offices, was ordered to stay open until midnight, and two shifts were put to work answering inquiries. Each office in the system was required to make daily administrative reports, noting the number of cases handled and the size of its backlog. OEP administrators could then monitor the performance of each office, if not in terms of the quality of its inquiry-responses, at least in terms of quantitative output.

When OEP regional offices complained of delays in answers to inquiries they had sent to the OEP national office, General Lincoln ordered that "turnaround time" on such inquiries be reduced to twenty-four hours, no matter how late the lawyers in the General Counsel's Office had to stay, and that he receive daily reports on GC's level of "production." Some attorneys objected to that approach and the disregard for quality it implied. "What are we doing, piecework?" muttered deputy general counsel Dick Murray. John Simpson, a former battlefield officer in Vietnam, referred to the daily reports as the "body count." Nevertheless they complied, rearranged office procedures to accelerate response time, and tried to make the body count "look good." Thus the stress on efficiency became a salient goal in each section.[2] Its effects on the nature of rule application were manifold.

Time Pressure, Informal Fact-finding, and Retreatism

Decision making in the judicial mode presupposes a determinate fact situation to which the "correct" rule or policy can be applied. If the decision maker has difficulty forming an opinion of what the facts are in a case, either because he cannot understand them or because of conflicting or distorted versions, he will be perplexed as to what rule to apply. Legal institutions, therefore, usually structure case presentation in order to produce comprehensive and reliable factual records. Some process cases only through standardized forms that call for relevant data and exclude the irrelevant. Some encourage citizens to communicate through lawyers, experts in translating their client's situation into the verbal categories of the bureaucracy. Some hold adversarial, evidentiary hearings and limit decision to facts adduced in the testimonial and documentary record. Some insist that information pre-

---

[2] On the tendency of organizations to adopt quantitative efficiency measures of self-assessment, see James D. Thompson, *Organizations in Action* (New York: McGraw-Hill, 1967); and Peter Blau, *The Dynamics of Bureaucracy* (Chicago: University of Chicago Press, 1955).

sented on an ex parte basis be verified and restated by quasi-independent experts, such as certified public accountants. As we have seen, the freeze agencies, in their rush to provide easily available and prompt responses, declined to establish formal case presentation, standardized inquiry forms, or fact-verification procedures. Conformity to the judicial mode of rule application was thus imperiled, and in a variety of ways.

One was that many inquiries were presented in an incomplete or rambling fashion, laden with extensive but irrelevant detail, omitting key bits of information essential for classification under CLC rules. Others contained relevant information but were all but incomprehensible to freeze officials because they were couched in the technical jargon of the inquirer's particular trade.[3] And because cases were presented in an unverified, ex parte manner, even when the freeze official could *understand* the inquirer's statement of his situation, he often was unsure whether he could trust it. Yet OEP lawyers and other inquiry-response officials were discouraged (although not forbidden) from calling the inquirer or other parties to get "all the facts," a process that tended to involve the official in long telephone conversations while the backlog of unanswered inquiries grew.

A common reaction to such situations was a form of retreatism—evasive and inconclusive responses. Moving as fast as he could through a stack of written inquiries, an OEP official would encounter an inquiry that seemed hard, because he had difficulty grasping the inquirer's problem or because he was suspicious that the facts were stated so as to mislead him. Without formal mechanisms to resolve such doubts and reluctant to slow down "production" by further investigation, the freeze official often dealt with the problem by sending the inquirer a noncommittal reply. Many ostensibly specific answers, on closer inspection, were actually quite vague, saying, "Based on the facts as stated in your letter, it appears that the following rules are applicable," without a statement of which clause in which of the several enclosed or quoted rules applied and what conduct was specifically required of the inquirer. Sometimes this was the best the official could do under the circumstances. Often, however, he just gave up. With a little more time, effort, consultation, and study of CLC policy, the official could have given the inquirer more specific guidance. To bounce the problem back to the inquirer in this way resolved the tension between the pressure to respond and the fear of making an incorrect answer, but it was extremely aggravating to the inquirer (who sometimes wrote back demanding a definite answer as to whether he could or could not charge a certain price for a new model outboard motor).

The absence of formal mechanisms in OEP for authoritative fact-finding

---

[3] Only 26 percent of the written inquiries answered by the OEP national office involved lawyers in their presentation. That percentage was undoubtedly lower at the regional office level.

also produced official paralysis when the agency faced a true adversary situation, where fiercely conflicting parties submitted different versions of the relevant facts. The following case provides a vivid illustration.

The Cincinnati Transit Case

A CLC regulation prohibited any reduction in the quality of goods or services to evade the freeze. In early September, Cincinnati Transit, a private bus company, sent OEP a letter and sworn affidavit stating that it had planned a new schedule, commencing September 5, which involved reduction in frequency of some service, but that 1) the reduction was insubstantial, and each rider would get "the identical quality of service" for the existing price and 2) the Cincinnati public utility director had approved the new schedule prior to the freeze, stating that it "would better meet public needs." GC's response on September 3 said that "based on your affidavit" and statements about the level of service, the rescheduling did not violate the freeze.

The bus schedule changes were put into effect. Within a few days, a Cincinnati city councilman called GC and claimed that contrary to the company's statement, a substantial decrease (13–18 percent) in frequency of service and operating hours had occurred. The Cincinnati city attorney called, too, contesting the factual allegations of the councilman (who, it emerged, was a Democratic candidate for mayor in the upcoming November elections; the mayor, city attorney, and utilities director were Republicans). The councilman then publicly charged the bus company with fraud and the city administration with collusion.

OEP, confronted with a factual dispute, quickly tried to duck it, saying the GC ruling would be reconsidered if new facts were presented to the IRS office in Cincinnati. That office, equally unprepared for fact-finding in an adversarial context, kept consulting the OEP regional office in Chicago, which kept calling Washington and sending along affidavits, transcripts, financial statements, and bus schedules that were being submitted by the conflicting parties.

Cincinnati Transit, its facts challenged, also made new arguments of law and policy: the freeze should not prevent minor, non-inflationary adjustments in service compelled by declining demand. Nor should the freeze compel the maintenance of services that exacerbated the company's deficit. (A planned municipal subsidy to the company had been cancelled in June due to the voters' defeat of a bond issue.) The freeze agencies, unable to deal effectively with the complex factual dispute, also began to characterize the problem as a policy issue. CLC issued a new rule stating that any reduction in frequency of service during the freeze required a proportionate price reduction "when the primary reason for the change relates to the return on investment of the company," but no price reduction was necessary "when the primary reason for the change is to adjust for changes in demand." The rule also stated (again attempting to avoid fact-finding by the agencies) that the decision on the "primary reason" for service reductions would be made by local regulatory agencies.

The next day, Cincinnati Transit threatened to defy any order compelling them to restore the old schedule. The mayor of Cincinnati called General Lincoln to protest CLC's rule, which "throws the decision back into my lap," and complained that "You've cost us the election." He wanted CLC or OEP to make the "primary reason" determination. At Lincoln's invitation, the mayor, the public utilities director, the Democratic city councilman, and the president and the attorney of Cincinnati Transit all assembled at OEP's Washington office; the Republican congressman from the area and assorted TV cameramen and reporters also showed up. It looked like OEP would have its first adversarial hearing on a question of fact.

But OEP officials were anxious, above all, to avoid such time-consuming, routine-disturbing adversarial proceedings.[4] The organization had no experience and no plans or procedures for structuring hearings. Moreover, in this case, a hearing threatened to be not only explosive and complex, but inconclusive: OEP officials belatedly realized that since a decline in demand had caused a reduction in Cincinnati Transit's rate of return, the schedule reduction was in response to *both* "primary reasons"; the CLC rule made no sense. Hence OEP officials decided not to hold a hearing or determine the "primary reason" for the service reduction and to insist, as the CLC rule stated, that the local regulatory agency decide. When the parties assembled, General Lincoln spent a lot of time fiddling with his pipe, reminiscing about his last visit to Cincinnati and gradually indicating, despite the impassioned pleas of the councilman and bus company president, that the decision would have to be made by the public utilities director, who sat glumly in the corner.

The mayor and utilities director went back to Cincinnati and, fearful of providing the Democratic councilman with more ammunition, stated that the rescheduling was primarily for reasons of return on investment and ordered Cincinnati Transit to resume its former level of service. Cincinnati Transit refused, demanded arbitration of its contract with the city, and sued OEP and CLC, challenging the CLC rule as an

---

[4] The delay associated with formal hearings has been the subject of much critical commentary. See, e.g., President's Advisory Council on Executive Organization (The Ash Council), *A New Regulatory Framework* (Washington: Government Printing Office, 1971); and for some concrete examples, Nicholas Johnson and J. Dystel, "A Day in the Life: The Federal Communications Commission," 82 *Yale Law Journal* 1575 (1973).

unconstitutional delegation of federal authority to the utilities director. The city attorney filed a complaint with the Cincinnati IRS office, charging the bus company with violating the freeze. Cincinnati Transit responded by saying it would come into compliance by a *fare reduction* commensurate with the service reduction. IRS consulted with OEP, which consulted with CLC, which decided that a fare reduction would be consistent with its policies, *provided* it reflected the entire savings to the company resulting from the service reduction. Again, this produced a new factual issue that IRS did not have the legal powers to resolve quickly: the company dragged its feet providing cost data, refused to allow IRS agents full access to all of its records (insisting on specific requests), and battled over appropriate accounting formulas. As the freeze ended, IRS was still investigating, Cincinnati bus riders continued to get less service at the original fare, the mayor was defeated in the election, and his replacement was the Democratic city councilman.[5]

Time Pressure and Careless Legalism

It has often been observed that time pressure jeopardizes rational decision making. In Herbert Simon's terms, the crush of time forces the decision maker into a stereotyped search for solutions to the problem, to selective perception of the situation, and hence to the first-discerned "satisficing" answer rather than the optimal answer.[6] The lack of time for deliberation has often been blamed for the callous and standardized treatment rendered defendants in urban criminal courts. Similarly, OEP General Counsel Elmer Bennett explained his frequent correction of answers drafted by his staff lawyers by citing, "Pressure of time. They just make errors, because of not reading the circulars carefully. They don't catch the exception to the general rule, or a later definition." My personal experience in the office confirms Bennett's observation. Dealing with a cryptic written inquiry, it would take a certain mental energy, a leap of the imagination, to visualize and truly comprehend the inquirer's situation. If I felt too hurried to stop to think about a case or was not stimulated to do so by some special argument, I was less likely to take note of potentially extenuating circumstances and more

---

[5] After the freeze, the company immediately instituted a fare increase without an increase in service, but this, the government contended, also violated Phase II regulations. The federal district court enjoined the company against further service cuts or fare increases. *United States* v. *Cincinnati Transit,* 337 F. Supp. 1068 (S.D. Ohio, 1972).

[6] James March and Herbert Simon, *Organizations* (New York: John Wiley & Sons, 1958), p. 116. See also Thomas Scheff, "Social Conditions for Rationality: How Urban and Rural Courts Deal with the Mentally Ill," in *Mental Illness and Social Process,* ed. Thomas Scheff (New York: Harper & Row, 1961); President's Commission on Law Enforcement and Administration of Justice, *The Challenge of Crime in a Free Society* (New York: Avon Books, 1968).

likely to classify the case under the first rule that seemed applicable rather than searching through the rule book for other relevant policy statements. The result might be called careless or unconscious legalism because the official, in his rush to judgment, simply fails to realize that he is applying an incorrect or unfair rule. As one GC lawyer told me, "It's not an easy job to tell what the easy ones are." He often thought a case was easy on first reading, he said, and was about to apply a certain rule automatically, but if he *took time* to read the inquiry again, it often seemed more difficult and the applicable rule less certain. Institutional pressures for quick response militated against "taking time."

More often than not, such instances of careless legalism produced inappropriately stringent outcomes. Because the general philosophy and pattern of day-to-day decision was to hold the line against recurrent arguments for accommodation, the freeze official was attuned to saying, "No. You're frozen." The most common legalistic mistake, therefore, was to apply a basic stringent rule in an automatic fashion, oblivious to the extenuating facts that would justify an exception under more specific, accommodative CLC rules.

Time Pressure, Inadequate Rules, and Inconsistency

The pressure for rapid response was also reflected in the decision-making process of CLC's Executive Committee, where most rules were made. Meeting every morning for two or three hours, ExComm concentrated on issuing as many rules as posssible, sometimes ten or twelve a day. At that pace, as noted in Chapter 2, ExComm members had little time to familiarize themselves with the policy issues raised by the cases referred from OEP, to think them through in advance, and to consider the consequences of draft rules. Discussion was very rapid and reasons for decisions usually were not stated in writing. Hopes for consistency rested largely on the memory and instant analytical ability of ExComm members.

This emphasis on speed sometimes resulted in over-broad rules. For example, when asked to rule on whether planned salary increases for teachers could be put into effect during the freeze, ExComm members were unaware of and unable to visualize the surprising variety of contractual and statutory arrangements for paying teachers that are used in the thousands of local school districts across the country. This lack of knowledge is a common problem faced by lawmakers; they often attempt to deal with it by consultation with experts or by holding hearings at which potentially affected parties can comment on a proposed rule's language and impact. CLC, responsive above all to the pressure to decide quickly, did not employ those techniques regularly or insist that staff members do so. It issued a teachers' salary rule based on one or two specific cases that had been referred to it and that it took to be typical. The hurried ruling turned out to be inappropriate, unclear, and unexpectedly accommodative with respect to many school districts that were not like the specific cases presented to CLC. Efforts to remedy the situation by issuing a revised and more stringent rule resulted in further confusion, along with vehement protests that teachers were being treated inconsistently and unjustly.[7]

One response to this kind of problem was for CLC to pull in its horns and restrict the scope of its rules to the facts in the specific cases brought before it, much as an appellate court restricts its holding to the case at hand. The key to the precedential, rule-establishing function of appellate court decisions, however, is the publication of an *opinion* wherein the court spells out the principles and policies that underlie the decision. But CLC and ExComm eschewed the time-consuming and somewhat threatening process of writing explanations for their numerous but narrowly cast rules. In consequence, many of their rules were poor guides; their applicability to analogous but slightly different situations was unclear, and they often appeared to be inconsistent. This was exacerbated by CLC's lack of attention to draftsmanship and by the minor role played by lawyers—perhaps the most distinctive aspect of legal training is its concentration on formulating decisions in precise language and its focus on problems of definition and possibly divergent interpretations of language. ExComm decisions, however, were generally made simply by checking off one imprecisely stated option in the issue paper prepared by the OEP Policy Analysis Office.[8]

Forced to deduce CLC policy from over-broad rules or from a series of detailed but unexplained and sometimes inconsistent rules, inquiry-response officials were often tempted to give up the search for CLC's true intention.[9]

---

[7] See pp. 54–55.

[8] Compare Victor Thompson's largely critical account of a lawyer-dominated regulation-drafting process in *The Regulatory Process in OPA Rationing* (New York: Kings Crown Press, 1950). Its emphasis, he claimed, was too much on legal precision; in consequence, the regulations could not be understood by the public.

[9] For example, CLC first ruled that wages of government employees could not be increased during the freeze, even when mandated by state or municipal law. Then it ruled that where states had minimum wage laws that called for an increased minimum as of a date that fell within the freeze period, wages could be raised to meet that minimum. Some states have statutes which prescribe minimum salaries for teachers, which local districts then may supplement; when it was learned that some states had enacted increases in that minimum wage effective in September 1971, CLC ruled that wages could *not* be raised to meet minimum wage laws applying to "specific occupational groups." Soon after, CLC ruled that wages for construction workers could be increased to meet the "prevailing area wage" minimums required by the Davis-Bacon Act for federally funded construction projects. When OEP was then asked whether construction workers could receive increases to meet minimums prescribed by *state* laws calling for payment of prevailing union rates, OEP officials were thoroughly and understandably perplexed as to which principle to follow and tended to slip into a highly legalistic discussion.

In those cases, there was little for the rule applier to rely on but a literal reading of the words of the rule. One consequence, therefore, was legalistic rule application. Another was retreatism. The corollary of both was inconsistency. To the extent that CLC was confused or its rules "taught" poorly, lower-level officials "learned" CLC policy differently. The *New York Times* called a series of agency field offices and asked the same questions to each. In many cases, the reporter received radically different answers. Practicing attorneys complained of their inability to discern freeze law reliably by reading the published rules or to get definitive answers from lower-level offices.

BUREAUCRACY AND LEGALISM

In OEP, as in many other bureaucracies, the internal social control system repeatedly directed the decision makers' attention to the body of rules themselves and discouraged the unauthorized (that is, non-rule-based) "giving in" to particularized pleas for relief from the freeze. These pressures increased over time: with each additional page in the growing manual of rules, it seemed to become more authoritative and more demanding of the freeze officials' attention. At the beginning of the freeze, it was possible for an official to "know" CLC policy as embodied in a relatively small number of rules, but this became impossible as page after page of rules added new policy specifications for a growing variety of commercial situations and employee compensation plans. Consequently, off-the-top-of-the-head decisions, based on one's memory or impression of CLC policy, became increasingly risky. The most likely source of error to be noticed and corrected by a reviewing official was failure to locate and cite a specific controlling precedent. More decision time, accordingly, had to be spent in searching through and analyzing the provisions in the rule book. The body of rules increasingly came to be regarded by OEP National officials as a closed system, a nearly complete expression of relevant policies, in which almost every contingency or possibly extenuating circumstance had already been taken into account.

One consequence was a tendency to deal with some inquiries wholly in terms of analyzing which rule category they best fitted into. For example, one discussion in GC dealt with whether the "points" charged by mortgage companies were really fees for a service (preparing and issuing the loan), in which case they were frozen, or really interest rates, in which case they would be exempt. The discussion focused on whether points were treated as interest rates under the income tax law and whether they fluctuated in step with interest rates. There was no discussion, however, of what the inflationary effects or the impact on the mortgage market and home buyers would be—either in general or with respect to the case at hand—depending on whether points were ruled frozen or exempt. Moreover, the continual mental attention to rule-based categories sometimes closed off the decision maker from sensitivity to the details of the inquirer's situation, unless the inquirer's dilemma happened to fit into a preexisting rule category. I found myself subject to these pressures, as this excerpt from my field notes indicates.

October 15. New York State Teachers' Association

Lou Neeb (an aide to General Lincoln) asked me to meet with the president, general counsel, and treasurer of the New York State Teachers' Association. The association, they told me, had planned a substantial dues increase for the 1971–72 school year to alleviate a serious deficit and hoped that the freeze would not prevent it.

I found myself extremely impatient with their presentation, which was made with great care and documentation. I was interested only in certain facts, those which would tell me into which rule-based category their case fell, e.g., what was their fiscal year, the proportion of members who had paid the increased dues before the freeze, whether services had been performed by the association during the summer, etc. Other facts which they stressed, such as the details of their financial situation and the nature of the services they provided, were irrelevant to me as an OEP lawyer, or so I felt. Hence, I was bored by the presentation of "unnecessary" detail and annoyed by their effort to elicit sympathy. I often interrupted to ask my own questions, and only the felt obligation to be somewhat polite and give them a "hearing" prevented me from rudely cutting them off and restricting the discussion to items of my own choosing.

This legalistic approach did not predominate in OEP during the freeze. Economic effects and issues of fairness were commonly discussed, equitable adjustments made in individual cases, and requests for rule reformulation sent to CLC, but the tendency of rule-based decision making to slide into legalism was real and powerful. Some circumstances during the freeze, as discussed in the previous chapter, helped to mitigate it. Conversely, some bureaucratic arrangements were conducive to the kind of legalism that is insensitive to justice-claims and the possibility of reformulating rules.

Insulation from Informal Contact with Citizens

In a decision system that is devoted to equal treatment of all applicants and to decision in accordance with rules, face-to-face, informal case presentation is often seen as something of a threat. Unstructured, private meetings between officials and regulated firms increase the risk of particularistic, idiosyncratic decisions. Confronted directly with citizens' personal and passionate statements of their problems, officials are more likely to see each case as unique, "different" from the situations dealt with in the formal rule, and hence to be swayed by the equities of the individual case rather than the overall goals of official policy and the necessity for uniform treatment. A familiar bureaucratic response is to insulate the decision maker from direct or informal contacts with citizens, to reduce such contacts to written case files, or to prescribe formal on-the-record formats for in-person presentation of cases.

So it was that the inquiry-response offices in the OEP national office sought to discourage conferences in which inquirers could present their cases face-to-face with agency officials. Some persistent inquirers still managed to gain in-person consideration of their cases, because they had political connections, because they had large-scale significance in the national economy, or because they were involved in situations in which the freeze was clearly threatening to disrupt normal economic functions, but such conferences were regarded as aberrant, time-consuming interruptions of routine. The participating OEP official was instructed to inform the inquirer that any in-person answers were unofficial. The only official response was a written one, which forced the official to deliberate, read the CLC rules, and draft an answer with appropriate citations, reviewable by his superior. And while the informality of written case presentation enabled some inquirers to tell their story in vivid detail and to make impassioned justice-claims, most written inquiries were not so articulate. And so in OEP, where face-to-face contact with inquirers was unusual and unwelcome, the human impact and economic consequences of rule application were often obscure to the decision maker, and the risks of legalistic patterns of thought and decision were correspondingly enhanced.

Separation of Functions

Systems of governance by rules usually entail four basic functions: making and amending the rules; enforcing the rules against and sanctioning violators; interpreting the rules (deciding which rule applies to particular cases); and making exceptions to the rules in particular cases where literal rule application would be unjust or inappropriate. The freeze administration, like many bureaucratic systems, chose to lodge those distinct but combinable functions in separate operating units. Inquiry-response officials in OEP were authorized to say what the rules required in specific cases, but were not primarily responsible for making or remaking the rules (that was for CLC), for enforcing them against violators (that was the job of the IRS), or for making equitable exceptions (a separate Office of Exceptions and Exemptions was established for that purpose). This division of labor in some ways increased the risks of legalism in the inquiry-response process.

The separation of "law" and "equity" enabled inquiry-response officials, on occasion, to close their eyes and ears to pleas of hardship. They could merely advise the oppressed inquirer to file an application for relief from alleged hardship in the Office of Exceptions and Exemptions, rather than taking the hardship as a signal to rethink the problem of which rule should be regarded as applicable or whether the rule could be amended. What I regarded as irrelevant information in the New York State Teachers' Association Case, I might not have regarded as irrelevant if my job definition had included express responsibility for equitable relief as well as application of preexisting rules.[10] Similarly, the separation of rule interpretation from enforcement meant that the decisions made by OEP inquiry-response officials were often made in bureaucratic isolation: the official did not have to explain and justify the rule in face-to-face conversation with the alleged violator, hear his excuses or expressions of remorse, gauge his good faith, or assess what it would mean to him to be dragged into enforcement proceedings. In sum, the inquiry-response official did not have to decide in a context that emphasized his own responsibility for the human consequences of his decision.[11]

In theory, the separation of rule application from rule formulation should not have caused any problems; the inquiry-response official need only be alert for and refer the troublesome case to CLC. However, several factors deterred OEP officials from referring even the perceived policy issue to a higher office. One reason was time pressure: a GC lawyer, for example, when confronted with an inquiry referred from a regional office that appeared to present a policy issue for CLC, also realized that to send the case "upstairs" would conflict with the directive to answer such inquiries within twenty-four hours, limit GC's "production" record, alienate the impatient regional office, and perhaps, because of the backlog in Policy Analysis and ExComm, produce an authoritative answer too late to be of much use to the inquirer (who might by then have decided to ignore the freeze anyway). The pressure for efficiency and quick turnaround time also induced higher offices to reject some referrals

---

[10] Of course, officials engaged wholly in questions of equitable relief may also become legalistic, as in the case of the rigid pleading rules developed by eighteenth-century British chancery courts. See C. K. Allen, *Law in the Making,* 7th ed. (London: Oxford University Press, 1964), pp. 380–382. OEP's Office of Exceptions and Exemptions, in fact, had a more formalistic set of procedures for case presentation than the inquiry-response offices.

[11] Again, there is no guarantee that enforcement officials will not become legalistic. I often heard OEP and Justice Department enforcement attorneys discussing whether or not to institute prosecution: the discussion usually focused on whether they could *prove* a rule violation, rather than on the impact of prosecution on the alleged violator or the fairness of the rules. However, as in the case of direct responsibility for equity, I would argue that face-to-face prosecutorial decisions are less vulnerable to legalistic tendencies than isolated, bureaucratic "rulings of law."

from lower ones. "Gatekeepers" turned away referred inquiries that they thought were insufficiently problematic; the lower offices in response were encouraged to assert themselves and decide more hard cases on their own. In addition, the fact that higher offices never reviewed the work of lower offices on their own initiative but relied upon lower-level officials to refer important policy problems upward increased the de facto discretion of lower offices. GC lawyers, for example, could avoid the time and effort of pushing a policy issue through the OEP Policy Analysis Office and on to CLC, and decide it themselves as a "matter of interpretation," trusting that CLC would almost surely never know.[12]

Yet another deterrent to referral of policy questions to CLC was the stratification and compartmentalization often associated with bureaucracy. Peter Blau has shown that the deference associated with consulting a bureaucratic superior induced officials in a wage-and-hour law enforcement agency to avoid such contact; they preferred to deal with the hard case by consulting with colleagues at their own level.[13] The same pattern could be noted in the freeze agencies. Most GC lawyers, for example, had little interaction with the Policy Analysis Office of OEP, ExComm, or CLC. Those bodies were seen as abstract and remote entities rather than a known group of people, and thus it was more comfortable for GC lawyers to try to resolve the policy issue by consultation with their immediate colleagues. Moreover, as each office came to believe in its own expertise in inquiry-response, reversals of its answers by superiors met with traces of resentment. "The General Counsel's Office is not the Supreme Court," the head of the OEP Correspondence Section told his personnel. On the other hand, status differences sometimes produced a reluctance to ask higher offices for further clarification of earlier rulings, for fear that they were "too busy" or "this isn't important enough to bother CLC about."

Barriers between lower offices and higher level rule-makers lead in some agencies to "unauthorized discretion," as lower officials amend or subtly defy official policy as applied to particular cases. That was rarely the experience in the freeze agencies. Multiple reviews and the belief that bureaucrats should

---

[12] This was facilitated by the narrow mode of communication of GC decisions and those of other lower offices: they were not published or distributed throughout the system, but sent as personal letters to the inquirer alone.

There is a parallel in other systems in which intra-agency or interoffice review depends on voluntary referral by officials. A frequently noted instance is police discretion to refer cases for prosecution, which gives them greater de facto discretion over search and seizure rule application. Courts cannot review Fourth Amendment violations in cases that never get to court. See Dallin Oaks, "Studying the Exclusionary Rule in Search and Seizure," 37 *University of Chicago Law Review* 665 (1970).

[13] Blau, *Dynamics of Bureaucracy.* See also Michel Crozier's discussion of the "isolation of strata" in *The Bureaucratic Phenomenon* (Chicago: University of Chicago Press, 1964).

not "make policy" constituted a strong hedge against decisions not authorized by the rules. More fundamentally, this loyalty to the authority of rules was encouraged by the fact that in the context of the freeze, unauthorized decisions would usually be accommodative, clearly visible to customers or workers in other businesses, and hence likely to result in public complaints or demands for analogous accommodative treatment. Accommodative exercise of unauthorized discretion by an OEP official, therefore, had a good chance of being detected by his superiors or by CLC. Finally, agency officials were inured to accept harsh results called for by CLC rules by the "definition of the situation" repeatedly asserted by CLC members and OEP leaders: "A freeze is bound to cause some hardship."

Consequently, if energy flagged and OEP officials were reluctant to refer a "hard case" to CLC for reformulation of a rule, the resulting de facto discretion was more likely to result in legalistic rule application than unauthorized policy-making. Officials in the lower office often would persist in efforts to "find" a "correct" answer solely by analysis of the concepts used in CLC rules or by analogizing the case to a previously decided one in order to maintain consistency. One final, if rather extreme, example from my field notes is illustrative.

October 7. Mt. Sinai Hospital Case

A hospital in Cleveland had planned a wage increase for its nurses and dietary workers. For administrative reasons, it had announced that half the staff would get the increase on August 12, the other half August 19. (It had done the same in a previous wage increase with the two groups reversed in time.) But the freeze intervened on August 15. Can "Group B," who didn't actually get their raise before August 15, now receive it? Or can Group B personnel be considered in the same class as Group A, so that their increase can be deemed "in effect" prior to the freeze? A long debate among several GC lawyers occurred.

I argued that they *are* in the same class (basically I was just plain sympathetic, thinking they shouldn't get screwed just because of an odd administrative practice). But Dave Beller said this would be inconsistent with our treatment of teachers. We say in those cases that unless a teacher actually worked at the planned new salary before August 15, he or she can't get the raise, even if other teachers under the same contract or plan worked and got paid at the new rate prior to the freeze. Finally we agreed there was something wrong with CLC policy here and took it to Elmer Bennett. After some discussion, he said that other wage earners should be treated like the teachers because only the teachers' policy was really clear in CLC rules. So the Group B nurses can't get their raise.

We all accepted this, rather than persisting and getting CLC to consider a policy adjustment. We seemed happy to have Bennett serve as a court of last resort, just to end the matter. I didn't feel *that* bad about the nurses. It's OK, I thought, because we got some more consistency. (Sometimes it seems we're getting so shell-shocked by the pace or the sheer number of cases or being cooped up in the office for long hours that we don't *care* about some of these decisions!)

This did not always occur, for as in the School Bus Contractors' Case, OEP officials often attempted to decide the hard case in terms of estimation and evaluation of consequences and by predictions of how CLC would deal with the matter (which was always based, in part, on how they thought CLC *should* deal with the matter). Moreover, the barriers of bureaucracy *were* permeable, counteracted by rewards for "taking things seriously." Some officials cultivated informal working relationships with officials in higher offices; they took hard cases to them in person for quick resolution, rather than debating whether or not to take the time to refer a case through routine channels.[14] A large number of requests for accommodative rule modifications were in fact referred to OEP's Policy Analysis Office and to CLC. For some OEP officials, however, isolated from direct access to information about the impact of their decisions, told that their job was to apply rules rather than to make policy, and urged to decide each case as quickly as possible, the legalistic pattern of rule application was a not uncommon reaction.

CONCLUSION

The most pervasive threat to the judicial mode of rule application in the agencies was the compulsion to decide cases speedily and efficiently as well as correctly and fairly. This compulsion was not the product of a bureaucratic love of efficiency for its own sake, or of a mindless organizational tendency to employ only quantitative measures of performance, or of the desire of inquiry-response officials to go home early. It was rooted in the notion that prompt decision making is an important component of doing justice— especially in a novel regulatory program that introduced new uncertainties

---

[14] The OEP national office established a relatively formal mechanism to facilitate inter-level communication as well. A Coordination Section was established, which included officials who worked in each operating office. The group met every day and, among other things, worked out methods of interoffice case referral. More important, however, were the informal relationships that developed, the familiarity that encouraged frequent trips between offices and lunches among officials from different offices. See generally, in this regard, Rensis Likert, *New Patterns of Management* (New York: McGraw-Hill, 1961) and Charles Perrow, *Complex Organizations: A Critical Essay* (Glenview, Ill.: Scott Foresman, 1972), pp. 32–52.

into economic behavior—and in the belief that rapid communication of the law's requirements to the public was essential to achieving compliance. These concerns, of course, are not unique to the freeze agencies. Nor are the inducements to legalism and retreatism that they engendered.

An emphasis on fast response to demands for legal decisions, the freeze experience shows, jeopardizes the quality of legal decision in several ways. First, if the rules themselves are formulated without taking enough time for consultation with affected interests or for good draftsmanship and articulation of the rules' purposes, the capacity of lower-level officials to comprehend and apply the rules intelligently and consistently is necessarily impaired. Second, time pressure encourages a pro forma, incomplete approach to fact-finding in the process of rule application, both with regard to adjudicative facts (determining the true situation or past behavior of the specific parties) and legislative facts (assessing the likely future consequences of alternative decisions or rule interpretations). OEP inquiry-response officials, for example, confronted with ex parte factual presentations which were often difficult to understand or of questionable reliability, did not undertake investigations or hearings to determine the facts; that, it was thought, would unduly slow response time. The result was sometimes retreatist decisions, in which rulings were left unspecific or reduced to meaningless form letters. Third, time pressure directly encouraged legalistic rule application, sometimes of a careless kind, in which the hurrying decision maker simply failed to grasp the essence of the case presented and applied the wrong rule, and sometimes of a more subtle kind, in which the decision maker failed to take the time to give full consideration to the alleged adverse effects of strict rule application or to undertake the effort of formulating and gaining approval for an exception or amendment to the rule.

The insulation and compartmentalization associated with bureaucratic organization also increases the risk of legalistic rule application. When decision makers are removed from face-to-face conversation with the people whose fate they are deciding, when the function of making exceptions to rules on grounds of individual case hardship is administratively separated from that of rule application, routinized and unsympathetic decision making is more likely to occur. When the authority to reformulate the rules is vested exclusively in a few high-level officials, but referral of problematic cases to those officials is left to the discretion of lower officials, bureaucratic limits on communication between hierarchical levels and ambivalence about deferring to higher officials seems to encourage the lower-level officials to persist in the effort to force even the hard case into existing rule categories.

The inducements to retreatism and legalism created by time pressure and bureaucracy are not irresistible. They can be counteracted, at least in part, by the supports for a consequence-oriented and more flexible judicial mode of rule application, as described in Chapter 7—formal and informal review of decisions, frequent collegial discussion, direct exposure of officials to citizens' justice-claims, intra-office leaders who engage in equitable rule modification and frequent referral of cases to higher offices, aggressive reporting of bureaucratic actions by news media, and a staff that is continually made aware of the social importance and impact of the program it administers. In large, high volume, overburdened decision systems, however, the inducements to legalism and retreatism can rarely be entirely overcome. They coexist with pressures for more responsive rule application. The result is likely to be different modes of rule application and different substantive outcomes, depending on the nature of particular cases and the way they are presented. The impact of case presentation is the subject of the next chapter.

CHAPTER 9

Case Presentation and Substantive Dispositions

Methods of legal decision making are important, in the last analysis, because they affect substantive outcomes for individual parties and the aggregate impact of legal policy. How did the clash of competing styles of rule application in the OEP national office affect the incidence of stringency and accommodation in the decision of individual cases? What determined whether a particular inquiry would be answered in the judicial mode or legalistically, stringently or accommodatively?

MODES OF RULE APPLICATION: SUBSTANTIVE IMPLICATIONS

The judical mode of rule application has no inherent tendency to produce any particular pattern of substantive outcomes, liberal or conservative, stringent or accommodative. It is responsive primarily to the substantive thrust of the rules it is called upon to apply, and secondly to the way those rules "work" in the context of the individual cases that happen to arise. The most to be said is that the judicial mode would tend to moderate extreme policies, those which favor one social objective to the virtual exclusion of other commonly held goals or values. In the case of the freeze, CLC rules favored one goal (stringent price and wage control) but not absolutely or intransigently. While inquiry-response officials in OEP employed a corresponding presumption in favor of stringency in deciding doubtful cases, that in itself did not dictate any particular pattern of results: pursuant to the judicial mode the presumption of stringency *could* be rebutted. The frequency with which that happened would depend on the nature of the cases presented to OEP officials. The more often those cases involved situations in which stringent rule interpretations appeared to produce undue hardship or disruption, then the more likely the judicial mode of decision would produce accommodative results.

It happens, however, that when the basic rules of a regulatory agency are stringent, normal mechanisms of case mobilization tend to thrust just those kinds of cases—the ones in which the stringent rules are arguably inappropriate or unfair—onto the dockets of agency officials, especially those at the higher levels of the bureaucracy. Secondary sources of knowledge about official policy, such as law firms and trade associations, develop in the community. Their job is to learn the rules and answer their constituents' questions about them, at least for recurrent problems, while directing the non-routine problems, including those in which the rules seem unfair, to the appropriate agency. During the freeze such organizations as the United States Chamber of Commerce periodically would send lists of increasingly specific questions to OEP, seeking answers for distribution to their members. Agency officials held question and answer sessions with such groups as the National Association of School Boards and congressional staff members. In consequence, after the first couple of weeks, the inquiries that flowed to the agencies in Washington tended to be more difficult, those in which there were plausible arguments for an accommodative answer. In the first two weeks of the freeze, only 20 percent of the inquiries answered by the OEP national office rated high on objective measures of complexity (factual detail and legal argumentation); a month later, 34 percent were complex; in the last two weeks of the freeze, 62 percent were.[1]

Moreover, the inquiries directed to the OEP national office were more significant than the average telephone call to a local IRS office. They were more likely to come from business firms and sizable organizations than from individual consumers and tenants, from inquirers with a larger stake in the outcome, and more likely to reflect a somewhat sophisticated understanding of existing CLC rules. Even so, the Correspondence Section rerouted to other agencies the written inquiries that seemed "simple," that is, obviously controlled by existing rules. Those that remained for decision by the OEP national office, therefore, were overwhelmingly from organizations rather

---

[1] These figures are based on a systematic sample of 447 cases from OEP's national office inquiry-response files, as described in the Appendix. Complexity was measured by means of a scale that included the following inquiry characteristics: number of pages; amount of legal or financial documentation; amount of factual detail concerning inquirer's situation; number of separate arguments; and length of argument. Inquiries that scored in the top one-third in at least three of the five characteristics were classified as high in complexity.

than individuals, from inquirers seeking an accommodative interpretation or modification of the CLC rules, with at least some argument in their favor.[2] With this kind of case load, the judicial mode of rule application in OEP National, even *with* a presumption in favor of stringency, might be expected to produce a substantial number of *accommodative* rulings.

Legalistic decision making, on the other hand, tended to produce stringent inquiry responses in OEP. The careless legalism that resulted from hurried decision making produced an insensitivity to complexities in the inquirer's case—complexities which, if recognized, might have stimulated a search for an applicable accommodative rule or interpretation. In such cases, the inquirer, in effect, was not given the opportunity to rebut the presumption in favor of stringency. The more subtle form of legalism that resulted from reluctance to refer perceived hard cases to higher offices or from the tendency to regard the CLC rules as a closed system also tended to produce stringent responses by rejecting more fundamental challenges to existing rules.

Retreatist decisions in the OEP national office—vague, incomplete, inconclusive inquiry-responses—cannot be classified as either stringent or accommodative in themselves. Inquirers who were seeking official permission to raise rents or prices and received inconclusive answers may have gone ahead and implemented the increases in many cases, but that is far from certain. What is more certain is that they felt frustrated and annoyed, and that arguments they had made for accommodation had gone unrecognized.

BREAKING THROUGH ROUTINE: AGGREGATE INDICATORS

How did the conflicting patterns of rule application interact or balance out? To what extent did tendencies toward legalism and retreatism overwhelm the judicial mode of rule application?

The interaction of the judicial mode and deviant styles of rule application can be summarized as follows. Pressures for rapid decision and bureaucratic insulation encouraged the routinization of decision. Inquiry-response officials tended to read inquiries more and more rapidly, through a set of lenses which picked out only the key words that enabled the official to place the

---

[2] Seventy-two percent of inquiries answered by OEP's national office were from organizations rather than individuals. In terms of function, 46 percent of all inquiries were from business firms (including landlords and farmers—7.5 percent were landlords); 10.5 percent from labor unions; 15.6 percent from government entities and nonbusiness organizations (school boards, municipalities, irrigation districts, private schools, colleges, clubs, and hospitals); and 27.8 percent from consumers, tenants, workers, or other individuals.

case into a routine category, screening out information about the inquirer's financial situation and what it would mean for him to be frozen. The arguments made by the inquiry, too, would be almost automatically fitted into a set of recurrent argument categories, for each of which there was a pat answer. These routine patterns, however, were repeatedly *broken through* in particular cases, in which officials suddenly became more sensitive to the consequences of decision. Sometimes, as in the New York State Teachers Association Case described in the last chapter, all that mattered to the official—in that case, to me—was how the case fitted into existing rule categories. At other times, something in the case or the way it was presented pierced that legalistic mind set and reminded the decision maker that a "real person" or organization was involved, that real problems would result from his decision, and that those should at least be considered and evaluated. The result, as in the School Bus Contractors' Case, might still be a stringent one. But Mr. Reynolds, in that case, did make an impact. I was moved to think about what would happen to the bus companies and their employees, the school children, and the school boards, and the freeze as a whole.

How regularly did that breakthrough occur, insuring consequence-oriented rule application and serious consideration of arguments for accommodation? I have no precise answers, but a few suggestive indicators with respect to OEP National.[3] Among the various offices in OEP's inquiry-response system, the Correspondence Section (CS) in Washington was particularly vulnerable to pressures for speed and efficiency. Its mission was defined as routine rule application rather than interpretation or policy making. The Correspondence Section was thought of as a sorting station, directing incoming cases to appropriate offices—transferring some to Exceptions and Exemptions, simple inquiries to other federal agencies, hard ones to the General Counsel's Office, retaining and answering inquiries of intermediate difficulty itself. Almost 25 percent of the inquiries examined in CS were identified as hard cases and referred to the General Counsel's Office

---

[3] Unfortunately, I can say little about rule application in the regional offices of OEP or the more remote IRS district offices. It is entirely possible that in those offices, removed from the policy-making center of the system, motivation was lower, understanding of the rules less complete, and adherence to the judicial mode weaker. The confusion and inconsistency encountered by some inquirers support this view. And for the first month or six weeks of the freeze, many field offices complained about insufficient guidance from Washington, indicating that they were consciously having difficulty. On the other hand, my own contacts with OEP regional officials (who sent over 2,000 individual inquiries to the national office for clarification or reformulation of applicable rules), the Cincinnati IRS office, and a visit to the IRS office in New Orleans all indicated that *motivation* to understand and apply the rules intelligently was quite strong. While inadequately explained CLC rules may have led to some legalism, retreatism, and even unauthorized innovation, I have no reason to believe these forms of decision making predominated in the field offices.

or OEP's Policy Analysis Office.[4] In all these cases, at a bare minimum, CS officials recognized something problematic, something that precluded routine rule application, legalistic or otherwise. There is little in the literature of legal agencies to provide a comparative benchmark, but in light of the pressures for rapidity of response and routine disposition, that would seem to be a high rate of upward referral, suggestive of a relatively low incidence of routine, legalistic case disposition.

Moreover, of the cases retained and decided by CS, almost one-third (30 percent) of inquirers *seeking* a price, rent, or wage increase were given accommodative answers.[5] Again, it is hard to say whether that is a high or low percentage, particularly in view of the fact that the General Counsel's Office issued accommodative answers in 46.7 percent of increase-seeking inquiries, and about 50 percent of ExComm's rule-making choices, as noted in Chapter 3, were accommodative. The increasing percentage of accommodative answers at progressively higher levels of the hierarchy might be taken as an indication that GC and ExComm had a less legalistic style or a more accommodative attitude than the Correspondence Section, but that is not necessarily the case. The dockets of the higher offices, it is more likely, were more heavily stacked with cases "deserving" accommodative answers. That is because lower-level officials were more likely to refer a doubtful case to a higher office if they thought an *accommodative* interpretation might be warranted. If they thought a stringent interpretation more appropriate in the doubtful case, they would be more willing to extend an existing rule by analogy and decide it on their own. As noted earlier, while the Policy Analysis Office in OEP issued a higher percentage of stringent decisions than ExComm, the Policy Analysis *attitude* was not more stringent than ExComm's; when ExComm disagreed with the Policy Analysis recommendation on proposed rules, it tended to choose a more stringent alternative than the one recommended. The cases that Policy Analysis retained and decided on its own were those with weaker arguments for accommodation than the ones it sent to ExComm. The same pattern—retaining the poor candidates for accommoda-

---

[4] Based on official records and my count of cases in the OEP national office files, about 8,150 inquiries were processed by the Correspondence Section (along with over 1,000 requests for exceptions and 3,600 complaints and expressions of opinion). Of the 8,150 inquiries, 4,600 were labeled "simple" and referred to other federal departments—Agriculture, Labor, Commerce, Treasury, HUD, and HEW; 1,700 were answered by the Correspondence Section itself; 1,650 were referred to the General Counsel's Office; and 200 directly to Policy Analysis.

[5] In 83.1 percent of the inquiries answered by the OEP national office, the inquirer was seeking a price, wage, or rent increase. In 16.9 percent, he or she was resisting or attempting to block an increase, in other words, seeking a stringent answer. These latter cases are difficult to interpret from the standpoint of mode of rule application and are therefore excluded from the analysis and tabular presentations which follow.

tive answers—may have been true in Correspondence. Hence a 30 percent rate of accommodative inquiry-responses in the Correspondence Section suggests that stringent legalism, while perhaps somewhat more common in Correspondence than in GC, was not the predominant style of decision in the OEP inquiry-response system.

Another indicator was my contemporaneous experience. For several weeks, my job in the General Counsel's Office was reviewing draft responses to inquiries that had come to the OEP national office from regional offices. The drafts had first been prepared by officials in the Operations Center and then reviewed by a GC lawyer. Most days, I judged about 25 percent to be wrong, or such incomplete explications of applicable policy as to require substantial revision. Some of these errors were accommodative in nature: the initial decision maker had extended an accommodative rule too far or had not sufficiently qualified his answer—and hence guarded against manipulation by the inquirer—by explicit reference to relevant stringent provisions. More often draft answers were simply too unspecific or ambiguously worded: the official could have done better. Perhaps half the errors, and hence about 15 percent of the answers I reviewed, I would estimate, were overly legalistic and stringent; they failed to apply applicable accommodative rules or to recognize a policy issue which consequence-oriented rule interpretation would have uncovered.[6] This experience indicates that insensitive rule application in OEP National was prevalent but by no means predominant. More likely than not, plausible claims to accommodative interpretations were at least considered.

CASE PRESENTATION AND SUBSTANTIVE OUTCOMES

What determined how a particular case would be handled? What characteristics of an inquirer, of a case, or of the way it was processed helped to break through the tendencies toward routine, legalistic rule application?

Discussion and Debate

For the majority of inquiries in OEP, the basic decision was made by a

---

[6] It is possible, of course, that along with my fellow officials I was so locked in a legalistic mind set that I did not detect most instances of legalistic rule application or detected only the most blatant examples. It is hard to disprove this possibility. Indeed, as some examples in the text demonstrate, I sometimes *was* guilty of legalism, especially of the more subtle kind, which devoted too much attention to conceptual consistency. On the other hand, because of my simultaneous role as researcher (by typing field notes each night, I did a great deal of retrospective analysis of my own decision-making behavior) and because of my frequent contact with the Policy Analysis Office, I feel I was rather sensitive to the policy issues involved in inquiries and tried especially hard to keep my own tendencies toward legalism within bounds.

single bureaucrat sitting at his own desk, without discussion of the case with colleagues, or with the inquirer, or with other economic actors who would be affected by the decision. The official simply selected the applicable rule and applied it. He then sent his draft answer through one or two reviews by superiors, and they too checked and approved most answers without discussion. That routine processing did not, of course, necessarily mean that the rules were applied legalistically, but the odds of avoiding legalistic treatment and of ensuring result-oriented rule interpretation in OEP were greatly increased by active discussion of a case among inquiry-response officials.

When different officials simultaneously addressed an inquiry, it seemed, different perceptions of the inquirer's situation were more likely to emerge. Ambiguities in the ostensibly applicable rule were more likely to be noticed. As a result of the attention focused on a case by discussion, an official was more likely to draw on his own experience and empathize with the inquirer's social world, to make that leap of the imagination that made a case "real" and the consequences of decision salient. As we saw in the Pruitt–Igoe Case in Chapter 7, policy considerations tended to be raised explicitly as the debaters sought support for the interpretation they favored. By becoming involved in discussion, an official—such as Wade in Pruitt–Igoe or Brock in the Vacation Pay Case—was more likely to develop a personal stake in its outcome and persist in getting the policy issue resolved. Finally, if discussion went on without producing consensus, it disrupted the pace of inquiry response and interfered with "production"; that made it more likely that someone would say, "Well, let's send it up to GC (or Policy or CLC) and let them worry about it."

When was a case likely to generate discussion and the more intensive consideration that ensued? The obvious answer, one might think, is when it was intrinsically hard or novel or important. Something about it created doubt in an official's mind and led him to ask a colleague's opinion or challenge a draft answer. There was, however, no guarantee that intellectual difficulty, as a property of a case, would be recognized, produce discussion, or result in referral to a higher office. The phenomena of legalistic and retreatist decision making indicate that decision makers sometimes fail to deal with the intrinsically hard aspects of a case. Moreover, it might be argued that virtually any case could be made to *seem* hard, at least initially, if only the inquirer made a good enough argument—by analogizing his situation to others in which an accommodative ruling had been made, or pointing out the adverse economic effects that would stem from applying a stringent rule. In *many* cases, the application of a stringent rule impinged upon values encompassed by the perfect competition theory or redistributive notions of social justice, and thus produced an arguably unfair result. The issue,then, is what made it more likely that a case would be *perceived* as hard or important and more likely to trigger discussion. A variety of case characteristics seem to have been significant in this regard.

In-Person Presentation

Whenever an inquirer arranged to present his case in person, he almost automatically broke through any propensity toward blatantly legalistic or retreatist case processing. The agency official who met the inquirer face-to-face almost unavoidably became cognizant of the inquirer's problems and was forced to attend to the fairness and economic impact of decision. Even when the decision maker tried to force the in-person presentation into rule-based categories, as I did in the New York State Teachers Association Case, he could not wholly screen "impact information" out of his consciousness; indeed, the emphasis on rules in such interactions was in part a defense against being unduly manipulated. In the Teachers Association Case, as in the Girl Scouts Case, I ended up—despite my initial impassive legalism—looking actively for loopholes in the rules that would provide financial relief to the inquirer.[7]

A survey of the OEP national office files confirms these observations. Table 3 deals with only those cases in which the inquirer was seeking (as opposed to resisting) an accommodative result—a wage, price, or rent *increase.* Based on a sample of OEP National inquiry-responses, the table displays the estimated numbers of cases in which the inquirer managed to present his case in person, as opposed to those presented in writing only, and the substantive outcome for each mode of presentation. While two-thirds of the relatively few cases (10 percent) presented in person received accommodative answers, only one-third of the many inquiries presented in writing had their prayers answered. Nor are these differences explained by other likely factors. It is not attributable to the office in which the answer was prepared: in both the General Counsel's Office and the Correspondence Section, cases presented in person received a much higher proportion of accommodative answers. Small inquirers as well as giant corporations and unions received more accommodative answers if they pre-

---

[7] See Peter Berger and Thomas Luckmann, *The Social Construction of Reality* (New York: Doubleday–Anchor Books, 1966), pp. 28–31: ". . . [I]t is comparatively difficult to impose rigid patterns on face-to-face interaction. . . . [T]he pattern cannot sustain the massive evidence of the other's subjectivity that is available to one in the face-to-face situation. By contrast, it is much easier for me to ignore such evidence as long as I do not encounter the other face-to-face." For further empirical confirmation of the significance of in-person as opposed to documentary decision making in the administrative legal process, see Robert G. Dixon, Jr., "The Welfare State and Mass Justice: A Warning from the Social Security Disability Program," 1972 *Duke Law Journal* 681. The Supreme Court's insistence that in some contexts "due process of law" requires oral as opposed to merely written presentation of evidence and argument, *Goldberg* v. *Kelly,* 397 U.S. 254 (1970), thus seems well-rooted in behavioral reality.

Table 3. In-Person Inquiry Presentation and Substantive Result

	Total Cases[a]		Presented In-Person			Percent Stringent Answer[b]	
	(In Sample)	Estimated Total	(In Sample)	Estimated Total	Percent[b]	In-Person Presentation	Written Presentation
All Cases	(359)	2896	(40)	293	10.1	33.9	65.5
Cases Decided By:							
Correspondence Section	(180)	1279	(10)	59	4.6	51.7	71.2
GC and Policy Analysis	(179)	1617	(30)	234	14.5	28.3	60.3
Cases from:							
Very large organizations[c]	(63)	549	(13)	98	17.8	8.7	66.9
Medium-sized organizations	(207)	1604	(24)	166	10.4	47.6	65.0
Small organizations and individuals	(89)	743	(3)	29	3.4	23.3	65.6
Cases Presented via:							
Lawyer or lobbyist	(130)	1011	(24)	181	17.9	39.6	63.9
No professional advocate	(228)	1865	(16)	112	6.0	26.0	64.8

[a] Cases in which inquirer was *resisting* or seeking to block wage, price, or rent increase omitted.

[b] Percentages computed on basis of estimated total cases to correct for weighting of sample, as described in the Appendix.

[c] "Very large organizations" were defined as business corporations listed on the New York Stock Exchange; international or national labor unions (as opposed to locals); state governments; governments of cities with over 500,000 population. Small organizations were defined as sole proprietorships and individual tradesmen or professionals. Medium-sized organizations was a residual category between small and very large.

sented their case in person. An inquirer whose lawyer or trade association representative presented his case in person to an OEP official was more likely to receive an accommodative ruling than an inquirer represented by a professional advocate whose case was presented in writing only.

It is possible, of course, that cases presented in person were more "deserving" of accommodative answers on the merits. Perhaps inquirers were more likely to take the trouble to go to Washington and seek an audience with freeze officials when they had especially strong arguments for accommodation or at least stronger on the average than those who only wrote to Washington. This is hard to prove one way or the other. To obtain an in-person conference, it took a great deal of persistence. Some kind of political connection was helpful—the assistance of a congressman, for example, or a lawyer with a friend high in the freeze agencies or in a cooperating federal department.[8] On a proportional basis, as Table 3 indicates, in-person conferences were also more often obtained by corporations or organizations with obvious economic importance—a major automobile manufacturer, the City of New York, or the Communications Workers of America. Inquirers in those categories, conceivably, husband their political resources and seek the aid of Washington connections only when they are pretty sure they have a legally justifiable claim; if that is so, one would expect a high percentage of the cases they presented in-person to "deserve" accommodative answers. But it is by no means clear that the politically well-connected and the economically powerful are more objective about their own deserts than the timid and obscure. Cases presented in-person, therefore, may not have been especially meritorious. And I *am* sure, from personal experience and observation, that given cases of equal merit, the one presented in person was less likely to be lost in the shuffle. Table 3 indicates that such cases were more likely to be considered by higher-level agency personnel—such as GC lawyers or Policy Analysis officials—closer to the policy-making process, with broader experience and a more sophisticated sense of their role as rule appliers than Correspondence Section officials. Inquirers who could arrange such a meeting thus had a better *chance* of having their arguments for accommodation carefully considered.

Other Special Contact or Advocacy

An interesting contrast is provided by analyzing cases that involved other forms of special contact with the agencies, such as inquiries presented by

---

[8] Almost one-quarter (24.4 percent) of inquirers represented by a Washington, D.C., law firm or a large, Wall Street-type firm (i.e., having a staff of at least twenty lawyers) obtained an in-person conference with an agency official. Only 9.4 percent of all inquiries and 26.8 percent of all inquiries presented by lawyers were from Washington or Wall Street-type firms. See Table 4, p. 156.

special advocates, but which did not involve in-person contact. These kinds of cases were more likely than routinely presented cases to be handled by higher-level inquiry-response offices, such as GC or Policy Analysis. To some extent, that alone increased the likelihood that they would be discussed or considered carefully. But unlike in-person presentation, special contact or advocacy was not strongly related to accommodative outcomes.

Some inquiries, for example, were not addressed to OEP but were sent to the White House or other high federal department officials or to congressmen. Those officials usually referred the inquiries to OEP's Correspondence Section. There they were tagged with a "VIP" label and were separately recorded and handled. VIP handling meant accelerated disposition, but there is no evidence that it resulted in substantively different treatment or even a greater likelihood of referral to higher levels in OEP.[9] Sometimes, however, such referrals were accompanied by a special personal request by the referring congressman that the matter be decided quickly or sent by the referring official directly to OEP's director or general counsel. Rarely was there any strong substantive recommendation, one way or the other, from the referring official, but his advocacy of prompt action often produced more careful, high-level consideration within the OEP inquiry-response system. A special routing slip or attached note designated the inquiry as non-routine. Similarly, Washington law firms and lobbyists often tried to avoid routine case-handling by addressing their clients' inquiries not to OEP as an entity but to specific, high-level CLC or OEP officials whom they knew or had somehow identified as strategically placed in the new operation. And regardless of whether special contact was made, presentation of a case by a professional advocate increased the likelihood that an inquiry would be referred to a higher office, as shown in Table 4.

Nevertheless, as Table 4 also reveals, the use of professional advocates did not result in more accommodative decisions. This pattern suggests that less "deserving" cases were identified as problematic and referred to higher levels simply because they were presented by high-powered advocates. Actually the reason goes a bit deeper. The significant factor in the identification of a case as hard was not so much *who* presented it, but *how* it was presented.

Complexity of Presentation

Just as in-person presentation tended to break through tendencies toward insensitive and retreatist decision, a breakthrough could also be achieved by certain kinds of written presentation. If the inquirer managed to pose his problem in a particularly vivid or articulate fashion, it became more real or at

---

[9] Of the VIP inquiries (which accounted for about 25 percent of the OEP national office case load) seeking accommodative answers, 38.2 percent in fact received accommodative answers, compared with 37.9 percent for non-VIP cases.

Table 4. Nature of Advocacy and Inquiry Disposition[a]

	Cases (In Sample)	Estimated Total	Percent[b]	Percent Addressed to Specific Official	Percent In-Person Presentation	Percent Complex Presentation[d]	Decided by GC or Policy Analysis	Percent Stringent Response	Percent Stringent Response Excluding In-Person Cases
Cases Presented via:									
Washington, Wall Street, other large law firms[c]	(28)	271	9.4	51.7	24.4	76.8	80.1	69.1	71.4
Other lawyer[c]	(66)	535	18.6	24.3	19.2	50.7	72.3	54.1	60.4
Trade association	(36)	205	7.2	29.3	5.9	24.9	66.3	60.8	62.9
No professional advocate	(228)	1865	64.8	10.7	6.0	15.0	46.2	62.8	65.7
	(358)	2876	100.0	18.1	10.1	27.8	56.3	61.6	65.5

[a] Excluding cases in which the inquirer was resisting or seeking to block a wage, price, or rent increase.

[b] Percentage computed on basis of estimated total cases to correct for weighting of sample.

[c] "Wall Street and other large law firms" includes any firm whose letterhead indicated twenty or more lawyers (partners and associates) in firm. "Other lawyers" includes house counsel and government attorneys, as well as smaller firms and solo practitioners.

[d] For definition of complex presentation see footnote 1 and pp. 00–00.

least non-routine to agency officials. Similarly, a case was more likely to be perceived as "different," harder to fit into existing rule categories, if it was presented in an especially complex way—if it included, for example, a great deal of factual detail about the inquirer's situation, or lengthy and multi-pronged arguments, or complicated legal references, or financial documentation. Table 5 illustrates this phenomenon. A sample of all inquiries answered by OEP's national office was rated on a complexity scale. The individual items coded were amount of factual detail, length of argument, number of separate arguments, and extent of legal or financial documentation.[10] The table shows that almost 90 percent of inquiries that scored high on this scale were extracted from routine handling, labeled a matter of interpretation, and referred to a higher-level inquiry-response office—the General Counsel's Office or Policy Analysis. Again, this is true for all kinds of inquiries. An individual or a large corporation or a law firm whose inquiry had the de-scribed indicia of complexity was much more likely to have it referred to a higher office than a similar inquirer who wrote a shorter, simpler inquiry.

Complex presentation, however, was no guarantee of a favorable substan-tive outcome. As Table 5 indicates, high complexity inquiries, surprisingly, were rebuffed more often than simpler ones, despite the fact that they were more often referred to GC and Policy Analysis and despite the fact that GC and Policy Analysis, in the aggregate, issued a higher percentage of accom-modative answers (44 percent) than the Correspondence Section (30 percent). This suggests that the operative factor in breaking these cases out of routine treatment and their designation as problematic was simply their presenta-tional complexity per se rather than "true difficulty" or "intrinsic merit." Complexity seems to have produced only an initial impression of difficulty, resulting in more careful and often higher-level consideration, but once that complexity was sorted out and analyzed, it did not necessarily reveal a meritorious claim.

Characteristics of the Inquirer

Despite OEP officials' avowed and sincere concern for strict equality of treatment for all inquirers, the characteristics of parties affected the likeli-hood with which their case would be seen as difficult, engender discussion, and penetrate to higher organizational levels. This was due partly to the predilection of some kinds of inquirers to employ special methods of case presentation and partly because the cases of some inquirers were thought to be more important. Confronted with pressures for "production" and some-times reluctant to refer cases to higher levels, most inquiry-response offices developed informal priority rules governing which cases were sufficiently

---

[10] See footnote 1, p. 146.

Table 5. Complexity of Presentation and Inquiry Disposition[a]

Nature of Presentation	Cases (In Sample)	Estimated Total	Percent[b]	Percent Decided by GC or Policy Analysis	Percent Stringent Decision in GC or Policy Analysis	Percent Stringent Decision, All Offices
All Cases						
High complexity	(86)	801	27.8	88.8	60.8	61.2
Low complexity	(269)	2077	72.2	43.8	50.5	61.8
	(355)	2878	100.0	56.3	55.4	61.6
Cases from:						
Very large organizations						
High complexity	(28)	309	56.3	91.9	66.9	63.0
Low complexity	(35)	240	43.7	69.2	20.3	51.0
	(63)	549	100.0	82.0	52.5	58.3
Medium-sized organizations						
High complexity	(54)	441	27.7	89.7	58.4	59.6
Low complexity	(150)	1149	72.3	52.7	58.2	62.9
	(204)	1590	100.0	63.0	58.3	62.1
Small organizations and individuals						
High complexity	(4)	51	6.9	64.1	37.5	60.8
Low complexity	(84)	688	93.1	19.8	46.1	63.8
	(88)	739	100.0	22.9	43.5	63.4
Cases Presented via:						
Lawyer or lobbyist						
High complexity	(56)	520	52.6	89.4	68.4	66.8
Low complexity	(70)	469	47.4	57.8	44.5	49.2
	(126)	989	100.0	73.2	59.4	58.7
No professional advocate						
High complexity	(30)	280	15.0	88.2	47.2	50.9
Low complexity	(198)	1589	85.0	38.9	51.4	64.9
	(228)	1869	100.0	46.2	50.0	62.6

[a] Excluding cases in which the inquirer was resisting or seeking to block a wage, price, or rent increase.

[b] Percentage computed on basis of estimated total cases to correct for weighting of sample.

important to be handled first and to warrant referral to higher levels.

One indicator of importance was the visibility of the inquirer and other affected parties. Once inquiries in any particular area, such as teachers' salaries, became the subject of controversy in the press, in Congress, or in other public arenas, an "incorrect" answer was sensed to be more dangerous, and hence inquiries in that field were more worthy of detailed discussion and referral to superiors. The same was true of inquiries from those whose prominence automatically made their price or wage behavior visible to the public, such as a giant, well-known company or union.

Another indicator of importance was the perceived economic significance of the inquirer and his request. One GC lawyer, discussing the handling of hard cases, told me, "You don't send it up as a policy question unless it's important. If it's just the problem of one company and it doesn't affect a lot of others, you tend to answer it." Unless, of course, the company was very large: an inquiry from IBM or A&P would be more likely to "affect a lot of others" than a conceptually similar one from the Royal Slide Fastener Company. As Table 6 shows, four out of five inquiries from very large corporations, unions, and government bodies were referred to higher levels of the inquiry-response system in OEP, while only one out of five inquiries from individuals and very small companies escaped routine handling in the Correspondence Section.

The higher rate at which inquiries from large organizations were referred to higher levels was not only due to their "importance" per se, but also because those inquiries disproportionately had other characteristics that led to the designation of cases as difficult, that is, they often were presented by professional advocates or contained a great deal of complex legal and financial detail. Over one-half (61 percent) of the inquiries seeking wage or price increases from very large corporations, unions, and government bodies were presented by lawyers or lobbyists, compared to 39 percent from medium-sized organizations and only 7 percent for small firms, such as proprietors and landlords, and individuals. Forty-five percent of the inquiries of very large organizations were addressed to specific higher-level officials, as opposed to OEP or CLC as an abstract entity; only 21 percent of inquiries from medium-sized organizations were, and 6 percent of inquiries from small firms and individuals. More than half (56.3 percent) of the very large organization inquiries rated high in complexity of presentation and argument, while only 27.7 percent of those from medium-sized organizations and 6.9 percent of those from small organizations and individuals were lengthy and detailed. Nevertheless, Table 6 shows that even when we control for complexity and the use of professional advocates, large organization inquiries—with or without these advantages—were still somewhat more likely than similar ones from smaller inquirers to break out of routine processing; this

Table 6. Size of Inquirer, Presentational
Advantage, and Inquiry Disposition[a]

Cases from:	Cases (In Sample)	Estimated Total	Percent[b]	Percent Decided by GC or Policy Analysis	Percent Stringent Decision in GC or Policy Analysis	Percent Stringent Decision, All Offices
Very large organizations						
Complex presentation and/or legal representation	(42)	404	73.5	87.6	58.2	58.7
Not complex/no legal representation	(21)	145	26.5	65.8	23.8	57.4
	(63)	549	100.0	82.0	52.5	58.4
Medium-sized organizations						
Complex presentation and/or legal representation	(110)	807	50.7	72.7	57.6	57.6
Not complex/no legal representation	(97)	783	49.3	50.9	56.7	66.4
	(207)	1590	100.0	62.0	57.3	62.1
Small organizations and individuals						
Complex presentation and/or legal representation	(8)	80	10.8	56.8	28.3	53.6
Not complex/no legal representation	(80)	659	89.2	18.7	54.0	64.7
	(88)	739	100.0	22.9	43.1	63.2

[a] Excluding cases in which the inquirer was resisting or seeking to block a wage, price, or rent increase.

[b] Percentage computed on basis of estimated total cases to correct for weighting of sample.

seems to confirm the importance of economic significance or visibility alone in the designation of hard or important cases.

However, Table 6 also shows that large organization inquiries were not treated significantly more leniently, in the aggregate, than inquiries from smaller organizations and individuals. Once they penetrated to higher levels, perhaps, inquiries from larger organizations were exposed to a stronger presumption in favor of stringency, simply because an accommodative ruling for them was both more visible and had a broader inflationary potential. In sum, the major advantages attained by the size and wealth of an inquirer were in achieving an initial breakthrough or escape from routine handling and more careful higher-level consideration. Only to the extent that such consideration increased the *chances* for accommodative treatment did the nature and manner of the inquirer affect the substantive outcome. Officials tended to discount or correct for the presentational advantages larger entities enjoyed. Whether this would be the case in other agencies, where officials were less committed to the success of the enterprise, is another question.

CONCLUSION

Where an agency is committed to equal treatment and a judicial mode of decision, but is compelled to decide most cases rapidly and routinely as well, there is a likelihood of differential handling of cases: some cases break through the barrier of routine treatment, with its risks of legalistic rule application; they evoke discussion, focusing official attention on the consequences of decision or inducing them to refer the case to higher levels of the organizational hierarchy. The likelihood of that breakthrough is enhanced, we have seen, by methods of case presentation that engage the rule applier's attention fully and impress upon him the uniqueness of the situation involved in the case. In the freeze agencies, that effect was achieved primarily by in-person as opposed to written case presentation or by written presentations that were especially rich in factual detail, diversity and amount of legal argumentation, or financial complexity. Those effects, moreover, were produced disproportionately by larger organizations, which were more likely to employ sophisticated legal counsel. Large organizations thus were more capable of inducing the official to perceive their case as hard, or as important because of the number of people affected.

The detailed discussion of a case, or its penetration to higher levels of the bureaucracy, was not a guarantee of a more favorable substantive decision. The lawyers in OEP's General Counsel's Office, for example, tended to counteract or discount the advantages of size and presentational complexity; they tried to protect themselves against being manipulated during in-person presentations by invoking the terms and categories of the rules. Nor did the retention and disposition of a case at a lower level mean that it would be decided legalistically and stringently; several indicators suggested that arguments for accommodation were regularly recognized in OEP's Correspondence Section.

But more generally, it would seem that penetration to a higher organizational level increases a party's *chances* for more favorable results. Lower levels of an organization are likely to be conservative in guarding against "mistakes" which jeopardize the organization's primary values and interests. At higher levels, more careful consideration of arguments is more likely. Higher-level officials are likely to have a more rounded sense of the agency's purposes in relationship to other governmental programs and values. They are also likely to have more authority to make exceptions or rule reformulations. Finally, higher levels of the hierarchy are more likely to be in the *habit* of making exceptions or innovations simply because mechanisms of upward referral of cases tend to send up those cases with the strongest arguments for changes or riskier interpretations of existing rules.[11]

Viewing legal organizations from the outside, such hierarchical effects may produce somewhat of an illusion of leniency, accommodation, or change. The conservatism of lower officials means that higher-level decision makers receive case loads disproportionately weighted with cases that include strong arguments for change. Even if they deal with that case load relatively conservatively, the top-level decisions, which are generally the only ones reported and visible to those outside the agency, will often appear to reflect a continuing tendency toward accommodation or change. This may not be true, however, for the decisions of the agency as a whole, taking into account the decisions of the part of the bureaucratic iceberg that operates beneath the surface of public visibility. In the freeze agencies, for example, while 50 percent of CLC decisions were accommodative, creating an appearance of a continuing drift toward leniency in freeze policy, the mass of inquiry-responses, such as those handled by the Correspondence Section and lower levels, were stringent in over two-thirds of the cases and showed no sign of becoming more accommodative in percentage terms as the freeze went on.

---

[11] Lower-level officials in the Internal Revenue Service audit system, for example, are less likely to "give in" to the taxpayers in disputed matters than their superiors. That is, in cases which are referred to higher levels of the IRS hierarchy, the agency settles for a smaller percentage of the claimed tax obligation than in cases settled at a lower level. Moreover, larger cases are more likely to go to the higher levels. See *Wall Street Journal*, February 5, 1973, page 1. The IRS official figures support the author's assertion that "despite the agency's claim that its staff administers the tax laws uniformly, the higher you go in the hierarchy the more generous settlement you're likely to get."

Similar effects have been described in the Social Security Administration and in private bureaucracies. See Dixon, "The Welfare State and Mass Justice"; H. Laurence Ross, "Insurance Claims Complaints: A Private Appeals Procedure," 9 *Law and Society Review* 275 (1975).

It is well recognized, of course, that higher levels of judicial hierarchies are more likely to innovate, to change or carve out new exceptions to rules, than lower ones. For some quantitative confirmation, see J. W. Howard, "Litigation Flow in Three United States Courts of Appeals," 8 *Law and Society Review* 33 (1973); Ronald Labbe, "The Role of State Supreme Courts in the Process of Constitutional Decision Making: A Study in State-Federal Appellate Process" (Ph.D. diss., Tulane University, 1973).

Conclusion

CHAPTER 10

Justifying Stringency

For governmental officials attempting to implement new policies, the law is both a resource and an impediment. When policies are implemented through the forms and procedures of the law, there is an implicit claim that those who disobey act in defiance of the rule of law itself and are legitimately subject to punishment. However, when they invoke the support of the law, governmental officials are also subject to the constraints of the legal tradition within which they operate—the obligations which that tradition imposes on official action, its standards of legal validity and fairness and rationality.

In the United States, standards of legality are complex and demanding. Administrators are expected to adhere faithfully to the positive law enacted by the elected representatives of the people. But there is also a strong tradition of pragmatism and natural law which suggests that there are implicit limits on positive law. Officials are expected to adapt positive law to the requirements of the particular case in light of competing public policies, constitutional principles, and commonly recognized notions of fairness, even if those values are not reflected in the words of an applicable positive law. Officials are expected to attend to the substantive consequences of rule application and to provide rational explanations and justifications for their decisions.

The emphasis on substantive justification of legal decisions exerts a profound influence on the regulatory process. It means that regulatory agencies cannot lightly disregard interests that are harmed by the implementation of their regulatory police mission. Characteristically, therefore, they are engaged in a process of seeking a rational reconciliation of conflicting values—balancing police-mission goals against considerations of economic continuity and fairness, balancing the formal justice of decision in accordance with general rules against attention to the substantive equities of each particular case. Consequently, variations in regulatory policy and legal method are likely to turn not only on organizational self-interest and political pressures, but also on the specific problems of *justification* faced by each agency in its particular legal and economic context.

This concluding chapter recapitulates the teachings of the freeze experience in this regard, noting the role of legal justification, among other variables, in determining the relative stringency of regulatory policy and the style of case-by-case decision.

SOURCES OF REGULATORY STRINGENCY

The members of the Cost of Living Council assigned to implement the wage-price freeze of August 1971 were men of a pragmatic cast of mind. They were Republicans, economically conservative, skeptical about the program they were called upon to administer, concerned about stopping inflation but also about maintaining the integrity of private enterprise and the values associated with a free market. One would expect them to take a broad rather than a legalistic view of the governing process, to adopt a role in which they attempted to do what they saw as right for the economy as a whole, rather than adhere mechanically to the literal terms of the freeze order. This attitude was in fact reflected in some of CLC's accommodative rules. CLC read the order as exempting exports and imports (noting that this construction would serve goals of trade policy). They exempted interest rates. They exempted wage increases under existing apprenticeship plans and under the Davis-Bacon Act (which required payment of prevailing union pay scales on federally supported construction projects). They exempted price increases pursuant to historically established seasonal variations and some contractual price-adjustment formulas. Nevertheless, these were only isolated exceptions from CLC's basic stance. By and large, the freeze was stringently defined and implemented. Businesses were not allowed to increase prices to compensate for unanticipated cost-price squeezes. CLC would not exempt price, wage, or rent increases that were small in amount, of little economic significance, or which had been promised in long-term contracts on which the parties had justifiably relied. CLC made no effort to deal with differences in merit or need which the freeze order ignored or exacerbated. While the freeze order was not implemented in an unthinking legalistic manner, with indifference to its consequences, CLC made little effort to investigate the consequences of its rules fully and carefully. Decisions were made rapidly, in private, with little input from those affected.

In analyzing why CLC leaned so strongly toward a stringently defined freeze, two sets of factors appear both important and of more general applicability. One set of inducements to regulatory stringency stems from the nature of the agency's legal mandate and the "definition of the situation" it suggests to regulatory officials. The second set derives from the power relationships set into motion by the promulgation of the authorizing law.

DEFINING THE SITUATION

When agency officials were asked by inquirers why a seemingly reasonable price or wage or rent increase could not be instituted, the officials would often reply, "That's what a freeze *is!*" A primary source of a stringent regulatory stance thus was a simplified *definition* of the law being implemented—a definition that did not allow for accommodation on the basis of other values. Yet that definition certainly was not dictated by the words of the freeze order itself, for CLC itself found sources of ambiguity and flexibility in that order. The sources of such a simple and stringent definition of the situation and indeed of the tendency to justify a legal ruling by reference to a definition, rather than a *reason,* are a bit more complex.

The Power of Metaphor

Laws usually make dull and difficult reading. They are encumbered with qualifications and ambiguities and complex terms. The president's executive order of August 15, 1971, for example, contained two densely printed pages of legal language. Its most important operative provision stated that prices and wages "shall be stabilized . . . at levels not greater than those pertaining to a substantial volume of actual transactions . . . during the thirty-day period ending August 14, 1971, for like or similar commodities or services." The president, announcing that order on nationwide television, however, used no such language. He simply said, "I am today ordering a freeze on all prices and wages throughout the United States."

One word—*freeze*—conveyed a simple but vivid definition of a complex program. Such simple metaphors can have a powerful effect on peoples' expectations. Proponents of regulatory programs often use them to develop popular support; the mass media use them to describe complex governmental actions. Indeed, it often seems that the more controversial or novel the subject, the more likely the law will be described in terms of a simple, unidimensional slogan or metaphor. The interesting result, the freeze experience suggests, is that such definitions affect not only the public but the administrators themselves. The image of a freeze—an absolute halt in all price or wage increases—dominated agency officials' own conception of what their mission was. They were reluctant to take steps that would disappoint the widespread expectations of an absolute freeze generated by the initial use of that term to publicize the program. Disappointing those expectations, they feared, would erode support. They, in a sense, were frozen too.

Simple metaphors often contain no clear policy implications and have no predictable influence on policy. Others imply compromise and accommodation. The metaphor of the "freeze," however, suggested a specific rule, an *objective numerical standard—zero* increases in prices and wages. As in the case of a red light, violations of such an objective standard would be evident to any observer. And because there were externally prepared unambiguous measures of the problem to be regulated—the monthly Consumer Price Index and the Wholesale Price Index—the extent to which the agencies made accommodative exceptions to the objective, stringent standard would be readily visible.

If the power of metaphor to define the agency's policy is linked to the expectations it engenders, that effect is intensified by the extent of the publicity it receives. In the case of the freeze, where the regulatory program was announced by the president himself, the idea of a "freeze" was transmitted to an enormous prime time television audience; it was printed in newspaper headlines across the country and on the covers of national news magazines. The audience of regulated entities was especially large and attentive. To agency officials, highly accommodative rulings would have seemed like a betrayal of a commitment their chief had made to the whole nation.

Limited Responsibility

The second critical component of agency officials' definition of their situation was that the program was of limited duration. That, too, was emphasized by the way it was announced to the public, as well as by the specific terms of the executive order. Any perception of hardship could be dealt with by saying, "Well, they'll only have to live with it for three months." The more generalized aspect of the short duration, however, was that the *responsibility* of the agency was explicitly defined, from the outset, as a limited one. To agency officials, the temporal limit on their jurisdiction meant that they were absolved of responsibility for unanticipated consequences, for adverse economic effects, and even for specific injustices. "The freeze necessarily entails some injustice," they said. Dealing with adverse economic effects was the responsibility of their successor agencies. Similarly, one would expect an agency whose sole responsibility, as stated in its authorizing legislation, is "environmental protection" to regulate pollution by electric power plants more stringently than a public utility commission assigned to limit pollution *and* assure adequate supplies of electricity *and* hold down electricity rates. Proponents of stringent regulation, therefore, might prefer narrow statutory statements of mission containing simple, objective rules; those concerned with values of economic continuity, long-range responsibility, and fairness may have cause to differ.

REGULATORY POWER

Regardless of how stringently an agency defines its police mission, it will have difficulty turning back the inevitable demands for accommodation if it lacks the objective power to resist them. One source of such power, of course, is coercion: a well-funded agency, with adequate resources for inspection and enforcement and effective sanctions at its disposal, may be able to deny even the most reasonable claims for accommodation. Regulatory agencies, however, are rarely well-endowed in terms of funding or coercive power. Regulated firms often have the capacity to complain effectively to courts or legislatures about "unreasonably" stringent policies which impair profitability and curtail employment and tax revenues. The power to impose stringent regulation, consequently, is largely *normative* power, the capacity to persuade regulated firms, the courts, the legislature, and the press that stringent regulation is *justified*. The freeze experience suggests several sources of that power.

Economic Slack

One important support for stringent regulation is the economic capacity of regulated firms to absorb the costs of stringent regulation, or pass them on in higher prices, without severe disruption of their basic economic function. The lesson of the second, sixty-day freeze imposed in June 1973 was that even strongly supported stringent regulations that drive important products or services out of the market or cause substantial loss of jobs are likely to be modified.[1] Pressures for the agency to "be reasonable" become overwhelming. The degree of stringency that is tolerable, therefore, varies with changing economic conditions, with the costliness and technological complexity of complying with specific regulations, and with the availability of products or services that can be substituted for those that are stringently regulated. Paradoxically, then, the greater the economic strength and adaptability of

---

[1] The situation may be somewhat different in such societies as Argentina where the dominant Peronist ideology holds that "an increase in popular well-being is incompatible with an increase of advantages for capital." But even there, unless the state has overwhelming coercive power, absolute and inflexible regulations which severely impair profitability must in time be relaxed. See Robert L. Ayres, "The Social Pact as Anti-Inflationary Policy: The Argentine Experience Since 1973," 28 *World Politics* 473 (1976).

the regulated businesses, the greater the regulatory agency's power to impose stringent regulations.

Jurisdiction Over Cost Factors

Comparison of the freeze agencies with the Price Commission during Phase II of the Economic Stabilization Program suggested an additional support for regulatory stringency. Compared to the Price Commission, and certainly compared to most regulatory agencies, the agencies had the legal power to control a broad range of potential cost increases for the firms they regulated. They could control their labor costs, their rents, and, except for imported commodities and raw agricultural products, the cost of all their material supplies. They could therefore control their prices more stringently. CLC, in fact, made its most accommodative rules (and had the most difficulty in adhering to stringent ones) with respect to cost-price squeezes stemming from transactions that were exempt from the freeze. For example, imported commodities and raw agricultural products were exempt; CLC ruled that firms that sustained price increases from those sources could increase their prices correspondingly, at least up to the point in the distribution chain where imported commodities were incorporated into other products or agricultural products were processed.[2] Hence the more complete the agency's control of the regulated firm's market environment, that is, the more it can protect that firm from cost increases or insure that it receives compensation for cost increases (whether by legally mandated price increases or by government subsidy), the greater its capacity to impose stringent regulations.

Political Support

In their pursuit of stringency, the agencies benefitted from the widespread popular approval of their program. Inflation has few overt supporters. The supporters of stringency, however, are often those least capable of exerting continuous pressure on an agency or supplying it with needed technical information. The rise of organized consumer and environmental groups and of public interest law firms, and the expansion of their rights of participation in the regulatory process, all reflect recognition of this problem and an attempt to remedy it. In the case of the freeze, however, the most powerful pressures for stringency did not come from the public at large or their self-appointed special advocates. The crucial sources of support for stringent regulation were the primary *regulated* groups themselves, business and labor.

---

[2] Similarly, taxes were exempt; CLC eventually ruled that property tax increases under net leases could be passed along in higher rents. A great deal of trouble was caused by CLC's attempt to prevent firms from passing along cost increases stemming from transactions beyond CLC's temporal jurisdiction—increases instituted before the effective date of the freeze.

There is a difference between the interests of business or labor as a class and that of individual firms or unions; any single firm or union may chafe under stringent controls, even if their class benefits from the regulatory regime as a whole. The individual firm or union's perspective is often predominant in regulatory politics. The agency is subject to pressures for accommodation from particular firms or unions, each seeking advantages over its competitors. A law such as the freeze, however, by virtue of its very breadth of coverage, emphasized the interdependence and common interests of all businesses. A concession allowing one business firm to increase prices would often harm another firm and induce pressures for wage increases as well. Thus, the freeze engendered strong and vocal support for equal treatment and mutual restraint. The willingness of organized labor to comply with the freeze (rather than striking to demand fulfillment of contracts) was publicly linked by labor leaders to stringency in price control. The willingness of business to comply was linked to stringent treatment of their competitors and workers and suppliers.

This support for stringency on the part of important regulated actors themselves is by no means unprecedented. There are many public programs, which, if successful, are likely to benefit business and labor in the aggregate by imposing restrictions or costs on both. The elite members of a profession or industry often support stringent regulation designed to prevent fraud or poor quality services on the ground that it will increase public confidence in *their* services. Regulation can remove the competitive disadvantage suffered by firms that invest in costly safety and environmental measures by forcing their reluctant competitors to undertake these investments as well. Here, then, is another apparent paradox: when individual regulated entities react to a regulatory law in terms of their *common* interests (and that is most likely to occur when the regulated industry is highly organized through trade associations or centralized unions or domination by large firms), the agency's prospects for stringent regulation improves, at least with respect to a considerable range of issues.

THE PROBLEM OF JUSTIFICATION

The inducements to regulatory stringency discussed above speak in terms of probabilities and the overall thrust of agency policy—the conditions under which it is more likely that the scores of policy decisions made by an agency, taken as a whole and weighted by importance, will hew closely to the stringent line. Regulatory agencies, however, generally must provide substantive justification for governmental impositions on *individual* citizens or business firms. Slack in the economy as a whole and the breadth of coverage may have *facilitated* a stringent posture during the freeze; but reference to those factors provided no reason for denying an exception in any one of the thousands of applications for relief from freeze-induced hardship. These were cases in which there *was* no slack, in which the breadth of regulatory control had proved inadequate to protect the regulated firm from a cost-price squeeze.

To prevent an originally stringent general policy from being eroded by case-by-case accommodative decisions, an agency must either ignore individual justice-claims by means of legalistic rule application or construct plausible justifications for imposing hardships on some in the name of benefitting many. The freeze experience suggests the conditions under which the concern for substantive justification is likely to be salient, even in a bureaucracy, and under which stringent policies can most easily be justified.

The Regime of Rules

The predominant activity of the agencies was responding to inquiries from the public concerning the requirements of the regulatory order. Businesses, unions, schools, and landlords requested official statements that a specific wage or price increase was legally permissible; they argued that exceptions should be made or rules changed to permit such increases. Responding to these requests transformed the agencies into a large, hierarchically organized bureaucracy, in which even the procedurally informal inquiry-response system emphasized decision in accordance with detailed written rules promulgated by the Cost of Living Council.

The emphasis on centrally promulgated rules, it should be noted, fulfilled important normative expectations. Citizens and businesses did not want informal advice from the agencies. They wanted authoritative and binding statements of freeze law that they could count on in planning their affairs and resolving disputes. They expected also that each inquirer would be treated consistently with similarly situated fellow citizens or firms. And finally, they wanted rulings that were prompt. In such programs as the freeze—broad in application, significant in financial impact, generative of a large volume of specific problems—prompt decisions can be assured only by delegating decision-making responsibility to a large number of officials and reducing most decisions to routine. Authoritative and consistent decisions can be assured only by instilling in those dispersed decision makers a common vision of organizational policy; such a vision can be communicated most clearly and rapidly by centrally promulgated rules.

The Problem of Legalism

An emphasis on prompt and consistent decision making, guided by rules, however, can easily deteriorate into legalistic modes of decision. One cause of legalistic rule application, suggested by the freeze experience, is rooted in the impulse to be responsive. To better allocate manpower to points of higher demand for legal decisions, bureaucracies establish quantitative bookkeeping systems, methods of measuring case loads and backlogs and turnaround time for each office. A stated backlog becomes a visible symbol of justice being delayed; it induces officials who are truly concerned with the quality of their decisions to decide as rapidly as possible. The attempt to decide quickly, however, jeopardizes quality. It deters officials from taking time to conduct investigations or hearings designed to gather complete and reliable information about the facts of each matter or the potential consequences of each decision. The attempt to decide quickly, we have seen, impels the decision maker to reduce cases to a limited number of routine categories; it thus increases the risk that he will neglect unique characteristics of the case at hand or apply the more general and frequently used rule rather than the rarely used exception. Pressure to decide rapidly induces officials not to bother to consult colleagues or superiors, not to refer a case to a higher office when there is an argument for the reformulation of the ostensibly applicable rule; one result is more discretion at lower levels of the hierarchy, where there is often less inclination or authority to adapt existing policy in an innovative way to competing values or new situations.

Tendencies toward legalism are also generated by the very bureaucratic forms designed to produce better legal decision making. When bureaucracies, in pursuit of efficiency and consistency of treatment, insulate decision makers from direct contact with those whose lives they affect, then citizens who are less adept at expressing their predicament vividly or understandably in writing are at a disadvantage. Their case is more likely to be shunted into a routine rule category without exciting the official's empathy or concern for the consequences of decision. The hierarchical division of labor characteristic of bureaucracy, where high-level specialists in policy formulation are separated from lower-level specialists in rule application, tends to curtail communication between levels; differences in social status and the lower office's interest in maintaining autonomy deter lower-level officials from consulting their superiors. Lower offices, accordingly, become less aware of the policy concerns of the higher levels, unconcerned about the threat of review, unwilling to question superiors about the possibility of changing existing rules, and out-of-touch with the thinking behind the policy makers' attempts to express themselves in the limited language of rules.

Counteracting Legalism

While these inducements to legalism were apparent in the freeze agencies, it also appears that they can be counteracted. A more flexible, judicial mode of rule application, concerned with the purposes behind rules and the substantive justification of the outcomes they produce, can be kept alive even in a bureaucratic setting. In the national office of OEP, for example, tendencies toward legalistic, routinized rule application were offset by in-person and informal case presentations, in which the official was inescapably confronted with information about the human and financial impact of his decision, and demands that he give understandable reasons for the agency's decision. Tendencies toward legalism were discouraged also by collegial discussion and debate among officials in the process of deciding cases. Multiple review systems and the grouping of officials in the same room invited debate and consultation; consultation, in turn, tended to focus attention on the purposes or policies implicit in CLC rules, and to generate arguments among officials concerning policy implications of alternative decisions. Interoffice barriers to communication were broken down by an informal system in which any official in office B, regardless of rank, could take a problematic case to higher office A and in which some officials became specialists in communicating between the offices. Responsiveness of the rule makers to requests for new rules or revisions of old ones emphasized the notion that existing rules were fallible and changeable instruments rather than immutable instructions. A high rate of upward referral or appeal in itself was a valuable aid to responsible rule application.

The most important support for the judicial mode of rule application and for its correlate—an adaptive, changing system of rules—was the high level of motivation that prevailed throughout the freeze bureaucracy, motivation to make decisions fair as well as legally correct. One source of this kind of motivation was the intensity with which the news media covered the agencies' activities. The resulting visibility increased officials' sense that they were engaged in an important and meaningful enterprise; that obvious instances of insensitive, legalistic rule application would become the subject of common knowledge; and that merely "correct" rule application was not justification enough for their actions. Perhaps even more basic to the concern for the "reasonableness" of decisions were the difficulties associated with enforcing the freeze order. The number of regulated firms was so large and the resources of the agencies were so limited in relation to the task that enforcement obviously could be achieved only by voluntary compliance. And voluntary compliance with the law, agency officials assumed, was conditioned on equality of application. Businesses, unions, landlords, and consumers could be expected to comply willingly only so long as the sacrifices required by the regulatory restrictions were equally distributed, so long as each particular firm or group of workers felt that it was being asked to bear no *special* burden in the battle against inflation.

The concept of equality of burden goes beyond formal equality, however. It relates to distributive justice. It calls for reformulation of rules of formal and equal application when they cause especially disruptive or harsh effects for some economic actors. The implication of the freeze experience, therefore, is that these considerations become more salient when the coercive powers of legal agencies seem inadequate. For agencies with insufficient enforcement powers, the primary hope of achieving compliance with their rules lies in continuing attention to the reasonableness of their rules, to the consequences they produce, and to the justice-claims they engender.

JUSTIFYING STRINGENCY

However desirable, the demand for substantive justification of rule application threatens the very foundations of such a program as the freeze, which attempts to achieve sudden, radical changes in human behavior through categorical, universally applicable rules, swiftly applied—regardless of incidental economic hardship, regardless of commitments and expectations based on lawful agreements, regardless of the differences in wealth or merit of those subject to the formally uniform rule. If agency officials were to take seriously the notion that the rules themselves must be substantively defensible, and they did, they would have to construct substantive justifications for the hold-the-line policy itself and the hardships it produced in individual cases. The way they attempted to do so—which suggests the conditions and limits of regulatory stringency in general—can be illustrated by reference to the school bus contractors case and an imaginary dialogue in which Mr. Reynolds, the bus companies' representative, pushes the agency official a bit harder than the real Mr. Reynolds actually did.

> *Reynolds:* I want to be sure you understand the situation. Imagine a school bus company which in March 1971 contracted to provide service, beginning in September 1971 at $40,000 per month. As soon as its bid was accepted and the contract signed, the company hired more drivers and granted a general pay increase. It repaired seats and bought new tires for its buses. It devoted many paid man-hours to recalculating routes and pickup points and checked different ones out through practice runs. Now the freeze order seems to say the company must charge last year's rates. That means it would lose money for the three months of the freeze, money that it could not recoup later on. The school district, meanwhile, which has budgeted $40,000 a month, gets a windfall. Why, in the name of justice and common sense, can't the bus company charge its contractual rate?
>
> *Freeze Official:* Because that's what a freeze is. The freeze order and the CLC rules interpreting it say no price increases are allowed.
>
> *Reynolds:* That's just being legalistic! I've asked you to *justify* applying those rules to this particular bus company—which is getting wiped out!
>
> *Official:* All right. *Every time* we block a contracted-for price increase, it defeats expectations and gives the other party a windfall. If we allow the price increase in your case, we would have to in other cases where there is a contract

calling for a price increase. That's only fair. But that would destroy the entire program. The whole problem of inflation—at least this inflation—is the expectation of continuing inflation, which leads people to build large price and wage increases into long-term contracts. If we let every contractual increase go through, we wouldn't have a freeze and we wouldn't be stopping inflation.

Reynolds: Nonsense! That depends on what is (or should be) frozen—*all* price increases or only unreasonable, undeserved, inflationary ones. You don't have to allow every contractual increase to go through; only moderate and necessary ones. In this case we're not talking about an inflationary increase. It's an entirely reasonable price increase—reasonable in amount, cost-justified, fair to everybody concerned. Why don't you just freeze unreasonable, inflationary increases?

Official: Well if we were starting from scratch, and in an ideal world, you might have a case—assuming you could prove to me that your bus company's increase is in fact reasonable in amount. But we're not in that position.

First, the executive order doesn't make any exceptions for "reasonable" increases. Everybody already understands a "freeze" to mean a freeze on all price increases, reasonable or not, deserved or not. To make such exceptions now would destroy the credibility of the anti-inflation program, because if we allow businesses to increase prices whenever the increases are "reasonable," we would have to allow reasonable increases in wages and salaries too—which seems only fair. And as soon as you start having movement in wages and prices, people would think the freeze was a fraud. Every business in the country would start pushing through the price increases it thinks reasonable or deserved, and every union or employee would put on the pressure to get the salary increase it thinks is reasonable.

But there is a second and perhaps more basic reason. We simply have no standards for determining what *is* an "unreasonable" or "undeserved" or "unduly inflationary" price (or wage) increase. Those are questions of value as well as economics, and they are politically explosive questions. To put together a set of rules that business and labor and consumers would all take as legitimate and fair would take a lot of consultation and probably a lot of participation by affected groups as well. The purpose of a freeze is to buy time to figure out and gain approval for those standards—yet without inducing a lot of "pre-emptive" wage and price increases while that consultation is going on.

Third, even if we had some guidelines on what constitutes a reasonable or non-inflationary price increase, they would be much more complicated than a flat freeze. It would be easier to cheat on them, and we don't have the mammoth organizational machinery it would take to enforce them or to resolve disputes about their application—because each dispute would involve finding out a lot about each firm or group of workers and its particular financial situation. If we made businesses apply in advance for permission to increase prices, most of them would still be frozen while the fact-finding process dragged on. Others would cheat. The virtuous would stay frozen while the bureaucracy ground on, and the unvirtuous would get away with it.

Reynolds: So at bottom, you're saying that because the government really doesn't know what it's doing—what reasonable and politically acceptable price and wage controls would look like—and because it didn't plan in advance and establish a bureaucracy large enough to decide individual cases and enforce the law against violators, then the bus company has to abide by a simplistic rule that is unfair in its case. Should it suffer because the government is inept?

Official: I'm afraid so. We can't always wait for perfect knowledge and organization before acting. Governments often undertake programs with insufficient foresight and planning, and the result—at least for a period of time—is a set of general rules which seem arbitrary as applied to particular cases. But if we now started making exceptions in every case where the rule seemed unfair—without general standards or machinery for making exceptions—it would be just as arbitrary and unfair. In fact it would be worse: there would be the injustice that comes from chaos *and* the success of the stabilization program would be jeopardized. At least now, people can plan on fixed rules for a specific period of time and try to adapt to it. If your bus company feels the pinch, at least the freeze is working and we have a better chance of stopping the inflationary psychology and coming up with a more stable economic environment.

Reynolds: Now you're saying that because it is working, it's OK to inflict hardship on some. Even assuming the evil of inflation is so great that it is justifiable to sacrifice some troops in a sudden assault on it (on the theory, perhaps, that the hardships of a freeze are less than those of a high-unemployment fiscal and monetary war on inflation), how do you know that this really will work? To inflict hardship in the course of a strategy of price and wage controls—which at least according to history are likely to fail—seems especially cynical and unjustifiable.

Official: Agreed, a sacrifice in a losing war is a shame, but I don't think it is necessarily unjustifiable, especially if it is a just war. I can't say that this is an unjust war or a clearly foolish strategy. The controls—beginning with the freeze—are not a certain strategy, but not a hopeless one either. Besides, they are the strategy that has been chosen.

Reynolds: Now you're saying that it is alright to inflict an unjust result on the bus company because the Congress and the president took a gamble that the controls would work and you're obligated to help them with their bet. In short, you don't have the authority to change the program, the law. So you enforce it without exception.

Official: That's not quite right. It's true that I don't have authority to change the rule or the strategy. But in my view we shouldn't. I am saying that to abolish or undermine the program by piecemeal exceptions would cause *more* injustice, while also disrupting the chance that the program *might* work.

In two respects, the freeze official's argument has a familiar ring. It is heard in other legal settings to justify categorical and stringent rule application. The first of these recurrent arguments relates to the problem of insufficient resources for more sophisticated law reformulation. The second involves the problem of prior commitments.

Insufficient Resources and the Justification of Stringency

When asked why the regulations should not prohibit only *unreasonable* price increases, one part of the freeze official's answer was that the agencies did not yet *know* what was reasonable, and they did not have the time or manpower to apply such a sophisticated standard to individual cases. This can be viewed as a claim that the agencies lacked certain important resources—knowledge, time, personnel. The complaint is a common one. Agencies often lack the empirical knowledge on which to base precise rules that discriminate among slightly different circumstances and strike an optimum balance between regulatory stringency and competing values. Agencies which might desire to adjust rules in light of their actual consequences often lack the time and personnel to do the requisite data-gathering and analysis. They lack money with which to finance studies of the regulated industries or develop alternate sources of information.

One response to such a paucity of resources is to evolve and enforce regulatory policy on a cautious, step-by-step basis. The agency or the legislature promulgates rules that employ very general standards, using such words as *unreasonable*. It enforces them only where the facts are obvious, where competing values are only weakly involved, and where there is a substantial consensus that the behavior involved should be prohibited or punished. The strategy is to move toward larger, more complex, or controversial problems only as the organization develops more knowledge and the resources to take on and deal with controversy. The contrasting approach is to jump into the fray with two feet, to enact and attempt to enforce sweeping rules that categorically condemn all manifestations of the evil, large or small. The agency deals with only the most obviously deserving applications for exceptions or those that can be adequately investigated within the constraints of time and manpower. In the second, sweeping approach, regulated firms that deserve exceptions bear the costs and inequities resulting from the agency's lack of resources. In the first, the cautious approach, the individuals that might benefit from more stringent regulation bear the costs.

The dilemma was posed clearly in Phase II of the Nixon administration's Economic Stabilization Program. By a four-to-three margin, the Price Commission decided, just a few days before the freeze ended, *not* to adopt a flat 2.5 percent ceiling on annual price increases. The arguments in favor of such a universal, objective, and stringent standard had been substantial. It would be clear and understandable. It would signal a determined effort to stop inflation. It would help inspire consumer confidence, thereby generating support from housewives, consumer groups, and organized labor. If strictly enforced, it would help both businesses and the Pay Board in holding wages to non-inflationary levels. It would be easily enforceable—customers could calculate price changes and complain of violations. A more sophisticated standard, requiring inquiry into the cost and profit levels of firms in order to determine a "reasonable" price, it was argued, would be beyond the capacity of the commission's limited staff to administer in light of the vast number of regulated firms and products.

The majority of the Price Commission, however, was ultimately persuaded that an absolute 2.5 percent rule would be too arbitrary in too many cases. Nor would it avoid the problem of inadequate resources: a flat rule would result in a vast number of requests for exceptions on grounds of hardship or inequity—too many requests, in fact, for the staff to verify and evaluate in an expeditious manner. Moreover, the majority was sincerely troubled by the problem of providing some intellectually convincing justification for a 2.5 percent figure—or a 2 percent or a 3 percent or any other figure that was arbitrarily pulled out of the hat. Instead, the commission adopted a more complex standard, relating the allowable prices to each firm's particular cost and profit structure. Moreover, the rule was to be self-executing for most firms. Only the very largest corporations would have to apply to the Price Commission in advance and present proof that projected increases were within the rules; the commission's limited enforcement and fact-finding resources, therefore, would focus only on the most economically significant business firms.[3]

The arguments made to Mr. Reynolds by our hypothetical freeze agency official were not unlike those advanced by the Price Commission's minority. At bottom, these arguments involved the assertion that under some conditions a sweeping rule is more effective and enforceable and hence ultimately fairer. There was a difference in context, however. When the Price Commission was debating, all prices and wages were frozen. The initial impact of the anti-inflation program had been made. It was widely regarded as successful. People were complying. The commission's greatest concerns were the wisdom and equity of its policy and its long-range effect on all aspects of the economy as well as on inflation. During the freeze, however, the primary

---

[3] In fact, the Price Commission, with a staff of about 400, had difficulty processing the applications of even the 250 largest corporations within the thirty-day time limit it set for itself. A longer processing time, the commission felt, was an unreasonable interference with pricing flexibility. Consequently, it negotiated agreements with many large firms, whereby in return for a pledge to keep price increases on a weighted average of all the firm's products to less than 2 percent annually, the firm would not have to pre-notify the commission and get its approval for any single price increase. The firms were thus willing to abide by potentially more stringent rules rather than endure the paperwork, legal expenses, and time lag entailed in applications to the agency under a complex set of rules. For an argument, however, that the agreements resulted in overly accommodative regulation, see Robert Lanzillotti, Mary Hamilton, and Blaine Roberts, *Phase II in Review: The Price Commission Experience* (Washington: Brookings Institution, 1975). On the formulation of the original rules, see C. Jackson Grayson, Jr., and Louis Neeb, *Confessions of A Price Controller* (Homewood, Ill.: Dow-Jones-Irwin, 1974).

concerns were compliance and the possibility of resistance, winning public confidence, and changing inflationary expectations. Categorical rules seem better designed to achieve those ends.

A simple, unqualifiedly stringent rule appears to stand on the high ground of moral principle or unified public purpose. Universalistic rules that treat everyone alike, regardless of their differences in wealth or desert, embody the most prevalent notion of equality before the law. Standards such as "need," "cost justified," or "reasonable rate of return," on the other hand, invite controversy. They are difficult for the public to understand and enforce. By definition, they produce objectively (even if justifiably) different results for ostensibly similar firms or citizens. Outcomes are thus likely to be perceived as unequal, the result of political pressure and favoritism. More complex, adaptive rules thus invite continuing political pressures on the rule-making and administrative process.[4]

Unmitigated stringency might seem substantively justifiable, therefore, and empirically more likely when it seems important to rally widespread public support for a new program or law, to generate commitment and energy, or to overcome ingrained practices and institutional policies.[5] Similarly, stringency often seems justifiable where the practice or condition to be regulated is rapidly *getting worse:* quick and effective government action then seems more important than the incremental additions to fairness that may result from taking more time for careful planning before acting. In cases, such as the freeze, where it is possible to conceive of regulation as a non-zero-sum game in which everyone, even the regulated firm, will gain if the effort is successful, harsh rules may be justified as unpleasant medicine for certain individual firms, but medicine that will ultimately leave even them better off than if the program fails.[6] The freeze also suggests that where regulation is based on a permit or licensing system, involving *applications* for price increases or other government action, it may be less disruptive of normal economic practices for an agency to promulgate stringent, simply applied rules than to use more sophisticated standards and fact-finding procedures that would make applicants wait in a long queue for agency action. Finally, where the rule maker mistrusts the capacity of primary rule appliers to adhere to the police-mission goal, either because of their lack of commit-

---

[4] Compare, for example, the administration of a flat percentage sales or excise tax with that of a graduated income tax.

[5] Compare the use of a sweeping, unqualifiedly stringent pronouncement designed to have such effects on public attitudes in *Brown* v. *Board of Education,* 347 U.S. 483 (1954), with the more adaptive, flexible enforcement section of the rule, the "all deliberate speed" formula announced in *Brown* v. *Board of Education,* 349 U.S. 294 (1955).

[6] This is analagous to the justification for inequalities proposed by John Rawls, *A Theory of Justice* (Cambridge, Mass.: Harvard University Press, 1971).

ment to those values or because of their lack of sophistication, and fears that a more flexible standard would result in undue concessions to competing values and traditional patterns of activity, it may seem justifiable to draw an overly wide protective arc around the value to be promoted.[7]

Prior Commitments

Another theme in the freeze official's argument in the hypothetical dialogue was that while the "rule of reason" Reynolds suggested was indeed reasonable, and that while the freeze might ultimately be counter-productive—never providing *any* compensation for those on whom it imposed sacrifices—it was *too late* to do anything about it. The course had been set. Unless and until it became clear that the course was disastrous, it would be more disruptive and unfair to try to alter its direction.

This is an old theme in the law. It holds that law should not change too fast or respond immediately to every piece of evidence that it is not working properly or causing unfairness, not because unfairness is good, but because injustice, more injustice, results from the anomie and confusion bred by rapidly changing law.[8] The lawmakers, accordingly, should not move too fast. They should give people a chance to work out ways of dealing with the unintended adverse effects of a law. The lawmakers should wait and see if the benefits a law produces outweigh the costs. They should wait until they gather enough knowledge to improve the law before undermining it and foreclosing the knowledge its administration generates. That can be done only if people can count on the law's continuation for a substantial or a fixed period of time. Moreover, changing a law too rapidly is unjust to those who have sustained losses in complying with it, as Mr. Hurd of OEP's Atlanta office argued against making an exception for the Girl Scouts.

Of course, arguments based on maintaining commitments and consistency of treatment are available to legal officials resisting *any* request for exceptions or changes in existing law. Law enforcement officials are perhaps prone to exaggerate the chaos and noncompliance that will result from weak enforcement measures or making exceptions. But the risk of abuse does not mean that those arguments are never justifiable, particularly in such cases as the freeze, where there is little contemporaneous evidence that the stringent rule is failing in its purpose or causing widespread disruption (as opposed to occasional hardships), where the sacrifices of the many who comply under the law are justifiable only if it is successfully enforced against all, and where compliance is so clearly conditioned on the perception of equal treatment.

---

[7] Consider *Mapp* v. *Ohio,* 367 U.S. 643 (1961) (the exclusionary rule) and *Miranda* v. *Arizona,* 384 U.S. 436 (1966), in this respect.

[8] See "Eight Ways to Fail to Make Law" in Lon Fuller, *The Morality of Law,* rev. ed. (New Haven, Conn.: Yale University Press, 1969), ch. 2.

The values served by stability and consistency of application of a law over time, therefore, create limits on the malleability of positive law and on the idea that laws should be justified in light of their consequences in individual cases. For this reason, even Cost of Living Council members—some of whom helped design the program, some of whom had argued strongly against the whole idea of instituting mandatory price and wage controls—took the stringent hold-the-line anti-inflation policy as essentially unalterable for the duration of the freeze. The president had made a public commitment to pursue a certain policy for a fixed period of time and had embodied that commitment in the specific words of an executive order. It was not for them, agency officials believed, suddenly to change that policy, even if they suspected that it would ultimately fail, even if its burdens were unequally distributed. They justified their position on grounds of an a priori principle: that the law, reasonably interpreted, should be consistently applied for the period that had been promised.

THE LIMITS OF STRINGENCY

If stringent regulation, strict adherence to a categorically stated police mission, can sometimes be justified, it cannot always be justified. If it is important to keep commitments, there is a greater danger that they will be maintained too long, long after the adverse and unintended consequences of a legal rule have become all too apparent to everyone but the administrators. A slavish devotion to consistency and formal equality of treatment is an obstacle to change. The difficult problems of gathering information about the consequences of decision and of reconciling the conflicting justice-claims of diverse constituencies should not be avoided or postponed too long. In the short span of the freeze, it was not clear who was gaining the most and who the least from the halt in inflation; the longer the regulatory program lasts, however, the real incidence of its benefits and burdens becomes more salient and standards for allocating them fairly—standards which generally entail departures from categorical, across-the-board legal rules or moral principles—must be developed.

The freeze, therefore, while providing an example of a successful regulatory program—intelligently run, on balance, and fairly administered—does not teach us that stringent regulation is always ideal or readily attainable. In fact, by teaching us that considerations of justice do play a major part in the regulatory process, it suggests that those very considerations—as applied in most other circumstances, in programs of longer duration and less extensive regulatory control—would call for a lighter governmental touch, the gradual development of rules which by their terms can more easily be adjusted to specific circumstances. As long as we demand justice, legal complexity will be our fate.

Appendix:
Notes on Research Methods

The agencies that administered the wage-price freeze of 1971 no longer exist. They have been dragged off to the secret bureaucracy burial ground. Their officials have moved on to other tasks; files are scattered; memories of informal conversations reported in this book have grown dim. The research reported here, in short, cannot be replicated. Basically, I can only ask the reader to accept on faith the veracity and objectivity of the descriptive material provided; but to provide some foundation for such faith and some insight into the process of participant-observer research in governmental agencies, I will describe some of the research methods I used.

OBSERVATION

My primary method of investigation was direct participant-observation. As noted in the Preface, I obtained a position as attorney on the staff of OEP's General Counsel's Office, beginning during the second week of the freeze. The director of OEP, as well as the general counsel and his immediate assistants, were aware of my identity as a researcher from the start, and I readily disclosed it to any other agency official who asked, "Where are you from?"—a common question in an agency filled with new recruits on loan from other federal agencies. But in their eyes, I am quite convinced, my identity as researcher was quickly subordinated to my role as co-worker. Most of my interactions with OEP and CLC officials were not in the form of interviews, but in the discussion of particular cases or operating problems in a high-pressure working atmosphere.

I worked in a variety of roles in the General Counsel's Office. Initially I served as assistant to John Simpson, the general counsel's aide in charge of office management and coordination with other offices. This position seemed ideal because it was not substantive work but administrative in nature. Rather than being tied down to a desk and specializing in one particular kind of legal problem, working with Simpson and accompanying him to daily coordination meetings quickly gave me an overview of the freeze administration and the problems of managing it. Daily administrative tasks also brought me into regular contact with all the offices in OEP National and enabled me to become friendly with at least a couple of officials engaged in each function. Simpson's work, it turned out, was also quite substantive. The job of routing cases to their proper office, for example, or deciding who in the General Counsel's Office should work on what problem, or when a problem was sufficiently important to consult the general counsel about it or refer it to CLC, all required a detailed knowledge of CLC rules. Gradually, therefore, I became drawn into discussions involving particular cases, answering questions brought to the General Counsel's Office by officials from other offices, helping to relieve bottlenecks by deciding some inquiries myself, and finally, reviewing inquiry-responses prepared by lawyers who were much newer recruits to OEP than I was.

Involvement in the decision of individual cases inevitably led to involvement in the rule-making process. When policy issues arose, I quickly learned I could expedite matters by taking them to OEP's Policy Analysis Office in person and by drafting issue papers for CLC myself. In addition, Elmer Bennett, OEP's general counsel, each day reviewed the stack of issue papers prepared by the Policy Analysis Office, checking them for legal problems (and adding his policy recommendations) before they were sent on to CLC. I often was assigned to take his comments and proposed revisions back to Policy Analysis, discuss them with Policy Analysis officials, and help draft new language. Repeated contact with those officials led to trust and confidence. On a couple of occasions, I was asked to attend meetings of CLC's Executive Committee when they were discussing issue papers that I had been closely involved with.

After about a month, I frequently became involved in a sort of troubleshooter role. Bennett or Simpson or one of General Lincoln's aides would ask me to sit in with them (or for them) in meetings with other OEP officials or CLC staff members or inquirers. I met with groups—school superintendents, constituents assembled by congressmen, New York City landlords— who had questions about the freeze. I was sent to New Orleans to help draft the complaint in an enforcement action. In consequence, I discussed cases with the general counsel virtually every day and had numerous interactions on agency business with OEP's director and his assistants, OEP regional office officials, and CLC's general counsel.

This, of course, was taking the participant-observer role to the extreme "participant" end of the spectrum. My initial strategy had been to play a more traditional "observer" role—to watch and listen to agency officials in action, to get them to talk about their work, to avoid "contaminating" their actions by my intervention, and to maintain the objectivity presumably protected by limited involvement.[1] Once on the scene, it appeared to me that maximum involvement offered distinct advantages over detachment.

The process of legal decision in an administrative agency is not easily susceptible to pure observation. It takes place at desks, in offices, in occasional conferences and telephone conversations, and in hurried conversations in corridors. The participants spend a great deal of time studying documents. To a very great extent, the process takes place inside people's heads. One must talk to them, ask them what they are thinking, *in the context of specific cases,* to find out how and why they decide cases as they do. In contrast, "interviews" at lunch or after work tend to produce general responses divorced from the immediacy of minute-to-minute thoughts and actions. Yet under the intense pressures of large-scale regulation, it is extremely difficult and ethically questionable to draw harried officials away from their responsibilities during working hours to ask them innumerable questions.

Active participation, conversely, meant that I did not have to interview agency officials about their roles or attitudes in the abstract, worry about the honesty of their statements, or divert them from important work. I talked with them in scores of casual conversations over a three-month period under the conditions of trust engendered by working together under pressure. I could discern their values and motivations in the course of mutual efforts at solving the same problem or complaining together about obstacles and unpleasant people we jointly had to deal with. Participation also meant that I *felt* the responsibility and pressures involved in the decision-making process, enabling me to penetrate the emotional and moral life of the agency in a way detached observation could not. Like other agency officials, I argued with my colleagues and inwardly blanched before the complaints of hostile members of the public. I experienced the kinds of anxieties, satisfactions, power

---

[1] See generally, W. R. Scott, "Field Methods in the Study of Organizations," in *Handbook of Organizations,* ed. James March (Chicago: Rand-McNally, 1965); George McCall and J. L. Simmons, eds., *Issues in Participant Observation* (Reading, Mass.: Addison-Wesley, 1969); Melville Dalton, "Preconceptions and Methods in *Men Who Manage,"* and Peter Blau, "The Research Process in the Study of *The Dynamics of Bureaucracy," Sociologists at Work,* ed. Philip Hammond (New York: Doubleday–Anchor Books, 1967); Sam Sieber, "The Integration of Field Work and Survey Methods," 78 *American Journal of Sociology* 1335 (1973).

drives, and feelings of boredom that were inherent in working in that agency. By systematically asking myself why I took any action, why I felt constrained to lean one way or the other in deciding a doubtful case, why I got angry at another official, or why I felt embarrassed on occasion, I was able to discover the unstated norms and values that permeated the decision-making process. By then casually asking other officials if they felt the same, I could verify those impressions.

There are hazards, of course, as well as advantages for a researcher to engage deeply in participation. One is that he will have too great an influence on the subject of his research and change the "natural" course of organizational conduct or the attitudes of his subjects. In one sense, I often did. I frequently changed an inquiry-response and attempted to persuade CLC to reformulate an existing rule. The agencies' decisions had real and far-reaching effects, and I felt it more important to try to alleviate disruption or injustice or prevent unequal treatment than to maintain the purity of my research effort, but this is actually an artificial distinction. The researcher does not distort the observed process so long as he acts within an established role within the organization. *Everyone* in the inquiry-response process in OEP, for example, was involved in the process of changing draft answers and suggesting changes in the rules. In a study of organizational processes, norms, and attitudes, it is not a distorting influence to change one particular decision out of the hundreds made each week, if that is done in accordance with standard organizational processes, norms, and attitudes. The participant-observer's responsibility is to insure that as a worker, his general approach, procedures, and attitudes are not markedly different from those of his colleagues—or if they are, to note precisely how. The best defense against that kind of bias is self-awareness, alertness to the possibility that one's actions and conclusions are influenced by idiosyncratic personal attitudes. My technique for detecting such effects was to type extensive field notes every night, in which I questioned my own motivations for decisions I had made and especially for any emotional reactions I had in the course of the preceding day. I specifically raised the question of whether those responses were the product of my own personal biography, attitudes, and dispositions, as opposed to responses generated by the overall culture of the organization.

A second problem of active participation is that it forces the researcher into specific roles or sections of the organization whose characteristic style and mode of operation may be different from that of other sections of the organization. I was prone, for example, to the sometimes-noted tendency to associate primarily with higher-level, more articulate officials in the agency, those who had greater perspective and overview of the agency's activity and participated in policy making as well as rule applying. One might expect these officials, however, to be more committed to the program and to adhere more closely to norms of the judicial mode than lower-level officials. (Actually, there was quite a bit of variation in this respect, even at the top.) The researcher, in turn, may be easily "captured" by the definition of reality and attitudes conveyed by the more high-powered, articulate, and important officials.

Again, the best antidote for this "elite bias" (or for the less frequently noted, but perhaps more common fault—the "anti-elite bias" engendered by associating with articulate dissenters and lower-level officials or those subject to the agency's activities) is self-consciousness. I used the process of recording field notes every evening as a device for systematically questioning whether any quotation by an official which I had recorded expressed a point of view widely shared in the organization, and I made it my business the next day to check it out with informants in other offices. For that reason, too, I tried to retain enough freedom and variety in my work assignments to have regular contact with all the offices of OEP and to cultivate contacts with a broad spectrum of agency personnel. Moreover, I eagerly seized upon any opportunity to undertake a new task that would bring me in contact with new officials, especially with field offices, with officials in Congress or other executive agencies, or with citizens in organizations who had complaints to make about the agency. On weekend trips to my home in New Haven, I talked with my dry cleaner and filling station operator and any other businessmen I knew about their reactions to the program. Such contacts with outsiders proved invaluable in clarifying the perspective of those inside the agency. Similarly, I gained valuable perspective by working for a time in' another agency with a similar role, the Price Commission.

Nevertheless, in the end, I had had relatively little contact with the field offices of the freeze agencies; I visited only one local IRS office in person—in New Orleans—though I spoke to officials in some others by phone. While I encountered nothing in contact with field offices that was discordant with my impressions of the Washington office, I cannot confidently assert that the spirit, the values, the concerns, and the practices observed in Washington prevailed throughout the OEP and IRS field offices. In addition, I believe that for some time after the freeze I perceived more orderliness and coherence in the freeze agencies than an outsider or a field office official did at the time and I tended to accept somewhat uncritically the justifications agency officials generated for their actions. The best solvent for that kind of bias, in my case, was the greater detachment and capacity for criticism born of the passage of time and especially the criticism of talks I gave and of draft chapters of this book offered by my academic advisors and colleagues.

Another hedge against the biases created by a particular perspective from inside an organization is to supplement participant observation with more systematic forms of research, conducted at a later point in time. Observations can be formulated into hypotheses to be checked by administering questionnaires to a carefully constructed sample of officials and strategically located outsiders or by systematic review and content analysis of the agency's files. In my case, the latter seemed the most valuable strategy.

ARCHIVAL SURVEY

After the freeze, I was granted access to OEP files, including 1) the records of the daily rule-making meetings of ExComm, including the issue papers and arguments concerning each problem that had been prepared by the CLC staff or the OEP Policy Analysis Office; 2) letter inquiries and responses prepared by the major inquiry-response offices in the OEP national office; and 3) teletyped inquiries to OEP National from regional offices and the answers thereto. These records facilitated substantive, quantitative analysis of case-by-case decisions in OEP National.

The file containing responses to letter inquiries answered by the OEP national office was helpful in testing hypotheses concerning the referral of cases to higher levels of the bureaucracy, effects of variations in case presentation on outcome, differences in decision making by hierarchical level or office, and other possible correlates of stringent as opposed to accommodative answers. My survey excluded, however, responses to inquiries by OEP regional offices, IRS, the CLC staff, and other cooperating government agencies.

Sampling was complicated by the fact that the OEP National inquiry-responses were stored in eighteen different files: there was a separate set of files for cases answered by each of three offices—Correspondence, General Counsel, and Policy Analysis; for each office, there were separate files for VIP cases (cases forwarded by governmental officials or congressmen) and ordinary cases, and within each of those categories, there were separate files for inquiries relating to prices, wages, and rents. In order to allow for comparison among each of the subfiles, I drew a stratified sample, sampling at a different rate from each subfile, so as to produce a reasonable number of cases from each subfile. The total sample was 447 cases out of a population of 3,502. For each case, I coded some forty different items of information, including 1) date and speed of disposition; 2) nature of inquirer (business firm, union, individual, etc.; large organization, small organization, etc.); 3) use of intermediaries (lawyer, politician, lobbyist) and special contacts within the agencies; 4) method of presentation (written only or in-person presentation as well; length, detail, complexity of written presentation); 5) type of issue; 6) nature and amount of argument advanced; 7) internal routing within the agency; 8) substantive decision by the agency. The coding form, as well as a table showing the sampling rates for each subfile, is available in Appendix C to Robert A. Kagan, "The Wage-Price Freeze: A Study in Administrative Justice" (Ph.D. diss., Yale University, 1974).

Information for each case was transferred to data processing cards and electronically tabulated. To correct for the "weighting" in the sample created by sampling at a different rate from each subfile, the sampled cases for each subfile were multiplied by the corresponding sample rate, creating an estimated total for each subfile. For example, in the *sample* there were thirty-five non-VIP cases dealing with wages decided by the General Counsel's Office and forty-one decided by the Correspondence Section; the sampling rate for CS was one for every ten cases in the file; for GC, it was one for every twenty. To learn, say, the percentage of stringent answers for all non-VIP wage cases for the whole agency, combining all offices, it would be distorting to merely combine those seventy-six sampled cases and compute the percent in which stringent answers were given. It was necessary first to compute the percent stringent for the cases sampled from each subfile, then *estimate* the result for *all* cases in the subfile by multiplying the sampled cases by the appropriate sampling rate, and finally combine the estimated totals of all subfiles. Consequently, all percentages noted in the tables in Chapter 9 are based on the estimated total cases.

One last point. The relative stringency or accommodativeness of inquiry-responses was measured by a combination of two coded items, as in the method employed with respect to ExComm rules described in Table 2 in Chapter 3. Stringent cases were those in which the agency's decision was "frozen" (no increase allowed) plus those in which the agency said, "It depends," or allowed the increase in part, but which I subjectively classified as stringent in light of my re-reading of the CLC rules and consideration of plausible alternative answers. Accommodative cases were those in which the agency clearly allowed the requested increase, plus "it depends" and "partly allowed" answers which I subjectively classified as accommodative. (Of the "it depends" and "partly allowed" cases in the sample, I classified 13 percent as stringent, 26 percent as accommodative, and 60 percent as "no judgment possible"; the "no judgment possible" cases constituted 22 percent of the total sample.)

Index

to **Authors, Government Publications, and
U.S. Court Cases** cited in the text

Page numbers in parentheses indicate author *edited*
book in which another author's article was cited.

General Subject Index